JEREMY BENTHAM AND THE LAW

JEREMY BENTHAM
AND THE LAW
A SYMPOSIUM

Edited on behalf of
The Faculty of Laws of University College, London

BY

GEORGE W. KEETON

AND

GEORG SCHWARZENBERGER

GREENWOOD PRESS, PUBLISHERS
WESTPORT, CONNECTICUT

Originally published in 1948
by Stevens & Sons Ltd.

First Greenwood Reprinting 1970

SBN 8371-2832-3

PRINTED IN UNITED STATES OF AMERICA

CONTENTS

PREFACE

THE bicentenary of Bentham's birthday on February 15, 1948, has offered an opportunity to the members of the Faculty of Laws of University College, London, to make some acknowledgment of the debt which the Faculty, and indeed the College, owes to one whose influence is still potent.

Bentham's contribution to legal thought and to the reform of law has been generously acknowledged in the past. In the words of John Stuart Mill, Bentham ' found the philosophy of law a chaos, he left a science; he found the practice of the law an Augean stable, he turned the river into it which is mining and sweeping away mound after mound of its rubbish '.

Sir James Stephen is equally emphatic. Bentham's legal writings, he says, ' have had a degree of practical influence upon the legislation of his own and various other countries comparable only to those of Adam Smith and his successors upon commerce '.

This collection of tributes may be concluded with Sir Henry Sumner Maine's praise of Bentham : ' I do not know a single law reform effected since Bentham's day which cannot be traced to his influence '.

Valuable studies exist upon Bentham's influence on particular branches of the law. What is still lacking, however, is a considered assessment of Bentham's contribution to the science of law as a whole and of his significance for the legal theory and practice of the present time. It may be that this appraisal of his work may best be undertaken by a single person. In the meanwhile, the members of the Faculty of Laws of University College, generously assisted by other writers, sought to assess Bentham's work in those fields of law which are most familiar to them.

The necessity of completing these studies by a definite date, in a transitional period such as the present, has necessarily limited the scope of the work undertaken. Furthermore, the Bentham Manuscripts in the possession of University College were removed for safe custody to Wales at the beginning of the recent war, and it was only with the assistance of the Librarian of the College and his staff, and with the co-operation of the Keeper of the Manuscripts at the British Museum, that a portion of the material was made available for use in the preparation of these essays. The Faculty of Laws also wishes to place on record its indebtedness to the Provost of University College for his constant encouragement and assistance, and to the Committee of the College for permission to reproduce the portrait of Bentham which appears as the frontispiece.

Finally, the Editors wish to thank Mr. Richard FitzGerald, who has acted as Assistant Editor, and upon whom has devolved the laborious task of proof reading and of compiling the index and the tables of cases and statutes.

THE EDITORS

University College, London,
   January, 1948

PART ONE

CHAPTER I

WAS BENTHAM A LAWYER?

H. F. Jolowicz

WAS Bentham a lawyer? The question is surprising with respect to an English legal writer famous here, and probably better known abroad than any other. But it is not new and it will probably always continue to be argued, for Bentham is one of the most original characters in the history of thought, and his nature is full of apparent contradictions. He was a scholar with no respect for scholarship, a jurist with no respect for law, a recluse who nevertheless enjoyed some of the best society of his time, and a dreamer of dreams, whose horse-sense criticised the abuses of his age with such effect that he became one of the chief agencies in the reforming period of the nineteenth century. Only a few of his works were published by himself. Generally he seemed to lose interest in what he had written and would not make the effort necessary to put his work into a fit state for publication. He preferred to go on writing something else, and constantly he so lost himself in detail that the work was never finished. In some ways he was careless, yet much of what he wrote is almost unreadable because, by striving for accuracy of analysis and expression, he obscured rather than explained what he had in mind.[1] Nevertheless he was the idol of his disciples, the founder of a most influential school, and no history of political or even philosophical thought can afford to neglect him.

Consider some of the facts of his life. He was born in London 199 years ago of well-to-do parents, and received a conventional classical education at Westminster School and Queen's College, Oxford, where he matriculated at the age of thirteen. Having far more than the ordinary allowance of brains he assimilated this with ease, wrote Greek and Latin verses with

---

[1] Even Dumont complained of his 'obscurity from too much precision.' See *Works* (Bowring's edition—hereinafter quoted by volume number only), Vol. 10, p. 451.

success and remained all his life perfectly able to comply with
the idiom of his time, if he so chose, by using classical tags and
references.   But he never mistakes a classical quotation for an
argument, and on his real mind the classics seem to have had no
effect at all.   While at Oxford he was set by his father the task
of translating Cicero's *Tusculan Disputations,* and, being a
dutiful son, did as he was told.   But schoolboy though he was in
age, he took up a perfectly independent attitude towards the
subject-matter.   At least it seems probable that his judgment was
formed then, though only recorded later, when he says that the
book ' like most of the other philosophical writings of that great
master of language, is nothing but a heap of nonsense '.[2]

Nor does his education appear to have aroused in him at any
time in his life the slightest interest in literature as such.   He
was extremely fond of music, but the other arts seem to have
left him entirely cold.   But he was far from dull.   Bowring's
Life of him has been said to be the worst biography in the
English language, and certainly it has many faults, but it has the
great merit of preserving for us much of Bentham's own conversation and many of his letters, some of which are calculated
to surprise those who know only his published work.   He is
sprightly, colloquial and full of interest in his surroundings.
From 1781 onwards he was frequently a guest at one of the
great country houses, Lord Shelburne's seat of Bowood, and
though he disliked dressing twice a day,[3] it is clear that he enjoyed
himself.   It is perfectly true that he was sometimes shy and
awkward there, and from a worldly point of view missed his
opportunities, as he did at the Bar, but he met distinguished and
interesting people.   He was a favourite with the ladies of the
house, and how it can be said that he—at any rate at this time
of his life—had no interest in women, I do not quite understand.
Not only did he fall in love, but his letters show that he could
make and enjoy a *risqué* allusion as well as other men.   Nor did
his shrinking from the outer world prevent him from undertaking an adventurous and uncomfortable journey by a roundabout route to Russia to visit his brother Samuel.

With respect to specific legal studies, he began in a sufficiently

---

[2] Quoted by Halévy, *La Formation du Radicalisme Philosophique,* I, 286–
287, from British Museum Add. MSS, 33, 537.
[3] Vol. 10, p. 97.

orthodox way. From his earliest years his father had cherished legal ambitions for him, which appeared to be justified both by his obvious abilities and the connections of his father with influential people in the law. No doubt he at first acquiesced. He was generally submissive to his father, and at a very early age can have known of no reason to object. In the same year in which he took his degree at Oxford (1763) he became a student of Lincoln's Inn, but he returned after some time to Oxford and there followed his amazing reaction to Blackstone's lectures, which he himself recounts:[4] ' I attended with two collegiates of my acquaintance. One was Samuel Parker Coke, a descendant of Lord Coke, a gentleman commoner, who afterwards sat in Parliament; the other was Dr. Downes. They both took notes, which I attempted to do, but could not continue it, as my thoughts were occupied in reflecting on what I heard. I immediately detected his fallacy concerning natural rights; I thought his notions very frivolous and illogical about the gravitating downwards of *haereditas;* and his reasons altogether futile, why it must *descend* and could not *ascend,* etc.'.

This boy's mind was already so tough and so impervious to authority that he could not help criticising the moment he first really began to hear about law. Authority meant nothing to him then, and it never meant anything to him for the rest of his life.

But he evidently not only listened to Blackstone, but attended other lectures on law. At least he says [5] that ' Blackstone was succeeded by Dr. Beavor, who read lectures on Roman law which were laughed at, and failed to draw such audiences as Blackstone drew '. This was presumably John Beaver, who was the author of some translations of legal works,[6] and of a book (which I unfortunately could not see, as the British Museum copy was destroyed in the ' Blitz ') called *Roman Military Punishments,* and illustrated by Hogarth. Clearly he was not a great man, but Bentham's subsequent contempt for ' Rome-bred ' law can hardly be laid at his door, for this contempt was no greater than that which he had for the English system, which he had all possible advantages in learning.

[4] Vol. 10, p. 45.
[5] Vol. 10, p. 45.
[6] See below notes 61 and 63.

When back in London as a student he was for a time assiduous in his attendance in court, as he makes clear when referring to his early idolatry of Lord Mansfield, and, though he says he never pleaded in court, he adds 'I have just opened a bill two or three times, saying a few words for form. When I had obtained my father's leave to give up pleading I heard that the bills were admired'.[7]

He also, for a time, did some conventional reading of law books, for once in his life evidently bowing to the advice of his elders, but he was afterwards sorry for it. 'I was', he says,[8] 'indeed grossly ignorant. Instead of pursuing sound studies or reading any modern books of law, I was set to read old trash of the seventeenth century, and I looked up to the huge mountain of law in despair. I can now look down on it from the heights of utility'. He must have been an exasperating fellow-student. In 1781, he tells us,[9] he was blind for two or three months and asked his friend George Wilson, who was reading Coke upon Littleton, to read aloud. 'I wanted ideas . . . their ideas were better than none. I made many observations showing him that their ideas were to be amended : he did not want them to be amended, but only to learn how he could make money out of them'. Similarly he says that Wilson 'admired Fearne prodigiously—I held him in contempt'.[10] This was no 'old trash of the seventeenth century', for Fearne's 'Essay on Contingent Remainders and Executory Devises' must have been quite new at the time of which he is writing. Wilson's admiration for it has been shared by lawyers generally since his time, but Bentham, already then, was evidently nauseated by logical refinements and what seemed to him to be an irrational basis.

In his later life Bentham continued to number lawyers among his friends, Brougham and Romilly particularly, and Brougham refers to his weight with 'even sound practical lawyers of the better school'.[11] He occasionally tried his hand at parliamentary draftsmanship,[12] and he had a long and unhappy experience of the parliamentary machine in connection with his Panopticon

[7] Vol. 10, p. 83. (Cf. Vol. 1, p. 247.)
[8] *Op. cit.*, p. 84.
[9] *Op. cit.*, p. 134.
[10] *Op. cit.*, p. 133.
[11] *Op. cit.*, p. 462.
[12] Vol. 10, p. 251.

scheme. Sometimes he even set out to argue about law ' as it is ',
instead of arguing about it ' as it ought to be.' Professor Halévy [13]
says that in his work on the Revolt of the American Colonies he
was more ' juridical ' and ' technical ' and less ' utilitarian ' than
he subsequently thought. He does indeed there reason rather
like a lawyer, and has clearly gone into the legal basis of the
matter in the Charters, but it is all in rather general terms. More
interesting in this respect is his ' Plea for the Constitution ',[14]
which concerns the illegalities committed in New South Wales.
Statutes as well as cases are cited with care, and historical argument is introduced. Nor is there much doubt that he was legally
right, for Romilly, whose opinion, as Bentham says, was ' not
lightly given ', agreed.[15] Later in *The King* v. *Edmund and
Others*,[16] he writes, according to the sub-title, ' Brief remarks
tending to show the untenability of this indictment ', and cites
statutes and cases, though the more general purpose of the
pamphlet is to attack the legal conception of conspiracy itself.

But in spite of such occasional excursions into the field of
law ' as it is ', he certainly in general cut himself off from practical legal work, and he often refers to himself as a ' non-
lawyer ' [17] or as no longer a lawyer.[18] In fact in the only case
in which I have noticed that he does call himself a lawyer—and
that is early in his life (1781)—it is in jest. ' Lady S. and
Miss F. . . they or either of them. . . . I speak as a lawyer '.[19]

Then should we take him at his word and answer our
question in the negative? Of course, as you have perhaps been
expecting me to say for some time, it depends on what you mean
by ' lawyer '. He was undoubtedly concerned with law throughout his long life, and he undoubtedly knew a great deal about
law. But to my mind that is not enough. To be a lawyer you

[13] *Formation du radicalisme philosophique*, Vol. 1, p. 362.
[14] Vol. 4, p. 249 sqq.
[15] ' What you state respecting Botany Bay . . . I take the law upon the
subject to be *exactly* as you have stated it.' Vol. 11, pp. 137–138.
[16] Vol. 5, p. 239 sqq.
[17] Vol. 7, p. 218 ; Vol. 10, p. 423.
[18] *E.g.* (Wilson) ' wanted to consult me on some point of law. I laughed
at him. He was a lawyer of eminence—I had quitted the law.' Vol. 10,
p. 134. In a review of Huphrey's *Real Property* in 1826 he says, ' For
my own part (ex-learned as I am, and therefore, if ever, no longer
learned—in the law in general, and in conveyancing law in particular,
never learned at all until I got this learning at the feet of my Gamaliel),
. . .' Vol. 5, p. 394.
[19] Vol. 10, p. 115.

must have some interest in legal technique, and you cannot have legal technique unless you are willing to acknowledge authority in something. Now Bentham, from his earliest years was, as we have seen, impervious to authority. This was the cause of his greatest triumphs, but it also resulted in some weaknesses. To begin with, it resulted in some impatience with detail in acquiring knowledge about actual systems of law, such as is not always noticed by his commentators. Professor Everett in particular says,[20] ' It cannot be too often insisted that Bentham, the enemy of *law as it is* was himself a lawyer and a scholarly one. His dislike came, not from prejudice, but from familiarity, he is equally certain of himself on systems not English. To Bentham, Gaius and Ulpian and Justinian were something more than names or Latin tags to quote with a solemn air. They were men who had written on law—as men they could be wrong . . . he insisted that whatever Roman law was it wasn't a system. . . . Acquainted with it, he dismissed it as almost useless for his purposes '.

I do not think he would have claimed an intimate knowledge of it himself, and I cannot recall finding much, if any, reference to individual jurists. In the first place he seldom makes any distinction between Roman law proper and the more modern developments from it, but commonly classes together under the name of ' Rome-bred ' or ' Romanigenous law ' all Continental systems together with English Equity and Ecclesiastical law. It was, of course, much more difficult to make the distinction in his day, when the Corpus Juris was still widely accepted as actually in force, than it is in ours, but if he had been interested in legal detail, his acuteness would have forced him to observe the difference. Secondly, it is fairly obvious that he relied very largely on Heineccius's *Elementa juris civilis, secundum ordinem Pandectarum,* which is an elementary book.[21] He seldom quotes

---

20 Introduction to *The Limits of Jurisprudence Defined,* pp. 19, 20.

21 The note published by Everett, *op. cit.,* p. 339, seems to show that Bentham had little acquaintance with Continental civilian literature. He there makes it a reproach that forty years after Heineccius had published a book in the order of the Pandects, ' Beyer ' published one in the order of the Institutes, both arrangements being those of an Emperor long dead and ' unconnected and incommensurable.' Actually there were many books of both sorts, Heineccius himself having published one in the order of the Institutes in 1725. ' Beyer ' is no doubt Eusebius Beger, for whom see Stintzing-Landsberg, *Geschichte der deutschen Rechtswissenschaft,* III, I (Notes) 167. Beger is quoted *e.g. Works,* Vol. 3, p. 162.

any other authority, and some passages in Heineccius he quotes several times, *e.g.* that on the division of offences into *delicta privata* and *publica,* and of the latter into *ordinaria* and *extra-ordinaria,*[22] and that on the different degrees of proof.[23] Here he certainly relied on Heineccius alone, for he says, ' Such, if Heineccius is to be believed, are the degrees of probative force that have been distinguished and received denominations in his school of fraud and nonsense '.[24] If he had looked at the texts themselves he would have found nothing about ' full ', ' half-full ' and ' less than half-full ' proof, for that is all due to later elaboration. In another passage [25] he takes the law of *stellionatus* and criticises it very justly as ' hodge-podge '. Although he goes into some detail, internal evidence shows, I think, that he looked only at Heineccius.[26] Elsewhere, speaking of the Roman rules of marriage he says they ' are a code of violence ; the man receives the lion's share '.[27] This can only be described as a blunder, for compared with the English law of his time, the Roman rules were very liberal to the wife. Perhaps here, too, he was relying on Heineccius, but had read the relevant passage,[28] which has a good deal to say of marriage with *manus,* too hastily.

If all this is correct, and if it had been pointed out to Bentham, he would not, in my opinion, have been in the least perturbed. He only cared for accuracy, even in matters of much greater interest to him, in so far as it was necessary to his purpose, and did not mind being known to be mistaken about detail. Writing to Wilson from Russia in 1787 concerning his pamphlet on ' The Defence of Usury ' he says, ' Don't let any flagrant absurdities go for want of correction or erasure : false or dubious law I don't so much care about, provided you correct it or clear it up in a note ', and again, ' All I am anxious to avoid is plying the public with false law ; the being seen to be ignorant or mis-

---

[22] *E.g.* Vol. 1, p. 139 ; Vol. 3, p. 172 ; quoting Hein. Pars., §§ 79, 80
[23] *E.g.* Vol. 6, p. 230 ; quoting Hein. Pars., IV, § 118.
[24] Vol. 6. p. 230. (Cf. Vol. 6, p. 302 on ' testimonial falsehood '.)
[25] Vol. 7, p. 18.
[26] Hein. Pars., VII, § 149. Bentham refers to *si quis imposturam fecerit in necem alterius* as the third out of six cases. This conforms to Heineccius, but can hardly be reconciled with D. 47, 20, 3, 1, and not at all with C. 9, 34.
[27] *Principles of the Civil Code* (Ogden's ed., 230. *Works,* Vol. 1, p. 355 (where the text is slightly different).
[28] Pars., IV, § 159.

taken in points of law at 1500 miles distance from all sources of information, gives me not the least concern. I have no opinion-trade to spoil '.[29] This is certainly not the language of a lawyer, but of a man who has very different fish to fry from those that come into the ordinary, or even the great, lawyers' pan.[30]

I have spoken above of the rare occasions when he does argue about law ' as it is ', which do show indeed that the Devil can quote Scripture to his purpose, but it is only right to add that the performance never rings quite true. In the New South Wales pamphlet, after triumphantly producing his cases, rather like a conjuror producing a rabbit out of a hat, he adds slyly, ' And who is there will deny that, in the scale of common law, a thousand unjudicial official precedents are not equal to one judicial one ' [31]—which is as much as saying to lawyers ' you see, I can handle your silly bag of tricks as well as you can your-selves, if I choose to give myself the trouble '. And of course it would be easy to show that in all these cases, it is not in fact law that he is concerned about, but policy.

More fundamental is his attitude towards legal technique and the problem of interpretation. Bentham's antagonism to professional lawyers goes deeper than his indignation at the self-seeking and corruption of which he constantly accuses them. It is a dislike for what they do ; and the characteristic thing about a lawyer is that he does not go into the ultimate constitution of the universe before discussing each case, but bases himself on some authority from which he proceeds to argue. In one form or another all lawyers are engaged on interpretation. Now Bentham recurs to the problem of interpretation a number of times,[32] and has some acute remarks to make on it. He even admits that a certain amount of it is unavoidable. But his object is to reduce the scope of it to the narrowest possible limits. One

[29] Vol. 10, pp. 174–175.
[30] What J. S. Mill says is no evidence for Bentham's attitude, but it seems to me that he never shows himself a truer Benthamite than when he says in his introduction to the *Rationale of Judicial Evidence* (Vol. 6, p. 202) ' The Editor has not thought it necessary to consult, on the state of the existing law, any other authorities than the compilations of Phillips, Starkie and others. These works were sufficiently authoritative for his purpose ; and if the state of the law be such that even these experienced lawyers can have misunderstood it, this simple fact proves more against the law than any remarks which the Editor can have grounded on the misconception '.
[31] Vol. 4, p. 261.
[32] *E.g.* Vol. 4, p. 312 sqq. *Limits of Jurisprudence Defined*, p. 252 sqq.

of the very few virtues which he finds in the English judicature is that in applying statutes they follow the expressed will of the legislator very closely [33]—a characteristic which does not find the same amount of favour with most theoretical writers to-day. His point of view is in fact, as every one knows, that of a legislator. In several places he quotes an alleged law of Bologna cited by Pufendorf to the effect that ' Whosoever draws blood in the streets shall be put to death ', and the unfortunate case of the surgeon who found a man ill in the street and bled him.[34] From this example he draws some important conclusions about the defects there may be in statutes and how a legislator should avoid them. But he says very little to help the lawyer who has to deal with a text which does in fact read in that way, and he does not say, as Aristotle does in an analogous case,[35] that from such laws arises the necessity for equity, and that equity is necessary precisely because of the difficulty in speaking correctly in general terms as a legislator has to do. He knows well the difficulty of speaking in general terms, and has advice for the legislator about how to get over it, but he is not interested in the lawyer's point of view.

I know that in thus separating the legislator rigidly from the lawyer I may be accused of adopting a typically nineteenth century point of view, and indulging in that ' legal pessimism ' which thinks of the lawyer as quite unconcerned with the activities of the legislator, and bound simply to ' construe ' what his sources say in accordance with the science of law. I know too that there are—especially today—many lawyers who are occupied in using their technical skill to produce legislation, whether supreme or subordinate, and that the process of litigation as conducted in the ordinary courts by barristers and solicitors holds a proportionately smaller place in legal life now than it did formerly. But I contend that the typical thing about a lawyer is that he is concerned with the application of rules to sets of circumstances. 'Even a legal draftsman has to keep his eye on the manner in which his words are likely to be applied by the technique, whether it be called legal or administrative, of his day, or he will fail in his function. Indeed if there were no such

[33] *Principles of the Civil Code* (Ogden's ed.), p. 156.
[34] Vol. 3, p. 207. *Limits,* p. 251. Cf. Blackstone's *Commentaries,* Vol. 1, p. 60.
[35] *Rhet.,* I, XIII, § § 13–14. (Cf. *Eth. Nic.,* V, X, § 4.)

technique to be known, there would be no justification for
having trained lawyers as draftsmen. This is bound to remain
true so long as we have any law—until in fact Plato's anti-legal
dream comes true and we are governed by philosopher kings,
who, being adept in the art of government, decide each case,
not according to rule, but as a good physician prescribes treatment, by ordering what will have the best results in the given
circumstances. This has not happened yet; there is still a
distinction between law and policy, which even the Soviet
Government has not found good to obliterate entirely. It consequently retains lawyers on its staff, although it may not give
them a very exalted position in the State.

To that typical function of applying rules, Bentham is, I
repeat, antagonistic. For him, as for his disciple, Austin, there
is no law but laws. In one place he speaks of ' monades of law ',
and actually says that you could count the laws in force at any
given moment [36]—a view which would leave no place for
general principles, standards and methods of interpretation, in a
word for legal technique. And his advice to legislators, which
is intended to avoid the necessity for interpretation, good though
it is in some respects, comes down in effect largely to great particularity in the provisions to be laid down. Even his researches
in language, which are coming to be honoured more in our day
than they were in his own,[37] did not convince him of the final
impossibility of saying exactly what you mean, or if that be not
impossible, at least of saying all that a legislator would have to
say within the compass of a manageable code. He still dreamed
the dream that the ordinary citizen would be able to read the
book and say ' Within this cover is the whole basis of my
rights '.[38]

Of course if he were successful there would be no need for
lawyers, or as he puts it himself, ' Expository jurisprudence, the
art of finding clear ideas to annex to the expressions of a man
whose ideas were not clear, instead of being the only branch
cultivated, would be thrown aside '.[39]

So set was Bentham on his own methods that he was ex-

[36] *Limits*, p. 262.
[37] See C. K. Ogden, *Bentham's Theory of Fictions*, and *Jeremy Bentham
1832–2032*.
[38] *Limits*, p. 331. (Cf. *Works*, Vol. 3, p. 193.)
[39] *Limits*, p. 330.

tremely critical of all codes produced by others which, even in the 'age of reason', relied in a greater or less degree upon traditional materials and were in fact the work of lawyers. For instance in his *View of a Complete Code of Law*,[40] he says, ' Of all the codes which legislators have considered as complete, there is not one which is so. The Danish is the most ancient code : it is dated 1683 ; the Swedish code is dated 1734 ; the code Frédéric 1751 ; the Sardinian 1770. In the preface to the Danish code it is expressly stated to be complete. However it contains nothing about taxes, no regulations relating to professions etc. . . . the code Frédéric, stated in its title page to be universal, is absolutely limited to civil law. . . . The Sardinian code recognises the Roman Law as its foundation, and frequently refers to it under the name of common law. It could not more effectually have plunged everything into uncertainty.' His judgment on the chief contributor to the French Code Civil is well known. ' Portalis is no more able than a pig to make a code with *reasons* to it. What mortal alive could be, who should take a code to make by a particular day, as a tailor would a pair of breeches? '[41] This was in 1802 before the code was ready. Another reference may not be so familiar. In a letter dated 1814 to the Emperor of Russia in which he offers his services in the department of legislation he says, speaking of the French and Bavarian codes, ' With mine before them, both these modern works took for their basis the jurisprudence of ancient Rome. Russia, at any rate, needs not any such incumbrance . . . codes upon the *French* pattern are already in full view. Speak the word, Sire, *Russia* shall produce a pattern of her own ; and then let Europe judge '.[42] About the best he can find to say of the French codes is that, whatever their individual merits, so great was the advantage of codified law that chaos would obviously have resulted if they had been abolished by the Restoration.[43] In fact, although almost any codification is better than none, his own method is by far the best. Yet this extraordinary man who invented the word ' codification ', who was its lifelong advocate, and who thought so highly of his own methods, never got within measurable distance of completing a draft, and his attempts seem

[40] Vol. 3, p. 206.
[41] Vol. 10, p. 396.
[42] Vol. 4, p. 514.
[43] Vol. 4, p. 500.

to show that if he had completed one its over-great particularity and probably its length would have made it hopeless from a practical point of view.

Negatively then my thesis is that Bentham was not a lawyer because he had no sympathy for, and indeed insufficient understanding of, legal technique, involving, as it does, at least some measure of submission to authority, and as the successful codes of modern times show, the employment in some measure of traditional materials.

Positively on the other hand, the fact that he was something other than a lawyer, and would have no truck with authority or tradition, meant that he could succeed where others failed, and gave him that insight which brushed aside all conventional explanations and all half-truths and went straight to the point in great matters and small. You may miss the half-tones, but you cannot deny the illumination.

The greatest example of his insight lies in his analytical work as a whole, of which it is obviously impossible to speak now. But take merely one fundamental point. We are accustomed now to the distinction formulated on the continent as that between subjective and objective right, and a high percentage of theoretical law books, especially of English books on Jurisprudence, go on the assumption that to say a man has a (subjective) right, can only mean that objective right, *i.e.* law, has imposed a duty on someone else. Austin has worked this idea into our bones. But Austin got it from Bentham, though he used rather different language, and Bentham claims priority for his analysis,[44] with at least some justification. Whether we agree or not, the power of penetration involved can hardly be exaggerated.

In more practical matters it is the same. One may be inclined sometimes to smile at his unrestrained strictures on lawyers, to whom he always attributes the basest of motives, and on the English legal system in general. But of his satirical description of Equity procedure,[45] Sir William Holdsworth says that it was substantially accurate, and is borne out by books of practice and the reports of royal commissions.[46] Again, he sees

---

[44] Vol. 3, p. 160; p. 180. 'This theory of services is new'.
[45] Vol. 6, p. 43.
[46] *History of English Law*, Vol. 9, p. 339. (Cf. *op. cit.*, p. 323, on Bentham's acuteness in perceiving the practical effect of the difference between the 'special' and the 'general' issue.)

straight through the usual talk about the 'sanction of nullity', and points out the absurdity of regarding it as a privilege to be absolved, *e.g.* in the case of wills, from rules of form. ' As if it were a favour done to a man to enable an impostor to dispose of his property in his name!—as if the exception could be beneficial, unless the rule were mischievous '.[47] Grand juries, which we have only recently got rid of, he calls ' purely mischievous ',[48] and he could see from his comparative studies what probably no one else saw until the great development of these studies in recent times, that English procedure is so different from Continental, that ' no other language affords anything like an equivalent for our word " trial " '.[49]

These instances are from the rules of judicial procedure, which were Bentham's chief legal interest, but let me end with an example from a different type of procedure—that of legislative bodies. His *Essay on Political Tactics*[50] was originally designed as practical advice to the French Assembly in the early days of the Revolution. It sets out Continental, especially French, as well as English methods, and the research involved cost Bentham a great deal of trouble.[51] Practically the effect of such recommendations as reached the French was negligible, for they were in no mood to be tutored by Englishmen.[52] But for the moment this is irrelevant. My point is that the arm-chair publicist shows here that for practical purposes all the great maxims of constitutional theory are not as important as the Standing Orders of the House of Commons. He who very seldom had a good word for the ' matchless constitution ' writes regarding such details of practice as follows, ' In this bye-corner, an observing eye may trace the original seed-plot of English liberty . . . the importance of these uninviting forms is no fine-spun speculation . . . political liberty depends everywhere upon the free action and frequent and genuine manifestation of the public will; but the free action and genuine manifestation of

---

[47] Vol. 6, p. 65.
[48] Vol. 6, p. 472.
[49] Vol. 6, p. 471.
[50] Vol. 2, pp. 299–373.
[51] Vol. 10, pp. 197, 219.
[52] 'Nous ne sommes pas des Anglais, et nous n'avons pas besoin des Anglais,' is said to have been the answer when a similar work by Romilly was presented. Halévy, *Formation du radicalisme philosophique*, Vol. 2, p. 24.

that will depend upon the mode of proceeding observed in going
through the several steps that must be taken before such a result
can be produced '.[53]

Today it is easy for us to see the truth of this, for we have
learnt it from our modern manuals of Constitutional Law.
Bentham saw it for himself, and to see it in his age required a
most uncommon power of penetration through form to essence,
and a remarkable freedom from inherited legal ways of thought.
He had indeed neither the typical virtues nor the typical vices of
a lawyer, but he had amazing horse-sense for a philosopher.

NOTES ON THE UNPUBLISHED MANUSCRIPTS

The lecture printed above was delivered at University College on
February 6, 1947. After the end of the Summer Term, I was
able to devote about a fortnight to the study of some of the
Bentham MSS. belonging to the College, which were kindly
made available in the Students' Room at the British Museum,
there being no place in the present condition (the result of
enemy action) of the College where they could be safely kept.
My object was to see if I could find any further evidence not
only, or even specially, of Bentham's knowledge of law, but of
the nature of his interest in it, of his technical equipment, and
of his method of work. I wanted to know what books he used,
and in particular whether there was any large number on
Roman and 'Rome-bred' law, and whether there was any
more evidence in the MSS. than in the published works of his
handling legal material as a lawyer does, with due interest in
exactitude and accuracy as well as wealth of citation. The
amount of MSS. I was able to look through in the time was very
small, but I was helped by a letter from Professor Everett who
recommended me a MS. called 'Critique of Criminal Jurisprudence'[54] on which Bentham worked from about 1774 to
about 1780, and by references to book-lists and similar material
in the catalogue compiled by Mr. A. Taylor Milne in 1937. On
the whole the little that I found seemed to confirm the ideas put
forward in the lecture.

First as regards book-lists. I found a few of these of different
sorts, some dating from about 1789 to 1809 of books to

[53] Vol 2, p. 332.
[54] Portfolios 69, 140, 159.

be bound;[55] the 'List of J.B's Books at Mr. Mill's' dated
October 16, 1826, which caused some coolness between the two
men, together with another connected list,[56] and a rather
pathetic note-book, inscribed on the cover 'Book Account
1801',[57] containing entries up to 1820. It has headings for
'Title of Book', 'To whom lent', 'When lent' and 'When
returned', and in the earlier years is neatly kept. But even then
the space for 'When returned' is seldom filled, and later the
entries become untidy, though there is an attempt to include
'books borrowed' and 'books desired'. It is of some interest
to note that in 1806 four books were lent to Dumont, and in
1805 five borrowed from Romilly. A letter of July 23, 1817, to
William Vaughan,[58] acknowledges the loan of books about the
U.S. and asks to be allowed to keep some. In particular
Bentham wants to have and pay for 'the fee-simple' of. the
*Philadelphia Gentleman's Annual Pocket Remembrancer for
1817*, though why does not appear. Another document which
gives some evidence of Bentham's reading, though not of books
which he ever necessarily had in his library, is dated '1827
Janvier 15' and headed 'Ouvrages en français que Mr. Bentham
prend la liberté de recommander à Mr. Herrera pour le compte
de Mr. Del Valle'.[59] It was apparently intended that the books
should be bought for the President of Guatemala to place in a
public library.

The general impression conveyed by these lists is, as one
might expect, catholicity, except that belles-lettres are excluded.[60]
There is even more history than perhaps some would expect, the
Herrera list especially including a number of French memoirs.
The lists of books to be bound are mostly divided under headings
(*e.g.* 'Poor', 'Prisons', 'Architecture', 'Ireland', 'America.')
among which 'Law' sometimes finds a place, sometimes other
legal titles, such as 'Juries', 'Libel', 'Penal Law', but the law
books are almost always considerably outnumbered by those on

55　Portfolios 108, ff. 115–120; 109, ff. 49–53; 169, f. 168.
56　Portfolio 10, ff. 187–188. Mill's letter, dated February 22, 1827, is
　　printed by Whittaker in his Report on the MSS. 2–3. (Cf. Halévy,
　　op. cit. (n. 50A), III, 473.)
57　British Museum Additional MSS. 33, 564. Correspondence and papers
　　of the family of Bentham, Vol. 28.
58　Portfolio 12, f. 12.
59　Portfolio 12, f. 370.
60　Unless one counts *Hudibras,* one of the books 'at Mr. Mill's'.

other subjects. Only one list[61] consists mainly of English Law books, and one other,[62] divided not by subjects, but into ' Folios and Quartos ' and ' Octavos and all under ', with ninety-eight items, consists to the extent of nearly half of Reports and other fairly technical legal works, such as *Palmer's Costs, 1796, Montefiores' Notarial Precedents, 1802* and *Bell's Bankruptcy Code, 1807.* Throughout the emphasis seems to be, however, on the working of institutions rather than on the ascertainment of legal rules, and this accounts not only for such items as the Lords' and Commons' Debates, but for the very high proportion of books on different aspects of public life in foreign countries.

Books on Roman law, even in its widest sense, are not many. The lists of those ' at Mr. Mill's ' include a Corpus Juris Civilis; Ferrières' *History of Roman Law,* translated by Beaver,[63] and Taylor's *Civil Law,*[64] as well as a Corpus Juris Canonici. Among books to be bound there are : Duck, *De usu et authoritate juris. civilis Romanorum,* 1689,[65] a copy of Justinian's Institutes dated 1643, and *Strykii Examen Juris Feudalis, 1689.* This last is no doubt the well-known work by the German civilian, Samuel Stryk, first published in 1675.[66] Pilati's *Lois civiles,* [67] which was one of the books borrowed by Dumont in 1806, is also concerned with Roman law, and was perhaps favoured by Bentham on account of its highly critical attitude.

There is a fair number of works on foreign, especially French, law, and Bentham's interest in Scots law is well in evidence. I have the impression that he was rather more at home with French law before than after the Revolution. One would, of course, expect considerable interest in the French codes, and

---

[61] Portfolio 109, f. 52.
[62] Portfolio 109, f. 49.
[63] *Supra,* n. (6). Claude-Joseph de Ferrière added this as the seventh volume to his edition of his father's translation of the Institutes. See *Biographie Universelle* (Michaud).
[64] *Elements of the Civil Law.* By John Taylor, LL. D., Cambridge, 1755. The author was more of a classical scholar than a lawyer, and expressly sets out to enrich the study of the law with a discussion of the manners and customs of the Roman people. The book is full of literary references both Latin and Greek.
[65] Translated into English by Beaver, London, 1774.
[66] Stintzing-Landsberg, *Geschichte der Deutschen Rechtswissenschaft,* III, 1. Notes, p. 44.
[67] No doubt *Traité des Lois Civiles* by C. A. Pilati di Tassulo, published at The Hague in 1774. I have not seen the book, which is not in the British Museum Catalogue, and take my information from Tipaldo's *Biografia degli Italiani illustri,* Vol. 6 (1838).

there is some evidence of it. Mr. Milne, in his 'description' on one folder,[68] even says 'an interesting fragment suggesting that Bentham had in mind a critical survey of the Code Napoleon', but if that is so he never got very far. The notes here include some maxims on draftsmanship[69] and some criticism of the arrangement of that part of the Code Civil which concerns 'Persons', especially marriage. An earlier set of notes of 1823 and the following year, is headed 'Procedure Code, Bonaparte's',[70] and in other places there are abstracts of code titles and notes on them.[71] If Bentham did intend anything like a commentary, it was probably the Code de Procédure Civile that he had in mind. In spite of his undoubted interest in criminal law, I did not come across any reference to the Code Pénal, and only a very few to the Code d' Instruction Criminelle.[72] The most coherent document is that of 1823. It begins with a familiar idea of Bentham's that the first step in procedure should be a free investigation by the judge. 'At the very opening the limit of the lawyer is apparent. The first title is[73] Summons . . . not initiatory audience. This summons is the act of the party : compliance with it is made obligatory. Thus the peace of every man is placed at the disposal of every other : why? only that (? suits) without ground may be (? instituted) and the number of suits be increased by the whole number of consciously groundless suits'. There follows more detailed criticism in the usual sarcastic vein on the system of serving the summons where immovable property is concerned. I am not sure that the system is completely understood. At any rate Bentham seems to have taken his information from the text alone, and not sought any explanation from books on French procedure, though he certainly had some in his library. Some comparisons with English procedure are interesting, but do not seem to include ideas outside his published works. ' In Bonaparte's system ', he says,[74] ' the aberrations are less enormous than in the English ',

---

[68] Portfolio 4, f. 2.
[69] E.g. ' 7. For completeness generalise ; ascending, proceeding in the way of ascent in the logical tree. 8. For correctness and clearness particularise ; proceeding in the way of descent in the logical tree '.
[70] Portfolio 54, ff. 193 sqq.
[71] Portfolios 31 and 97 ; dates 1827 and 1828.
[72] There is a table of headings of this code in a copyist's hand. Portfolio 97, f. 218.
[73] I.e. of the Code de Procédure Civile : ' Des Citations '.
[74] Portfolio 54, f. 202.

but the advantages are not all in favour of the French. His
objections to the system of collecting evidence are quite John
Bull-ish. 'Judge, sole evidence collector, and reporter of dᵒ,
between parties and witnesses and ultimately—decreeing Judges:
they knowing nothing but what he has pleased to give them: he
not responsible but to *them,* to whom his manner of conducting
himself is unknown'.[75] Another typical touch is in a comment
on § 42 of the Civil Procedure Code,[76] which deals with expert
witnesses: 'Gens de l'art instead of science: named by the
Judge not as anglicè by the party'. Here a trivial verbal criticism
is followed by one which goes to the root of the matter. This
difference between French and English procedure is now a commonplace, but may not have been so when Bentham wrote.
Throughout, the main interest is certainly in procedure and
arrangement. In one document concerned with 'nomography'
and contrasting Brougham's methods unfavourably with his own
he actually says 'Law reform means particularly procedure
reform',[77] and even when he is dealing with the Code Civil he
seems chiefly concerned to criticise the arrangement, as witness
the remarks already quoted on marriage and others on the
sections dealing with 'absence' (§§ 112–143), where he comments 'In J.B.'s Code the effect of these provisions will be
produced under the head of title by succession by the addition
of presumed death to actual death'.[78] So also opposite the
heading of Livre II (Des Biens et des differentes modifications
de la Propriété) he notes 'This should have come first'.[79]
Evidence concerning codes other than the French is slight in the
papers I have seen. There are a few interlinear notes in a list
of titles of the Belgian Civil Code,[80] a Table of Contents (in
English) of 'Carmer's Prussian Code'[81] and tables of Austrian
codes in their Italian form.[82] A date '1832 May 9th' on one
of these might be in Bentham's hand, but there is nothing more
of his.

[75] Portfolio 54, f. 194.   In a copyist's hand, but no one is likely to doubt
  the authenticity.
[76] Portfolio 31, f. 226.
[77] Portfolio 4, f. 93.
[78] Portfolio 31, f. 230.
[79] Portfolio 31, f. 221.
[80] Portfolio 31, f. 222.
[81] *I.e.* that of 1794.   Portfolio 97, f. 220.
[82] Portfolio 97, ff. 222–224.

Bentham in fact was not meant to be a commentator. He could never follow any other person's train of thought for long, but would always be off on his own. The exuberance of his own ideas, joined with that streak of indolence, which made it so difficult for him ever to complete his own works for publication, resulted also in a certain impatience of documentation. He had neither the lawyer's instinct for quoting authority, nor the scholar's (or pedant's) habit of exact references, while, on the other hand, his passion for exact statement of abstract principle led him to neglect 'exemplification'. He had, of course, learnt the ordinary English lawyers' method of citation in his early years, and can use it when he chooses. He also, of necessity, gives references to Bracton, Fitzherbert, Coke and others when he is dealing with historical questions, such as frankpledge [83] or the meaning of 'felony'.[84] But any one who looks in the MSS. for more evidence of exact research and documentation than is to be found in the published works is, to judge by the samples examined, doomed to disappointment. It was interesting too, to come across a fairly elaborate 'Apology for non-exemplification' in the 'Critique of Criminal Jurisprudence', in which he says, in effect, that he has endeavoured to make his work so clear that examples are unnecessary.[85] Giving examples does, as he remarks, involve a great deal of time and labour, and he had so much to say that he was always in a hurry. This trait comes out pretty clearly in his correspondence, but the list of books recommended to the President of Guatemala [86] furnishes some new examples. It is headed by the note 'On n'a pas eu le tems de les ranger selon l'ordre des matières' and, although purporting to be a list of works in French, contains several entries like this: 'Mill. Histoire de l'Inde Britannique, traduit de l'Anglais, s'il y en a'. Even vaguer is 'Dictionnaire de Chymie— Demandez à M. Dumeril par le moyen de M. Say lesquels sont les meilleurs, les plus recents'. But the cream is, I think, provided by the following: 'Mably: ses oeuvres ne valent rien hormis peut-être un qu'on ne se rappelle pas' and 'Mémoire (? à l') histoire de Madame de Maintenon par l'homme que Voltaire a critiqué'. One wonders whether the list was ever used, and if so what Mr. Herrera made of these entries.

[83] Portfolio 140, f. 85.
[84] Portfolio 140, f. 112.
[85] Portfolio 140, f. 21.
[86] Above, note 57.

PART TWO—ENGLISH LAW

CHAPTER 2

BENTHAM AND ENGLISH PENAL REFORM

Margery Fry

' I do not know a single law reform effected since Bentham's day which cannot be traced to his influence '—SIR HENRY MAINE : *Early History of Institutions*, p. 397.

BENTHAM AND HIS GROUP

BENTHAM'S contributions to the reform of penal law, procedure, and sanctions were largely conditioned by his own very unusual personality. His greatest successes were gained when he worked with the grain of that personality, his vexatious failures arose when he failed to recognise the nature of his own powers and limitations. ' It would be easy ', writes Leslie Stephen, ' to make a paradox by calling Bentham at once the most practical and most unpractical of men '.[1] This easy paradox does not probe far enough into the contradictions of his nature. In the arrangements of his daily life, at any rate in his later years, he was methodical to the point of fussiness, but an extreme dependence upon routine is often rather the leaning upon a crutch than the more flexible activity of a person who is thoroughly at home in the business of living. Some of his excursions into the arrangement of life, whether in his steam-heated house with special arrangements of pipes under his own seat, or in the extremely detailed plans into which he entered in his description of his ' Panopticon ' and other projected institutions, reveal a curious delight in mechanical contrivances which one may guess to have been due rather to his close intimacy with his engineer brother, Samuel, than to any natural gift for handling matter.

When Bentham moves into the world of abstract thought his mastery is at once apparent. Here he is completely at home. It was in a flash of real self-knowledge that he marked out for himself, at the age of twenty, the career which he followed, with extraordinary pertinacity, into extreme old age.

[1] Leslie Stephen, *English Utilitarians*, I, p. 233.

20

Between six and seven years old [2] he had been humiliated by his inability to answer the question ' What is genius? ' sprung upon him in learned company by his too-proud father. The question haunted him for years. At twenty, relying on an etymology of his own, he discovered the word to mean invention or production.

' Have I a genius for anything? What can I produce? ' That was the first inquiry he made of himself. Then came another, ' What of all earthly pursuits is the most important? ' Législation, was the answer Helvetius gave. ' And have I indeed a genius for legislation? I gave myself the answer, fearfully and tremblingly—Yes! '

It is in the realm of human relationships that Bentham's strength and weakness are most strangely intermixed, and his knowledge of his own qualifications seems most uncertain.

He was in no sense a systematic student of psychology; one gets the impression that his picture of human nature is largely a mirror image of his own mental make-up. And the very fact of his being an exceptional person falsifies his estimate of more ordinary people. It could hardly be otherwise, in so far as he judged human nature by his own. Never quite a child, yet never quite growing out of childhood, reasonable to the point of analysing such remnants of unreason as still remained in him (his fear of ghosts, his minor jealousies, for example), devoured by intellectual curiosity from earliest childhood, so that, his material needs being always more or less adequately provided for, he lived largely in a world which the average man hardly guesses at, he can never have known what it was to meet on terms of intimacy the common run of humanity. In the few such minglings which he made, with the teasing servants of his infancy, with bullying undergraduates, or with the trio of rogues with whom he journeyed to Russia—in such contacts there is an incongruity which seems almost shocking.

Neither the apathetic mentality nor the over-mastering passions of the ' average ' man found any place in his character. And if this is true of the average it is even more significant when we compare Bentham's picture of the criminal evolved out of his inner consciousness, with the actual types which drift through the law courts into the prisons. The Second Rule of his ' Moral

[2] *Works,* 10, pp. 26, 27.

Arithmetic' tells us [3] that 'no man engages in a career of crime, except in the hope of impunity . . . in all cases of offence there is a calculation of the chances for and against'. A statement like this reveals Bentham as a student of man in the abstract rather than of men.

We may say then that Bentham was not well qualified for day to day relations with people of little ability and less education. His proposal to become himself the Manager of his own Panopticon never, mercifully for him, came to the point of acceptance. One is aghast at the thought of what such hourly contact with the criminal classes of London would have brought about. But with those of his own calibre things were far otherwise. He was the founder and leader of a group of men of great intellectual ability, many of them of outstandingly noble and disinterested characters. If Bentham had not left a single written word we could have deduced something as to his mental eminence and his complete sincerity from the records of those who were not only content, but proud to acknowledge him as their master. Romilly, the two Mills, O'Connell, Dumont, Brougham and, of a later date, Macaulay and John Austin make indeed a brilliant constellation of which he was the α star. And it was as his ideas passed, whether in written form or in action, through the hands of these men, that they leavened the lump of English thought.

That his personal relations with his friends and followers were not uniformly easy seems to have made little difference to the reverence—no other word is strong enough—with which they regarded his teaching. But his intimates seem sometimes to have felt a mixture of exasperation with their admiration. This is vividly expressed by Brougham. Brougham had passed [4] from being the object of an embarrassingly jocose partiality on the part of the 'dear grandpapa' who nourished his 'dear sweet little poppet' (who was about to make a great speech upon law reform) with the 'pap' of the true doctrine, through facetious scolding and the verdict that the mountain had been delivered of a mouse, to the hardly more embarrassing position of being the object of a disparaging pamphlet,[5] yet he was not turned by

[3] *Theory of Legislation* (ed. Ogden), p. 325.
[4] Leslie Stephen, *English Utilitarians*, 2, p. 226, and Bentham, *Works*, 5, p. 555.
[5] Lord Brougham *Displayed. Works*, 5.

wounded vanity from his esteem for Bentham's intellectual greatness, however it may have tinged his view of him as a man. In
the introduction to his speeches [6] published six years after the
philosopher's death, he seems to relive the whole range of his
emotions towards his former mentor.

His description begins with a fanfare of enthusiasm : ' The
age of Law Reform and the age of Jeremy Bentham are one
and the same. He is the father of the most important of all
the branches of Reform, the leading and ruling department of
human improvement. No one before him had ever seriously
thought of exposing the defects in our English system of Jurisprudence '.[7]

' He might be said to be the first legal philosopher that had
appeared in the world '.[8]

But after describing the intellectual eminence and the ' un-
remitting perseverance ' of the philosopher and his wide learning,
Brougham passes on to an unflattering account of Bentham's
character.[9]

> ' His honesty was unimpeachable, and his word might,
> upon any subject, be taken as absolutely conclusive, what-
> ever motives he might have for distorting or exaggerating
> the truth. But he was, especially of late years, of a some-
> what jealous disposition. . . . His impatience to see the
> splendid reforms, which his genius had projected, accom-
> plished before his death, increasing as the time of his
> departure drew nigh, made him latterly regard even his
> most familiar friends only as instruments of reformation, and
> gave a very unamiable and indeed revolting aspect of
> callousness to his feelings towards them. . . .
> ' Into all these unamiable features of his character, . . .
> there entered nothing base or hypocritical. If he felt little
> for a friend, he pretended to no more than he felt. If his
> sentiments were tinged with asperity and edged with spite,
> he was the first himself to declare it ; and no one formed a
> less favourable or a more just judgment of his weaknessess
> than he himself did, nor did any one pronounce such judg-
> ments with a severity that exceeded the confessions of his

---

[6] *Speeches of Lord Brougham*, Vol. 2, pp. 287 and 299.
[7] *Ibid.*, p. 287.
[8] *Ibid.*, p. 288.
[9] *Ibid.*, pp. 297, 298.

own candour. Upon the whole then he presented an object of admiration and gratitude, in his private character he was formed rather to be respected and studied, than beloved '.

The strange coldness which Bentham showed in valuing the reforms of Romilly find their explanation in this biographical note. It is true that Romilly died almost without achievement, yet posterity sees in his labours the necessary spade work for the cause of humanising the ferocious penal laws of his time, and there is something rather painfully ungenerous in Bentham's reference to his ' reformuncules ' and his statement that ' Romilly had the ear of the Chancellor, . . . and so he got some of his little miniature reforms adopted. Had they been considerable they would have been resisted with all Lord Eldon's might '.[10]

BENTHAM'S THEORIES AND PLANS FOR LAW REFORM

In fact Bentham's plan of law reform was not to press for a series of ' reformuncules ', dealing with scandalous injustices or cruelties one by one. Yet it would be altogether wrong to conclude that Bentham was indifferent to even partial reform. Both his books and his correspondence show the intensity of his hatred for each separate cruelty, as well as his distrust of the whole lack of system under which they were perpetrated.

If then we observe a certain undervaluing of piecemeal reforms in his references to them, we should attribute it more to his impatience to see a comprehensive attack upon the whole condition of the Law than to a petty vanity.

After a first frustrated hope [11] of going into Parliament for one of Lord Lansdowne's pocket boroughs, Bentham never made any attempt to enter political life. We have then the strange picture of a man whose long life was almost wholly spent in projects of legislation who yet himself took no active part in the public life of his time. He lived apart, secluded, surrounded by followers of great ability whom he regarded, perhaps too much, as tools for the achievement of the great work to which he had dedicated himself, as apostles to whom he confided his absorbing doctrine. He tolerated no back-sliding, no complacence over partial victories. For him nothing less than the embodiment in

---

10 *Works,* 10, p. 186.
11 *Works,* 10, pp. 229 *et seq.*

law of his whole philosophy of the relation of the State to the citizen could be success.

He was a man of great originality, yet the outlines of that philosophy came ready to his hand in the work of a far less subtle thinker—the young Italian nobleman whose book *Dei Delitti e delle Pene* appeared in 1764. Its influence spread rapidly; the times were ripe for a reconsideration of the theory of legal penalties.

Beccaria held that laws should be based on public utility, not, as hitherto, on the passions of the few; he laid great stress upon the 'greatest happiness' principle, as the foundation of legislation. Promptness and certainty of justice; clear laws in the vernacular, known to the people, are essential to good government. The measure of criminality should be the injury done to society, offences toward God which do not endanger the public security should be left to His judgment alone. A prisoner should have time and opportunity to prepare his defence, he should not be forced to take an oath—'no oath has ever yet made any criminal speak the truth'.[12]

Such was the foundation upon which Bentham began to build, and whose main lines he always followed, though he held that even in Beccaria's work there was some reasoning drawn from false sources.[13] He was in particular horrified at Beccaria's suggestion that the right of property is 'a terrible right, which perhaps is not necessary'.[14] Where he criticises, however, it is generally with a suggestion of apology to the predecessor whose 'arms were of celestial temper.'[15]

It would be impossible within the limits of this chapter to give an adequate account of the theory of legislation which Bentham elaborated upon the simple lines of Beccaria's short treatise. Nor would it be useful for a far less skilled hand to attempt to do again what has been finely done by Leslie Stephen and Halévy. Bentham himself, beginning with the study of the penal law, was carried by the logic of this thinking, since both 'rights and obligations are the children of the law',[16] into an

---

[12] For Beccaria's views see Farrer: *Crimes and Punishments*, containing a translation of the treatise.
[13] *Principles of Legislation*, p. 67.
[14] *Op. cit.*, p. 114.
[15] *Op. cit.*, p. 76.
[16] *Works*, 3, p. 166.

analysis of the whole structure of government. But the mass of his writings upon the penal code alone is large, though in its published form it contains many repetitions.

Here we must restate some of his outstanding contentions; leaving aside the question as to whether Bentham regarded the 'utility principle' as a finished philosophy of ethics, or simply, as Maine thought,[17] as a working rule of legislation, and without attempting to probe exactly what he understood by it or discuss its final validity.

Bentham adopted from Beccaria the doctrine that what the earlier writer had called (in a phrase of which the mathematical vagueness is maddening), 'the greatest happiness divided amongst the greatest number', but which Bentham usually prefers to call the 'utility principle', must be the foundation of penal law. When once this is accepted it is no longer possible to regard the whole apparatus of judgment and penalty as existing for 'the punishment of wickedness and vice'.

> 'The degree of sinfulness of an action', wrote Beccaria,[18] 'depends on the unsearchable wickedness of the heart, which cannot be known by finite beings without a revelation'

and Bentham declares that whilst

> 'morality and especially religion . . . form the necessary complement to legislation'[19] they have different functions and cover a different area of human actions. 'Legislation has the same centre with morals, but it has not the same circumference'.[20]

'It is indisputable truth'[21] (he represents an objector as saying), 'that no act should be punished criminally without a criminal intention. Is it not so? I don't know. In the first place I don't understand you. I suspect you don't altogether understand yourself. Settle with yourself what you mean by the word "intention"; and then state your question to the principle of utility. If you get an answer that is fit to satisfy you it must be from that'.

In his consistent desire to prevent the law from taking

[17] Maine, *Early History of Institutions*, 1890 ed., p. 399.
[18] From translation by Farrer: *Crimes and Punishments*, p. 201.
[19] *Principles of Legislation*, p. 65.
[20] *Principles of Legislation*, p. 60.
[21] *Works*, 10, p. 141.

cognisance of moral guilt, as being a matter upon which it is quite incompetent to pronounce, Bentham establishes his own criteria for the gravity of an act. The evils produced by an anti-social action are elaborately classified.[22] They are first grouped according to the persons who suffer from them : *viz.:*

1. Private offences against assignable persons other than the offender himself.

2. Offences against oneself—but as these are later swept into the limbo of imaginary offences they have little importance in the general analysis.

3. Semi-public offences which threaten danger to a portion of the community.

4. Public offences which produce some common danger to all the members of the State.

After the further classification of offences according to their nature, Bentham proceeds to a consideration of their bad effects. The ' evil of the first order ' which an act produces is the same whether it was done ' knowingly and willingly or unwillingly and undesignedly '. ' But the alarm which results is very different '. It is in this cleft between danger and alarm that Bentham finds the place to graft his theory that the character of the offenders justifies the State in its gradation of penalties even where two crimes appear identical. It must be admitted that in describing ' character ' he sometimes wavers from the use of purely neutral names, and such words as ' wickedness ' and ' depravity ' creep in. His evaluation of the gravity of various crimes is interesting, though sometimes questionable. Under the circumstances which make alarm greater or less are listed *inter alia* the intention of the delinquent, his motive, his character (including relapses) and the position which has furnished him an opportunity to commit the offence. Rather oddly, as it seems to us, Bentham considers that an offence committed by a person in a position which gives special opportunity for its commission causes less alarm than one which anybody may commit. He argues that the extortions of an officer of police cause less alarm than the robberies of a highwayman (but *judges* undertaking to rob, kill or tyrannise will cause an alarm proportioned to the

---

[22] For this classification, see *Principles of Legislation:* Principles of the Penal Code, Part 1.

extent of their powers).[23] It is to be inferred that punishments
for failure in positions of trust will in general be lightened,
though to most modern people such crimes will seem eminently
calculated to undermine the sense of confidence in human relations.

It is on this analysis of evil that the legislator should base the
decision as to what acts must be treated as offences and what
punishment allotted. ' Legislation, which hitherto has been
founded in a great measure only upon the quicksands of prejudice
and instinct, ought at last to be built upon the immovable basis
of sensations and experience. It is necessary to have a moral
thermometer to make perceptible all the degrees of happiness and
misery. This is a term of perfection which it is not possible to
reach ; but it is well to have it before our eyes '.[24]

' The whole of government is but a tissue of sacrifices ' [25]—
a balancing of greater and lesser evils, of greater and lesser satis-
factions, the suffering of a punished criminal goes duly down on
the debit side, and must be balanced by some greater good in the
credit column ; even the gratification of revenge, within legal
bounds, on the part of the injured person is entered as a ' good '.
' Everything which implies a manifest pain to the offender,
implies a pleasure of vengeance to the party injured '.[26]

But whilst the natural feelings of an injured person are
allowed for, Bentham warns us that the object of the law is not
vengeance.[27] Punishment alone is not sufficient for ameliorating
the evil, satisfaction is required.

And since pecuniary penalties are on the whole less painful
than the others, and pecuniary redress is more satisfactory than
mere vindictiveness, compensation of the injured party stands
very high in Bentham's estimation as a valuable instrument, it
' will answer the purpose of punishment but punishment will not
answer the purpose of compensation. By compensation therefore, the two great ends of Justice are both answered at a time,
by punishment only once '.[28]

' Laws are everywhere very imperfect upon this point—

[23] *Op. cit.*, p. 246.
[24] *Op. cit.*, p. 102.
[25] *Op. cit.*, p. 124.
[26] *Op. cit.*, p. 128.
[27] *Op. cit.*, p. 281.
[28] MS. Portfolio 98, f. 4.

. . . Punishment, which, if it goes beyond the limit of necessity, is a pure evil, has been scattered with a prodigal hand. Satisfaction, which is purely a good, has been dealt out with the most evident parsimony '.[29]

Even in the case of homicide satisfaction is due to the heirs of the victim.[30] Where there is a clash of interests, ' What is due to an injured party under the title of satisfaction ought to be paid in preference to what is due to the public by way of fine '.[31]

Bentham even suggests that where only inadequate satisfaction can be obtained from the offender, the state itself should provide restitution.[32]

But though compensation is Bentham's favourite remedy for crime, he is under no illusion as to its being the only sanction necessary.

In fact, the allocation of punishments occupied him continually. The duty of the legislator is, on his theory, to secure immunity from crime by offering to the potential law-breaker a calculation in which the probable pains following illegal action will just over-balance the probable pleasures which it may procure him. The process is as follows (though here described in reference to capital crimes only) :

' When a person feels himself under temptation to commit a crime punishable with death, his determination to commit it, or not to commit it, is the result of the following calculation :

' He ranges on one side the clear portion of happiness he thinks himself likely to enjoy in case of his abstaining; on the other he places the clear happiness he thinks himself likely to enjoy in case of his committing the crime, taking into the account the chance there appears to him to be, that the punishment threatened will abridge the duration of that happiness. I do not say that this calculation is made with all the formality with which I have represented it. But however, well or ill, the calculation is made; else a man could not act as he is supposed to do '.[33]

In order that the calculation may be truly made the penalties

[29] *Principles of Legislation*, p. 284.
[30] *Op. cit.*, p. 283.
[31] *Op. cit.*, p. 321.
[32] *Op. cit.*, p. 317.
[33] Fragment on Government. *Works*, I, pp. 445, 446.

to offences affixed by law must be clearly laid down. The law must also decree certain grounds upon which the punishments should be modified, it must leave a certain latitude to the tribunals (but not an unlimited freedom) to proportion their judgment to the particular circumstances.[34]

Bentham undertakes an inquiry into the nature of the penalties which the law may prescribe, with their advantages and disadvantages.

Seven qualities [35] are described as desirable in a punishment: it should be *susceptible of more or less, equal to itself* (*i.e.* be made to correspond to the different circumstances and sensibilities of different offenders so as to produce equality of result); *commeasurable* (so that the prospective offender may make his calculations between greater and less offences); *analogous to the offence* (offences of cupidity, insolence and idleness would be punished respectively by fines, humiliation and compulsory labour or forced rest); *exemplary* (everything must be done to render it impressive to the populace); *economical* (*i.e.* of severity only just necessary to answer its end); *remissible* or *revokable*.

It will also be a merit if it can reform the offender, can take away his power of doing injury, or furnish an indemnity to the injured party.[36]

The legislation must avoid such punishments as shock established prejudices.

In the light of these principles Bentham examines different types of punishment and in the course of this examination the essential humanity of the man comes out clearly though somewhat erratically.

His strongest condemnation was reserved for the infliction of death as a sanction.

' The more attention one gives to the punishment of death ', he writes,[37] ' the more he will be inclined to adopt the opinion of Beccaria—that it ought to be disused '.

> ' Whence originated the prodigal fury with which the punishment of death has been inflicted? It is the effect of resentment which at first inclines to the greatest rigour;

---

[34] *Theory of Legislation*, Part 3.
[35] *Theory of Legislation*, pp. 336 *et seq.*
[36] To these Dumont later added Simplicity. Leslie Stephen, *English Utilitarianism*, I, p. 267.
[37] *Theory of Legislation*, pp. 353, 354.

and of an imbecility of soul, which finds in the rapid destruction of convicts the great advantage of having no further occasion to concern one's self about them '.

And again, two years before his death, he writes to his ' Fellow-Citizens of France' that the question is one which has been familiar to him for ' three-score years or thereabouts' and explicitly affirms his view that the death penalty should be abolished for all offences.

We must not overlook the real courage that was needed to formulate and declare his opinion of capital punishment so unequivocally in an age when it was one of the almost universally accepted sanctions of the penal law. The levity with which Parliament passed laws involving its use was illustrated by Mackintosh, who wrote ' Every Member of Parliament has had it in his power to indulge his whims and caprices on that subject; and if he could do nothing else he could create a capital felony . . . '.[38]

' Mr. Burke once told me that on a certain occasion when he was leaving the House one of the messengers called him back, and on his saying that he was going on urgent business replied, " Oh, it will not keep you a single moment; it is only a felony without benefit of clergy " '.

It was such callous indifference which sharpened the edge of Bentham's indignation.

Yet there were elements in the setting of the most horrible of public executions, those carried out under the Inquisition, which Bentham would gladly have borrowed for his criminal code.

Believing intensely as he did in the force of deterrence, in ; the motive power of fear, he was constantly searching for punishments which would appeal to popular imagination without the infliction of real injury. ' It is the real punishment which does all the evil; it is the apparent punishment which does all the good '.[39] An *auto da fe* with a dummy victim, if only the secret could be kept, would be an ideal punishment. With something of gusto he describes the imposing and terrifying ceremonial, with the scaffold spread with black, the officers of justice in mourning and the executioner covered by a mask.

---

[38] Mackintosh, *Miscellaneous Works*, 3, p. 371.
[39] *Theory of Legislation*, p. 399.

In an unpublished manuscript note Bentham carries this idea to still further lengths. It would appear probable that here, too, the 'execution' is to be a symbolic one, avoiding death but *not* discomfort!

'PUNISHMENT MURDER by Poison

'In the procession to execution the condemned might have hung in each ear transparent bottles filled with a black fluid with a label being tyed to each, marked in large letters " POISON ".

'He might be compelled in part of execution to drink a dose of the Poison with which the crime was perpetrated, proper remedies for the producing of an evacuation being at hand to be administered after a certain interval '.[40]

The desire to devise punishments which should fulfil the triple object of being at once 'analgous to the offence', 'exemplary' and not *too* painful to the offender led Bentham into some strange and rather grim inventions which are however abandoned in his later plans; one gains the impression of an increasing hatred of all cruelty as he grows older.

The punishment which occupied far the largest place in Bentham's consideration was that of the 'ordinary prison'. He wrote of it as 'a school in which wickedness is taught by surer means than can ever be employed for the inculcation of virtue '.[41] Into his schemes for its reformation we shall have to inquire later.

We must never forget that the whole complex structure of Bentham's scheme for the prevention of crime rests upon his demand for a complete reframing of the penal code in accordance with the principle of utility. To moderate or alter penalties was not enough: the Augean stable must be rebuilt rather than cleaned.

'The mildness of the national character is in contradiction to the laws, and, as might be expected, it is that which triumphs; the laws are eluded; pardons are multiplied; offences are overlooked; testimony is excluded; and juries, to avoid an excess of severity, often fall into excess of indulgence. Thence results a system of penal law, incoherent, contradictory, uniting violence to weakness, dependent on the humour of a judge, varying from circuit to circuit, sometimes sanguinary, sometimes null '.[42]

[40] MSS. University College, London, Library, Portfolio 96, f. 10.
[41] *Theory of Legislation*, p. 352.
[42] *Op. cit.*, pp. 354, 355.

Such a state of affairs, he thought, could never be remedied until the uncertainties and contradictions of 'judge-made' or common law were reduced to nothing, and the confusion of the Statute Book brought to the order of a coherent code.

In face of this vast design, to which he had consciously devoted his life and his 'genius' and which he fondly hoped to see fulfilled in his own lifetime, we can understand Bentham's impatience with partial reform, his disappointment in minor successes of his lieutenants. In fact, the first great inroads into the jungle of English Criminal Law were achieved by a man who could certainly not be reckoned as one of his disciples.

THE WORK OF PEEL

As in still better known incidents of his political career, Sir Robert Peel recognised popular items in his opponents' programme and lifted them, unburdened by acknowledgments, into his own field of action. No mention of the labours of Romilly or Mackintosh, still less of the name of Bentham, occurs in his speeches, though it is easy to interpret as a hit at Bentham his reference to its being 'the fashion to impute to' the legal profession 'an unwillingness to remove the uncertainty and obscurity of the law, from the sordid desire to benefit by its perplexity' 'This is a calumny', he added, 'which I know to be unfounded'.[43] It was perhaps unfortunate that Bentham's feelings about judges and lawyers had been so freely and uncompromisingly expressed! It is difficult to read today, without a sense of exasperation, the ponderous speeches, with no spark of warmth about them, in which Peel urged the 'nicely calculated less and more' of his reforms, which crept forward, 'going on' said Bentham, 'but at such a pace, that after some hundred years employed in doing it the business will be still to do'.[44]

Peel successfully opposed Sir James Mackintosh's motion as to the expediency of removing the death penalty in a large number of cases on the ground that the House might find itself committed by so general a motion to approval of all its points.[45]

To us today it would not seem (as it certainly cannot have seemed to Bentham) that Parliament would have been pledged to a dangerous leniency if it had accepted them all.

The implications of the speech in which Peel opposed the

[43] Peel, *Speeches*, I, p. 409.
[44] *Works*, 5, p. 595.
[45] Peel, *Speeches*, I, p. 243.

motion were that if the matter were left to him the Government would itself take action in most of these cases but would resolutely oppose the abolition of the death sentence for larceny or forgery. All the resolutions were negatived.

To us the principal interest of this abortive debate is the clarity with which it marks the descent of Peel's subsequent reforms, through Mackintosh, who took over as a solemn duty the continuation of Romilly's work, from Romilly's acknowledged leader, Bentham. It seems to have been this debate which finally decided Mackintosh that he, in opposition, could do nothing.

With rare self-forgetfulness he was ready to hand over the work to his more powerful opponent. He was however, wise enough to feel that his labours were not wasted. ' His own failures he knew had been as necessary a part of the complex process by which truth is diffused through the public mind as the frosts of winter to the fertility of the natural soil '.[46]

Even Bentham in his calmer moments admitted some advance in Peel's reforms. Whilst reiterating, in 1827, his view of their inadequacy, he adds, ' . . . it is now no longer considered as a mark of disaffection towards the state, and hostility to social order and to law in general, to express an opinion that the existing law is defective, and requires a radical reform. Thus much Mr. Peel's attempts have already done for the best interests of his country; and they will in time do much more. A new spirit is rising in the profession itself '.[47]

However much we may regret that Peel failed to acknowledge his debt to his predecessors, the links between Bentham, Romilly, Mackintosh and Peel sufficiently indicate the direct descent of his activities from the Utilitarian philosophy, and in estimating the influence of Bentham upon our criminal law we must admit the great importance of Peel's work. His *Five Acts,* consolidating and amending the laws relating to larceny, malicious injuries to property, offences against the person, forgery and coinage offences were all, he said with justifiable pride, in 1828, comprised in one small volume, yet contained the substance of what was before spread over one hundred and thirty acts of parliament.[48]

[46] R. T. Mackintosh, *Life of Sir J. Mackintosh,* 2, p. 391.
[47] *Works,* 6, p. 203.
[48] Peel, *Speeches,* 1, p. 529.

The *Five Acts* greatly diminished the number of capital offences, although, in spite of the efforts of Mackintosh and others, death was still retained for many crimes. It was not until 1861 that the offences punishable by death were finally reduced to their present number.

Peel not only carried out the mitigation of the savage penal laws of this time ; he followed also, however grudgingly, Bentham's teaching as to the need for clearing the tangle of the Criminal Law. As we have seen, the mere consolidation of existing provisions, accompanied by the cutting away of dead wood and ' sleeping statutes ' and some small measures of actual reform, was far from fulfilling Bentham's dream of a logical coherent code of law, based upon a ' moral arithmetic ' of pleasures and pains, yet it was a matter of no small importance to have the main elements of criminal law reduced to something like order. Then, as now, the vast majority of crimes—as opposed to minor offences—were those against property. They were dealt with by no less than ninety-two statutes. Many of these enactments dealing with some particular form of theft or injury to property were spatch-cocked into Acts dealing with quite other matters. Thus one Act dealt with the transport of sugar from the American colonies, frauds by bankrupts, importation of naval stores from the American colonies, the measurement of coals in the city and liberty of Westminster, and the preventing the stealing or destroying of *madder roots!* [49]

The receiving of stolen goods was dealt with by twelve statutes.[50] Such multiplicity of laws left a number of loopholes, since each covered but a certain class of offences, whilst others fell between. It was not an offence in the eye of the law to rob a ready furnished house, though it was a very serious one to rob a ready furnished lodging.[50] Whilst you might not steal or destroy fish in a stream passing ' in or through ' an estate you could do so with impunity where the stream passed along the boundary between two estates.[51]

A man indicted under an act against stealing from ships on navigable rivers escaped because the barge from which he stole was aground.[52]

[49] Peel, *Speeches*, 1, p. 400.
[50] *Op. cit.*, p. 401.
[51] *Op. cit.*, p. 401.
[52] Leslie Stephen, *English Utilitarians*, 1, p. 204.

A notorious receiver of stolen goods could be severely punished for buying a glass bottle or a pewter pot, but would get off if he received £10,000 or £20,000 in cash, bank-notes or bills.[53]

Offenders might also escape on the ground of minute technicalities in the matter of trial. 'Ought the murderer to have all the benefit of acquittal?' asked Peel, 'because the murdered man had three Christians names, and only two of them are set forth in the indictment?'[54] The reduction to order of this mass of incoherent legislation was indeed an achievement of which any statesman might be proud. Peel is careful however to disclaim any far-reaching intentions of subverting ancient institutions, or relinquishing what was practically good 'for the chance of speculative and uncertain improvement'.[55] The lawyers needed not to be apprehensive lest a Bentham come to judgment!

SOME LATER LAW REFORMS

No one can have failed to see the influence of Bentham, together with that of Romilly and Mackintosh, in the shortened list of capital offences, and the removal of some of the worst anomalies of the statute law which resulted from Peel's legislation. In these instances the pedigree of reform seems fairly clear. It is obviously more difficult to assign Bentham's exact share in developments of the criminal law as we get further away from him in time, yet very competent authorities are decisive in affirming its force. Thus Dicey wrote that 'the name of one man, it is true, can never adequately summarise a whole school of thought, but from 1825 onwards the teaching of Bentham exercised so potent an influence that to him is fairly ascribed that thoroughgoing though gradual amendment of the law of England which was one of the main results of the Reform Act'.[56]

Sir William Holdsworth indicates the political track of this influence: 'When the age of reform began in the nineteenth century the leaders of thought were the new Whigs who had learned from Bentham, and not the old Whigs who had learned from Burke'.[57]

[53] Colquhoun, *Treatise on the Police of the Metropolis* (1806), p. 9.
[54] Peel, *Speeches*, 1, p. 407.
[55] *Op. cit.*, 1, p. 409.
[56] Dicey, *Law and Opinion in England* (1914), p. 126.
[57] Holdsworth, *Some Makers of English Law*, p. 246.

It may be interesting here to note the subsequent history
of a few of the changes in the list of crimes advocated by our
author.

In particular it is tempting to trace his influence in a very
special degree in the series of Acts in 1822, 1833 and 1835 which
for the first time brought cruelty to animals within the scope of
the criminal law. At any rate this legislation must have caused
him lively satisfaction; his fondness for animals was one of the
most engaging traits in his character. It was their 'love of
pussies' that first brought Bentham and Dumont together, and
the historic friendship between Bentham and Romilly had as a
bond of union their respect for animals.

Bentham explicitly urges the need of extending legislation
to the interests of non-human beings. 'It is proper', he says,
'. . . to forbid every kind of cruelty to animals, whether by
way of amusement or for the gratification of gluttony. . . .
Men must be permitted to kill animals; but they should be forbidden to torment them. . . . Why should the law refuse its
protection to any sensitive being?'[58]

To a man with Bentham's sense of justice any punishment
of which the suffering was multiplied by its effect on innocent
people was abhorrent. He protested strongly against those which
were made to bear upon the innocent for the sake of an oblique
effect upon the guilty.

Such were the 'corruption of blood'[59] of which the effect
was that descent could not be traced through the person whose
blood was corrupted, and the forfeiture depriving the family of
a condemned man of the very means of subsistence. Both these
punishments, mainly applicable in cases of treason, awaited the
year 1870 before they were abolished,[60] in spite of Bentham's
reasoned attack upon them.

The Infanticide Act of 1922, eighty-six years after his death,
at last abolished in law the possibility of what Bentham had
described as 'the barbarous infliction of an ignominious death
upon an unhappy mother, whose very offence proves her excessive sensibility'.[61]

No such humane legislation has yet removed from the

[58] *Principles of Legislation*, pp. 428, 429.
[59] *Theory of Legislation*, pp. 71, 331 and 332.
[60] Stephen, *History of Criminal Law of England*, 1, p. 487.
[61] *Theory of Legislation*, p. 265.

criminal law the offence of attempted suicide, of which Bentham argues that ' the alarm ' (caused by the attempt) ' cannot be very great when the offence cannot be perpetrated except with the consent of him who suffers by it '.[62]

Nor has the law been altered with regard to offences of a homosexual character, though it becomes increasingly obvious that the usual penalties attached to them are as a rule worse than useless. Bentham devoted considerable attention to this subject.[63] His general argument is that the whole question is one which regards the individual rather than the community, and would properly lie outside the field of penal legislation.

CODIFICATION

If, however, Bentham were able to fulfil his desire to return to this world once in every hundred years (and his first centennial visit is now some sixteen years overdue)—if he could step out of his glazed box at University College, London, and confront the jurists of today, it would not be particular omissions from his programme with which he would reproach them. He would indubitably be bitterly disappointed to find his life's ambition unfulfilled, and some of the fruits of his lifelong industry lying still in MS.

Codification (to use the word he himself invented) was the passion of Bentham's life. He followed it as other men follow wealth or art or science with whole-hearted devotion. ' To be without a *code* ', he wrote in his old age, ' is to be without justice '.[64] For him ' the power of the lawyer is in the uncertainty of the law ' [65] and lawyers were the last people from whom he expected justice. It is not surprising that the bitterness with which he expressed his feelings towards the legal profession made him enemies. The real ends of English procedure he thought were ' the power, wealth, factitious dignity, ease at the expense of official duty, and vengeance at the expense of justice ', which constituted ' the good of the judges '.[66] Nor did the lower ranks of the profession escape more lightly.

' All the industry of lawyers has been hitherto employed to

---

[62] *Theory of Legislation*, p. 256.
[63] See appendix, *Theory of Legislation* (ed. Ogden).
[64] *Works*, 10, p. 597.
[65] *Op. cit.*, 10, p. 429.
[66] *Works*, 2, p. 11.

prevent the grounds of law being canvassed, almost as anxiously as that of divines to prevent the grounds of religion from being examined '.[67]

' It is as impossible to a lawyer to wish men out of litigation, as for a physician to wish them in health '. Bentham had himself in calmer moments admired the judgments of Lord Mansfield, and reckoned lawyers amongst his personal friends. Perhaps his antagonism to the profession may be partly traced to the insistence with which his father urged upon the precocious boy his own ambition to see him Lord Chancellor. The Great Seal was, one may say, dangled before him in the cradle, towards this prize he was continually exhorted to ' push, push '. Thus he was early forced to formulate his own attitude towards that British Justice which Blackstone was so highly praising, and already, when called to the Bar, he had little respect for it.

The two causes which were ' at nurse ' for him and should have brought in his first legal earnings he advised should be abandoned to avoid throwing good money after bad. Yet it was impossible for him to overlook the terrible importance of the law, and specially of its criminal side.

The condition of crime in England, and particularly in London, at the end of the eighteenth and beginning of the nineteenth centuries must indeed have horrified any thinking person.

Crime was rampant and impudent, and the motley crowd which attempted before the introduction of Sir Robert Peel's ' peelers ' to deal with it, both inadequate and incompetent, struggled in vain against a population of criminals, whose yearly gains were calculated at two million pounds a year.

Highwaymen infested the roads, foot-pads the streets and squares of London. More than half the hackney-coachmen were flashmen, or accomplices of thieves—thousands of coiners were employed in the manufacture of false money, and ' scarcely a waggon or coach ' [68] left the metropolis which did not ' carry boxes and parcels of base coin to the camps, seaports and manufacturing towns '.[69] And all the time the manufacture of criminals went busily on.

Children were enticed to steal before they knew it was a

[67] *Works*, 10, p. 74.
[68] Colquhoun, *Treatise on the Police of the Metropolis*, p. 105.
[69] *Op. cit.*, p. 98.

crime. Samuel Rogers, born fifteen years later than Bentham, reported seeing ' a cart load of young girls, in dresses of various colours, on their way to be executed at Tyburn ' [70]; between 1787 and 1797 ninety-three children were transported to Australia, but most of the budding criminals went to complete their apprenticeships in gaol, where urchins of five could be found sentenced for the most trivial ' crimes '.

At Oxford Blackstone's lectures had an immense effect on young Jeremy's mind. The easy optimism of the teacher disgusted him, yet his very repugnance moved him to that detailed consideration of legal questions which later formed the subject matter of his ' Commentary on the Commentaries '. He applied the touchstone of the ' greatest happiness ' principle to the matter and the administration of English law, and found them wanting; instead of happiness they produced misery, instead of justice, ruin.

If this state of affairs were to be mended, the inconsistencies of statute law, the uncertainties and complexities of the common or ' judge-made ' law, and the danger of ' sleeping ' laws, must all, Bentham thought, be swept away, and a clear statement of the law made available to all citizens.

But it was no mere restatement in orderly form of the current law of England that Bentham proposed to undertake. The vast scope of the task he had set himself is well shown by Brougham.

' None ever before Mr. Bentham took in the whole departments of legislation. None before him can be said to have treated it as a science, and by so treating, made it one '.[71]

Bentham's science was to be a world-basis of good government. His hopes were raised when in 1811,[72] on Lord Sidmouth's coming to office, he had an exceedingly satisfactory interview with the new Minister, who expressed to him a desire to be favoured with his suggestions for the reform of the law. Bentham in consequence proposed that he should be encouraged, with no pecuniary reward, to prepare a Penal Code for England. Of course nothing came of it.

In 1814, undiscouraged by this rebuff, he hoped to be used for codifying the Russian law. The Emperor Alexander [73]

[70] Quoted Calvert, *Capital Punishment in the Nineteenth Century*, p. 5.
[71] Brougham, *Speeches*, 2, p. 291.
[72] *Works*, 10, p. 468.
[73] *Works*, 10, p. 478.

acknowledged his zeal by the gift of a diamond ring, which Bentham returned with the seals of the package unbroken. But when a Commission for the revision of the Russian Code was appointed it was, Bentham considered, so incompetent a body that he refused to work with it.

For the most part his offers to draw up complete legal systems for one country after another met with a rather pathetic lack of success, though Dumont reports in 1815 the assembly of the newly liberated city of Geneva as deliberating on ' our penal code '.

To the United States, to the State of Pennsylvania, to the National Assembly of France, to the King of Bavaria, to the Legislative Committee of the Spanish Cortes, to ' all nations professing liberal opinions ' he made offers, or sent proposals, all with the same fate. The one successful result of these endeavours, the influence of Bentham's work on the Indian Penal Code, will be traced elsewhere in this book.

Though we have several versions of the principles upon which he intended to draft it, and its main lines are clear from many of his works, Bentham never completed the penal code which was the first of his great projects, and which in fact led on to all his other efforts at codification.

Perhaps no one man could ever have carried out the task which Bentham had undertaken, and to which he gave the best part of his life.

The youth who wrote to his father that he was ' codifying like mad ', in his late thirties reports that on his Russian visit ' code was going on at a very pretty jog-trot, till Sam's inspection-house came upon the carpet ' [74]; at 79 he was optimistic, ' When I have written my code '; at 82 he was still ' codifying like any dragon '.

Though it was partly the very magnitude and profundity of his plans which prevented their completion, there were elements in Bentham's own nature which mitigated against success. He had a zeal for perfection—' I have seen him ', says Dumont, ' suspend a work almost finished, and compose a new one, only to assure himself of the truth of a single proposition which seemed to be doubtful '.[75] He was to a remarkable degree the

---

[74] *Works*, 10, p. 167.
[75] Ogden, *Theory of Legislation*, p. xlix.

slave of a natural dislike of reviewing and revising his own work. He was almost indifferent to publication and seems to have relied largely on his disciples to get his writings into final shape. He had a restless curiosity which drove him from one enterprise to another. George Wilson, with the unflattering perspicuity of a friend, reproached him in 1787 thus: '. . . your history since I have known you, has been to be always running from a good scheme to a better. In the meantime, life passes away and nothing is completed '.[76]

Where Bentham failed no one has yet succeeded. In 1878 a Royal Commission prepared a Draft Criminal Code, but it was never passed into law. English law remains what it was when Lord Justice Greer in 1932 described it, 'a sprawling and unwieldy mass' containing 'a number of anachronisms and anomalies, such as the now valueless and inconvenient distinction between felonies and misdemeanours which hardly a lawyer in the land would be prepared to defend '.[77]

Today so far as consolidation and codification of the statute law are concerned, the long inertia is breaking down. The Lord Chancellor (Lord Jowitt) announced, on July 30, 1947, his plans for reducing to order the chaotic state of the statute book.[78]

If Bentham's influence is too remote to be regarded as operative in this decision, at least his arguments are vindicated just before his bi-centenary year!

THE SANCTIONS OF THE LAW

Although Bentham's ideas regarding the codification of the law have so far failed of success, much, though not all, of what he urged regarding its sanctions has passed into practice since his time. We have seen that his detailed analysis of the Theory of Punishment inclined him to concentrate his attention on the treatment of offenders. In much of what he says humanity, good sense, and a reforming spirit stand out. If the modern reader at times differs radically from him it may, in the main, be attributed to the fact that we no longer pin our faith blindly to the working of the moral arithmetic; we neither attribute its

---

[76] *Works,* 10, p. 171.
[77] Quoted in C. K. Allen, *Law in the Making,* Clarendon Press, 3rd ed. (1939), p. 296.
[78] *The Times* newspaper, July 31, 1947.

calculations to all would-be law breakers, nor believe so naïvely in the power of fear.

We have seen that Bentham recognises clearly that in allotting punishment the character, physical and mental, and all the circumstances of the offender should rightly be taken into consideration, and there are moments when the more modern theory (by no means yet entirely accepted) of *treatment* seems about to oust from his mind the theory of *punishment*—he seems ready to accept the German proverb, ' Punishment should be like salad dressing—more oil than vinegar '.

In this spirit, as we have already seen, he took up a firm stand against capital punishment, and we have already dealt with the diminution in its use which can so largely be attributed to his teaching.

Next to the death penalty he abhorred the use of transportation, all too often resulting in the death, through hardships and neglect, of its victims.[79]

The independence of the Colonies in America had put a stop to transportation thither, and the newly found Australian continent seemed to offer an acceptable substitute. The first convoy of eleven ships conveying convicts to Australia sailed in May 1787, when Bentham was about twenty years old. With officers, marines, their wives and their children, with 742 convicts, male and female, it set sail on ' a nine months' journey to a destination six months away from the nearest source of food '. Clothing for the 190 women had been forgotten; so too, apparently, had medical stores. Almost naked, hungry, sick, without shelter and without hope, life seemed to lose all value for the wretched prisoners. ' If the natives shot at them with arrows, they simply sat still, hoping to be killed '.

The seed-wheat had gone mouldy on the voyage, and refused to sprout; when fresh seed was obtained it was eaten by rats as soon as sown. The second fleet sailed with some thousand more convicts; 261 died on board and fifty more shortly after landing. The men were confined on board by old slave irons and when a man died in his fetters the convicts concealed the corpse in order to draw his rations. On arrival ' great numbers were not able

[79] For details of transportation to Australia and Norfolk Island, see Wilson: *The Crime of Punishment* (Cape, 1931) and Bentham's own pamphlets, ' Panopticon *versus* New South Wales ' and ' A Plea for the Constitution '. *Works*, Vol. 4.

to walk, nor move hand or foot; such were slung over the ship's side. . . . Some crept on hands and knees '.[80]

In 1799 out of 300 convicts on one ship, 101 died on the voyage.[81]

Even when food became a little less inadequate moral and physical suffering continued unbearable.

The ' worst ' convicts were sent to Norfolk Island. Of their lot the Chief Justice of Australia said that if the choice were offered to him ' he would not hesitate to prefer death, under any form it could be presented to him, rather than such a state of endurance as that of the convicts at Norfolk Island '.[82]

It was no wonder that Bentham protested against this ghastly state of things. It was a punishment which he described as ' having all the faults which a punishment can have, and none of the qualities which it ought to have '.

We are justified in supposing that this strong protest had influence upon the decision to end deportation to New South Wales in 1840. In 1852 the system was abandoned, but as late as 1890 the British Government was still paying for the support of convicts in Australia.[83]

The pillory Bentham dismissed as being ' of all punishments the most unequal and unmanageable ' [84]—sometimes a scene of buffoonery, sometimes an exhibition of popular cruelty. This punishment was last used in 1830 and was finally abolished in 1837.

His attitude to whipping was equally uncompromising. We know that the calm of the family home at Queen's Square Place was often horribly disturbed by the screams of soldiers being flogged in the barracks nearby, and it is not surprising to find Bentham opposed to the punishment, not only on account of the atrocious—and even sometimes fatal—torture it inflicted, but also because of its uncertainty—the executioner being susceptible to bribes where the condemned could afford to purchase a mock infliction.[85]

Bentham's denunciation of mutilation as a punishment was,

[80] Bronwich, *The First Twenty Years of Australia,* quoted by Wilson, *op. cit.*
[81] *Works,* 1, p. 498.
[82] Wilson, *op. cit.,* p. 120.
[83] Wilson, *op. cit.,* p. 127.
[84] *Principles of Legislation,* p. 350.
[85] *Op. cit.,* p. 347.

so far as his own country was concerned, already flogging a dead horse. The last trace of it in English law disappeared with the abolition of branding for felony in 1779.[86] Curiously this practice was not altogether disapproved of by Bentham [86] who feels that it might be used to mark a criminal already condemned to perpetual imprisonment to prevent his escape, or for a dangerous offender who would no longer be dangerous if recognised as such. With characteristic detail he adds that the marks should not be made with a hot iron, but 'imprinted by coloured powder pricked into the skin'. The whole question of tattooing exercised a queer fascination over Bentham. Part of his plan for the Panopticon was that he would himself submit to be decorated and so reconcile his prisoners to an identification mark which would render escape difficult. He would really like to see every one marked with his personal names, after the fashion of sailors, indelibly printed on the wrist. If great men wore print marks upon their foreheads public opinion might be changed from its actual opposition to such a scheme. Branding was already often reduced to a more or less merciful farce; being either carried out with a cold iron, or, if a hot one was used, by the interposition of a slice of bacon between the branding iron and the criminal's skin. 'To keep up the farce, the supposed sufferer puts forth loud cries of agony and pain. The spectators, who understand the whole game, only laugh at this parody of the law'.[87]

But after all, he reflects, how many persons in the French revolution owed their safety to disguises which this kind of imprint would have made impossible. Twentieth century Europeans can, alas, see the force of this objection as clearly as Bentham did, and neither our criminals nor our babies' wrists will as yet wear national registration numbers.

We have already seen how greatly Bentham favoured pecuniary penalties; in his views on their administration he was once more well in advance of his own, and in some respects, of our times.

By an Act of 1870 the court may, on convicting any person for felony, award compensation not exceeding £100 for loss of property on the application of the aggrieved person.

[86] *Principles of Legislation*, pp. 347 *et seq.*
[87] *Op. cit.*, pp. 400, 401.

By the Acts of 1861 compensation for injuries to property may be awarded instead of conviction for a first offence. The same principle is embodied in the provision of the Probation of Offenders Act, 1907, that a court in making a probation order may order the offender to pay damages for injury or compensation for loss—the limit of such payment ordered by a court of summary jurisdiction being, in general, £25.

For cases of wilful damage to property amounting to less than £20 compensation for damage may be ordered in addition to fine or imprisonment.

Some provision exists under the Pawnbrokers Act, 1872; the Protection of Animals Act, 1911; and an interesting provision of the Factory and Workshop Act, 1901, gives power for a fine imposed for neglect in observing the provisions of the Act, which has resulted in death or injury to any person, to be employed, wholly or in part, for the benefit of the injured person or his family.

But in general it still holds true that any one who is injured by the criminal act of another will have to seek redress through a further process in a civil court. Bentham's desire to see 'satisfaction' made part of the penalty under the criminal law has thus only been partially fulfilled, and it would be difficult to prove that even this is a direct result of his teaching. It is, however, interesting to observe in this as in many other matters a definite trend of modern thought along the lines he laid down with such clarity a century ago.

For purposes of compensation and punishment a person's 'place in the scale of affluence' ought to be considered. His dependants, including wife, children as yet not grown-up, grandparents, etc. should be taken account of. An estimate would be made of his annual net income, and the judge would declare the ratio of the penalty to it.

This kind of consideration for the difficulties of the poor had long to wait for legal recognition. The Criminal Justice Administration Act, 1914, requiring time, in most cases, to be given for the payment of fines, brought the annual figures of imprisonment under this head down rapidly, and a further decrease followed the passing of the Money Payments (Justices Procedure) Act, 1935, which directs a further inquiry into means before imprisonment is carried out for non-payment of a fine imposed by a court of summary jurisdiction. These figures ran to an annual average of over 83,000 for the five years before the first of these Acts came into force; for 1945 they were under 39,000, a very striking instance of the useful effect of what might be called ' imaginative ' legislation.

In the matter of giving preference to restitution or compensation to the injured person over the payment of fines to the State, or indeed in the provision of such satisfaction at all, little progress has been made, though some recognition of the rights of the injured person to compensation without having recourse to the civil courts has been secured since Bentham wrote.

PRISON PLANS

Of all his considerations of the sanctions lying behind the penal law none cost Bentham so much thought, or unfortunately, so much worry, unhappiness and even financial loss, as his study of the prison question.[88] His first detailed study of prison conditions is contained in his *View of the Hard Labour Bill* (1778). It comes as rather a surprise to find him to a large extent favouring a measure proposed by his bugbear, Blackstone.

Indeed the measure was, for its period, in many ways an enlightened one, embodying a number of the reforms which Howard's researches had shown to be urgent. If many of the miseries of nineteenth century prisons indirectly resulted from it, they were not, except in a few instances, such as the use of the treadmill, envisaged by it.

The directions for the choice of site of the labour-house, near but not in a ' trading town ', for the buildings, including chapel and infirmary, for the segregation of the sexes, the allocation of a sleeping room for each prisoner, the provision of work, the compulsory appointment of a surgeon or apothecary, grants to discharged prisoners of not less than £2 and not more than £5, all these show a very definite advance upon anything that had gone before.

Bentham's own suggested amendments to the Bill are so characteristic that some must be mentioned here.

The labour-house is to have a committee of management; ought not its members to have their expenses paid? There

---

[88] For the details of Bentham's plans of Prison Reform, see Vol. 4 of his *Works*.

should be a garden, to supply vegetables and give work; on Sundays the convicts should walk in this as far as its limits allow, but should be restrained by a 'slight chain' linking couples chosen by lot to prevent 'insurrection and cabals'. The convicts should have some share in the profits of their labours, and should be allowed to spend their earnings, even on drink, if 'spirituous liquors' were excluded. The Governor too, though getting a fixed minimum salary, should receive augmentations from the profits of prison labour. The problem of the use of Sunday (still a thorny question in prison administration) occupies Bentham greatly. The Bill would allow men to employ themselves in reading 'the Bible or other books of piety'—this Bentham thought they would only pretend to do, and wished to see *permissive* work on such things as knitting, spinning or weaving, with a small profit to themselves. 'Devotion, it is true, is better on such a day than industry; but industry is better on every day than total idleness, that is, than despondency or mischief'. Moreover he favours the introduction of music on Sundays, he would allow of 'suitable discourses' as well as two religious services. He would have wished every inmate to have the benefit of spiritual consolation in his own way but thinks the complications would be too great. Jews and Catholics were the worst off—could there be a special labour-house for Jews, run at the expense of their community?

Bentham's preoccupation with health, one might almost say comfort, came out in many details. Besides 'coarse blankets', sheets and a bedstead should be provided; the use of sheets had caused a diminution of leprosy. The cells must be large enough —they should be warmed by flues or lateral chimneys. He had heard that steam might be used for such a purpose, perhaps the bread-oven or the copper in which victuals are boiled might supply it. Lights must be arranged, for the provision of the Bill that labour should continue throughout the daylight hours divided toil too unevenly according to the time of year. Laborious and sedentary work must alternate.

The infirmary should be high up, with a flat roof for exercise; it should be raised on arcades, allowing for exercise in wet weather. There were times when Bentham's belief in fear led him to some conclusions which seem to us to contradict his benevolence; dungeons must be called by no less intimidating name (a better error than the habit of giving pleasant names to unpleasant facts); they were to be dark to inspire terror, and might be removed from the main building to ensure silence.

He was inclined, perhaps wisely for his age, to favour such marks as a shaved eyebrow or chemical stains, to obviate the use of chains in preventing escapes.

Bentham's most curious suggestion for inspiring awe was for the outside of the labour-house. A bas-relief or painting was to represent a wolf and a fox yoked to a heavy cart, and a driver whipping them. ' In the background might be a troop of wolves ravaging a flock of sheep, and a fox watching a hen-roost '. Perhaps a monkey might be added, symbolising mischief. If these bas-reliefs were made in artificial stone one mould would suffice to cast one for every labour-house. A motto should be added—Bentham suggested ' Violence and knavery are the roads to slavery '

His fairy godmother, though bestowing on him some humour, did not add an acute perception of the absurd.

When Bentham next occupied himself with the question of prison reform it was no longer as a commentator and a critic of other people's suggestions but as the joint author with his brother of a brand new proposal.

' Sam's inspection house ', which became later the Panopticon, was ' a simple idea in architecture ' which Samuel Bentham had intended to employ for his Russian workshops. Jeremy became obsessed by it; its possibilities seemed to him endless. It was ' applicable to any sort of establishment in which persons of any description are to be kept under inspection, and in particular to

Penitentiary Houses,	Manufactories,
Prisons,	Mad-houses,
Houses of Industry,	Lazarettos,
Workhouses,	Hospitals and Schools '.
Poor Houses,	

By means of this ' new mode of obtaining power of mind over mind ' we should see ' morals reformed, health preserved, industry invigorated, instruction diffused—public burdens lightened—economy seated, as it were, on a rock—the gordian knot of the Poor Laws not cut, but untied '.

It is true that Bentham was sometimes joking in his own elephantine manner; when he proposes the securing of virginity 'by transferring damsels at as early an age as may seem sufficient into a strict inspection school', and adds, 'With what eagerness gentlemen who are curious in such matters would crowd to such a school to choose themselves wives is too obvious to insist on ', the reader should turn back to the point where the author confesses that in applying his invention to schools he has perhaps, under a flow of spirits, indulged in a *jeu d'esprit*. But most of his plans are, even where they border on the ridiculous, put forward in absolute earnest, in immense detail and at rather wearisome length. The great idea was of a building of circular (or, as later suggested, polygonal) shape with an outer ring of cells separated by an annular open space from an inner block or tower. The functions of this inner block or tower seem rather numerous for its size, or else they were varied in succeeding plans as these flowed from Bentham's pen. The top floor is to be the chapel, to which the public are to be invited, and by every means induced to come. There will be common-rooms for the staff, men and women together, but most important of all, there is to be an inspection lodge which must be large enough to serve as ' a complete and constant habitation for the principal inspector or head keeper and his family '. The more numerous the family the better; they will all share in the job of constantly watching the unfortunate prisoners.

Very elaborate plans are made for preventing prisoners from looking into the lodge and seeing whether they are in fact observed, including blinds which would have served to shut out some of the already scanty light and air of the unfortunate chief inspector and his brood. By day each cell would be under full inspection by the direct daylight coming in at its window, by night a small lamp with a reflector affixed above each window of the central lodge would light them enough for safety. With every cell the inspector could communicate directly by means of a speaking tube about the size of a pea-shooter.

In the first plan each prisoner was to be alone in his narrow radial cell, so that to the benefits of perpetual observation the curative effects of solitude should be added. It is much to Bentham's credit that, evidently influenced by Howard's precepts, he entirely renounced this idea in his second version of the scheme and is unsparing in his condemnation of the use of solitude beyond two or three days at most; 'Solitude when it ceases to be necessary becomes worse than useless ', and ' There are ways enough in the world of making men miserable without this expensive one '. So in the revised plan cells are to be twice the size originally intended. In them, two, three or exceptionally four men are to be confined. Bentham seems oblivious of the evils which would inevitably arise when a forced companionship, possibly lasting for years, had to be endured within the bounds of a narrow cage, exposed not only to the nerve-wracking sense of perpetual observation from the central lodge but to the humiliation of the curious gaze of the public who are to circulate freely through the building, though possibly kept away from the actual bars by a second railing. The provision in the latest version of the Panopticon, as set forth by James Mill,[89] of screens to cut off part of the cell from view can hardly be said to improve matters.

After a great discussion of the evils of employing human labour merely for producing rather than directing power, it is startling to find that the tread-wheel is still to be used perhaps for two periods of an hour a day for each prisoner, partly for its power production, partly as exercise in the open air. Bentham seems to have been under the illusion that treading the wheel was no more strenuous than walking up-hill, and holds it therefore to be permissible for women as well as men. In general he desires to see his prisoners employed as far as possible on work that they like. But the choice of occupation would not be large, and would, after all, be entirely dependent on the whim of the contractor-governor.

For the most dangerous part of Bentham's scheme was its financial side. The prison was to be farmed out to the person who, if otherwise unexceptionable, offered the best terms. He was to control, almost in his absolute discretion, the whole concern. Some ' reward ' for their labours the prisoners were to have, something would be set aside for their time of discharge, but also it would be only from their earnings they would obtain any food beyond bread and water *ad lib*. Obviously the allocation of the profits thus handed over to the workers, the provision of the food and other comforts upon which they could be spent,

[89] James Mill : article on Prisons and Prison Discipline in the *Edinburgh Review*, reprinted from the *Supplement to the Encylopædia Britannica*, *c.* 1825.

and the conditions of work in general, would offer terrible opportunities for injustice. The chief safeguards proposed by Bentham were two; first, the enlightened self-interest of the contractor, who would wish to maintain his workers in physical fitness, and secondly an ingenious form of fine in case deaths or escapes were over-numerous. The *probable* annual deaths were to be estimated at one in twenty (a sufficiently horrifying figure but moderate compared with the transportation losses), the contractor was to receive a sum arrived at by multiplying £10 by this number, and to be docked at the end of the year of £10 for each death or escape.

But not only would the ' felons ' be terribly at the contractor's mercy during the time of their sentence; their liberation after it had expired was hedged round with conditions which, if unfulfilled, left them for the rest of their lives as his ' boarders '.

As a fact merely incidental to the distance between the bars, Bentham states that boys of little more than ten years were often sent to prison. Would even these poor little wretches be doomed to life-long servitude, redeemed only by occasional marches to (cheap) military music, and Sunday school with the singing of hymns and the drawing, engraving or colouring of pictures illustrating the Bible or the Book of Common Prayer? The history of too many institutions proves that the contractor would not facilitate the release of his best workers.

In criticising Bentham on this score it must not, however, be forgotten that he was trying to persuade the government and the public to accept his Panopticon as a substitute for transportation. From transportation but few convicts came back, and those that did were not welcome since almost all returned perforce to a life of crime. The harsh provisions of the scheme so far as it related to liberation may be attributed to the desire to reassure a timorous public accustomed to see all serious criminals shipped away safely out of the country.

The long and hateful story of contract labour in prisons and elsewhere warns us only too clearly of the inevitable scandals which would have attended the realisation of Bentham's scheme. In fact, though clearly conceived in a mood of rather frigid humanitarianism it would, from its complete lack of understanding of human nature, have inevitably worked out as an engine of terrible cruelty. One surprising mitigation of suffering is suggested; indeed a hint is thrown out that prisoners from the two sides might be permitted to marry and the cell partnership become that of man and wife. Into the preliminary selection of brides or the probable subsequent complications of family life the inventor discreetly refrains from entering.

Such in brief outline were Bentham's plans for the scheme upon which he spent so much energy and which brought him so much frustration and unhappiness. Some modifications of it—particularly as to the conditions for release, the arrangements for visitors and the feeding of the prisoners—were made in the agreement subsequently drawn up, but never actually signed, between him and the Treasury Commission.[90] His hopes were high that with Samuel's help he would be able to put it into practice, and become himself the first governor. After many difficulties he bought a site for the prison, and with his brother made expensive and extensive preparations for beginning to build. The delays, the opposition and the final rejection of the plan he attributed (apparently without any real grounds) to royal antagonism. ' But for George the Third all prisoners in England would, years ago, have come under my management '.

The Committee which finally rejected the scheme certainly does not seem, from its careful report, to have been actuated by any unfair motives; its decision was supported by arguments which, whilst acknowledging fully the disinterested zeal of the originators of the plan, were based upon the insufficient safeguards of the prisoners' welfare in the hands of less high-minded governors who might follow them.[91]

At last, in 1812, an Act of Parliament was passed providing for the building of a penitentiary at Millbank, not on the Panopticon plan, ' and for making compensation to Jeremy Bentham, Esquire for the non-performance of an agreement '.

He received £23,000, which may have enabled him to recoup the money he had spent, but can have been but small consolation for the wreckage of his hopes. It is difficult to disentangle the complicated story. Bentham's friends were clear that he had been very badly treated. Bentham himself never quite got over his disappointment and chagrin. ' I do not like ', he would say, ' to look among the Panopticon papers. It is like opening a drawer where devils are locked up '.[92]

[90] *Works,* 11, p. 148.   [91] *Works,* 11, p. 96.   [92] *Works,* 10, p. 250.

However satisfied, for the sake of his reputation and his calm old age, Bentham's posthumous friends must be that the scheme never came to fruition, it is impossible not to sympathise with his very human distress at its failure.

There is a further cause for regret about the whole affair. As we have seen, even when his mind is most distracted by his own fatal ingenuity, flashes of good sense remind us of Bentham's fundamental wisdom in his theory of the relation of society to its recalcitrant members. His insistence that work should be productive and not, like the capstan, blindly punitive, that if prisoners can find amusement in their work so much the better, it should be as interesting as possible, that conversation should be allowed, that long solitude was dangerous and evil, his constant preoccupation with the subject of prisoners' health, his hope of introducing music into their lives; all these convictions and many others like them point him out as a real reformer. In spite of its rather naïve form his plea that normal human mating should not be indefinitely denied even to ' felons ' was far ahead of his time, as it still is of ours. In these and other ways Bentham had it in him to make a great contribution to the prison system of his day. On the whole it cannot be said that he made it. It is true that in 1815 a Bill was passed making illegal the atrocious system of charging fees for their keep to prisoners, whether convicted, untried or even acquitted, by which people were still held by their gaolers after the law had intended their release. This system was one which Bentham had vigorously attacked. True also that Peel's Acts of 1823 and 1824 had initiated other reforms in prisons, making it the duty of Justices to visit them, and requiring sufficient sanitary accommodation, classification of prisoners and a reformative regime. But no inspectors were provided, the Acts had no teeth, and were largely disregarded. They did not apply either to debtor prisons or to the 150 or so squalid local gaols and bridewells. These latter were swept away shortly after Bentham's death.

So, perhaps because the Panopticon scheme ended in smoke, Bentham's valuable ideas seem to have had on the whole very little effect upon the prisons of his times or of succeeding years. The nineteenth century, which opened when Howard's fame was at its height, which saw, in its earlier half, the concentrated zeal of Bentham and the warm-hearted mission of Elizabeth Fry, closed in a period of public apathy so far as the welfare of prisoners was concerned.

LOOKING BACK TO BENTHAM

For in his attitude towards criminals and crime Bentham was essentially of his age, though his lack of reverence for the past, his determination to re-think accepted conclusions, his humanity and his courage carry him often to form opinions far in advance of his own, sometimes alas! of our, time.

Perhaps in some ways it is regrettable that he never practised in the courts. He knew well enough, and hated profoundly, the complexities of a procedure never tested against the common sense of the 'utility principle'. He was all for simplification. But besides the artificial elaborations of the law, he would have seen in the courts—and perhaps have been readier than his fellow barristers to recognise—something of the infinite intricacy of human nature and human motive.

For all the subtleties of his analysis, he lived in a far simpler world than ours. It was, as it were, a purely Euclidean universe, with axioms unqualified and unquestioned, filled with people who could be classified, and whose actions could, it was supposed, be understood and predicted in accordance with a few elementary rules. For us the area of the conscious life, the realm of conscious will, is but a film over the surface of the depths of primitive mind-stuff subject to the forces of unconscious impulses. We realise that overt acts seemingly almost identical may derive from widely different causes. Arson may be the result of astute calculations for obtaining a high insurance value for dubious goods or the blind outlet of adolescent unrest. The sexual attraction which in one man results in the tenderest consideration may take homicidal form in another. Bentham's theory that the State is concerned not with motives but with deeds of omission or commission threatening the common welfare fulfils well enough the requirements of this more modern view; it is when we consider the methods which the State must employ for the protection of its members that his precepts need remodelling to match with modern knowledge. All he says of the value of 'indirect prevention of offences', even though some of the methods he proposes would seem today unlikely to succeed, brings him extraordinarily close to the modern view that crime

is at least as likely to be diminished by the provision of decent
social conditions—with Bentham's insistence on ' enlightenment '
(which we should call education) and the encouragement of
' innocent amusements ' among them—as by measures based on
fear.   Nevertheless, Bentham does seem to place what seems to
us a quite exaggerated trust in deterrence by fear of punishment.
In this he closely follows Beccaria who, however, in an illuminating passage, denies any consistent ratio between the severity of
punishment and its power of preventing offences.

There are springs of human action below, and perhaps above,
the plane of conscious calculation.   It is at our peril that we
ignore this fact, the peril of increasing crime by the very means
intended to check it.   Here is the problem which modern knowledge sets to the penologist of today.   It is interesting to note
that the people who have most to do with administering the
penalties dictated by the law are just those who are most aware
of the need for further research into the infinitely complex causes
of crime.   We are being forced away from the tariff punishment
handed out to the ' average ' man, and towards the treatment
suited to individual cases.   Bentham himself shows at moments
a foreknowledge of the way in which, after many years delay,
penal science was to move.

He had admitted in his principle of equality of punishments
a far wider variation of treatment than the practice of his time
would have allowed.

Attention, he says, must be paid to ' age, sex, condition, fortune, individual habits and many other circumstances ' if the
penalty is to be so adjusted as to correspond to different measures
of sensibility.   Read ' treatment ' for ' penalty '—and who
could wish for a better prescription?   It is when he comes to
discuss the meaning of sensibility that Bentham, half playfully,
gives his most astonishing glimpse into the future.   ' This
difference of sensibility [93] depends upon certain circumstances
which influence the physical or moral conditions of individuals,
and which, being changed, produce a corresponding change in
their feelings.   This is an experimental fact.   Things do not
affect us in the same manner in sickness and in health, in plenty
and in poverty, in infancy and in old age.   But a view so general
is not sufficient: it is necessary to go deeper into the human

[93] *Principles of Legislation*, p. 33.

heart. Lyonet wrote a quarto volume upon the anatomy of the caterpillar : morals are in need of an investigator as patient and as philosophical. I have not courage to imitate Lyonet. I shall think it sufficient if I open a new point of view—if I suggest a surer method to those who wish to pursue this subject. . . .

' The foundation of the whole is temperament, or the original constitution. . . . But although this radical constitution is the basis of all the rest, this basis lies so concealed that it is very difficult to get at it, so as to distinguish those varieties of sensibility which it produces from those which belong to other causes.

' It is the business of the physiologist [94] to distinguish these temperaments; to follow out their mixtures; and to trace their effects. But these grounds are as yet too little known to justify the moralist or legislator in founding anything upon them '.

It is the striking of sparks such as these last words give which makes Bentham such a fascinating writer. Yes, even though he would undoubtedly lash the shortcomings of our generation with his unsparing tongue, we would give a great deal to have him back amongst us and to see that amazing mind at work upon the problems of our time.

---

[94] Note ; can this word be a slip or a misprint for *Psychologist,* a word used elsewhere by Bentham and surely demanded here?

CHAPTER 3

BENTHAM AND THE POOR LAW

M. I. Zagday

IT was in 1795 that Jeremy Bentham first appears to have seriously begun writing on the subject of the poor law.[1] What exactly drew him to it is uncertain. But he had on many occasions shown sympathy for the poor and defended their interests,[2] for according to him they constituted 'the greatest number' of his famous utilitarian formula. He also admits that 'the relief of indigence is one of the noblest branches of civilisation'.[3] More positively, what influenced him was the actual maladministration in the existing poor law system as evidenced by the lamentable condition of the poor, their mendicity and refusal to work, and the panic that resulted from the scandalous expenditure on the relief of such paupers. Indeed, the commotion that prevailed attracted the attention of many other contemporary writers, each of whom set out to propound a scheme of his own on poor law reform. Of such writings that appeared immediately before Bentham began his own contribution, and without going too far back, mention ought to be made of Richard Burn and John Ruggles, who had published histories of the poor law in 1764 and 1793 respectively. Joseph Townsend's work on the poor law appeared in 1785 and 1788. Bentham had made his acquaintance in 1781 and must have discussed the subject with him.[4] Bentham was also aware of Sir F. M. Eden's *State of the Poor,* published in 1797.[5] Malthus's *magnum opus* appeared in 1798, a little too late for Bentham to make comments on it. But Bentham appears to agree with the view that most of the evils of excessive population are directly due to the maladministration of the poor law, but disagreed with

[1] *Catalogue of MSS. of J. Bentham* in the library of University College, London, p. 52.
[2] *Works,* Vol. 2, p. 574; Vol. 9, pp. 15 sq. 489.
[3] *Works,* Vol. 2, p. 534.
[4] Sidney and Beatrice Webb, *English Poor Law History,* Part 2, Vol. 1, p. 8.
[5] *Catalogue of MSS.,* p. 54, Contents of Box 149.

Malthus and Townsend regarding the abolition of the poor
law itself. The legislature, too, by attempting at repeated
intervals, and without much success, to remove some of the evils
of the system by piecemeal legislation, had attracted the attention and criticism of the public.

Bentham's writings on the poor law stretch from 1795 to
1798. A great number of these are still in manuscript and are
carefully preserved. Some are written in the neat hand of a
copyist and are much more legible than Bentham's own hand.
The earliest important work is his ' Essay on the subject of the
Poor Laws,' dated April 28, 1796. This essay, which has still
to be published, is essentially theoretical and stands in marked
contrast with his other works. Here he works out the definition,
object and theory of a proper poor law. The other important
work is the ' Outlines of a work entitled Pauper Management
improved '. This was published in parts in consecutive numbers
of the *Annals of Agriculture,* a well-known journal starting from
1797, as ' Situation and Relief of the Poor ', in order that readers
of the journal might supply Bentham with detailed information
about the state of the poor in various parishes by filling in the
' Pauper Population Table '. After he had obtained this
information he intended, he said, to publish ' two independent,
though connected, volumes : Pauper Systems Compared, and
Pauper Management Improved '.[6] The *Outline* itself is later
' To be filled up and the work published in one volume octavo,
as soon as sufficient number of the communications solicited in
Vol. 29, No. 167 of the *Annals of Agriculture* have been
obtained '.[7] The response was negligible, as the type of information asked for was too detailed, and in any case neither the
overseers of the poor nor the superintendents of the workhouse
or poorhouse kept any records or statistics of the poor [8]—an
oversight which Bentham did not fail to criticise severely in his
plan of reform. And so the contribution stopped at Book 4,
Section 6, as did any further designs for publishing any other
work on the poor law. The *Outline* was reprinted in 1798, and

[6] *Works,* Vol. 8, p. 361.
[7] *Works,* Vol. 8, p. 369.
[8] In this connection two interesting letters are preserved in his manuscripts.
One of these is a letter dated March 17, 1797, from the overseers of the
parish of Bloomsbury to Patrick Colquhoun, regretting inability to give
the information asked.

again in 1812, and in the collected works in 1843. A translation of this work in French by A. Duquesnay appeared in Paris in 1802.[9] The only other printed work by Bentham on the subject of the poor law is the *Observations on the Poor Bill introduced by the Rt. Hon. William Pitt*. This was written in February 1797 but was not printed until 1838, six years after Bentham's death, when Sir Edwin Chadwick found it among his papers and had it printed for private circulation. So that the *Outline* is the only work which was published before the Royal Commission's Report on the Poor Law appeared in 1834. And yet Bentham's influence, direct and indirect, on the subsequent development of poor law policy is indeed remarkable. He turned out to be the prophet of the new Poor Law of 1834, many of whose reforms he had anticipated many years previously.

What characterised the sad state of the poor law of that time was a singular absence of a general theory of poor law, both in the contemporary writings and in the sporadic reformatory attempts of the legislature. The poor law had been the work of amateurs and had grown up instinctively in tradition or had been moulded by immediate questions of policy. There was no reference to general principles. Bentham's contribution in this connection is therefore the more significant. With him legislation on the poor law, as with everything else, was an inductive science and the work of specialists who ought to arrive at general principles on the basis of ' observation and experiment which compose the basis of all knowledge '.[10] He set out therefore to collect factual ' account of the Paupers needing public assistance in as many parishes as I may be able to obtain it ',[11] by means of an elaborate Pauper Population Table and Table of Cases Calling for Relief, with a view to discover the causes of their destitution and the way to assist them. This technique of legislative reform of the poor law found acceptance with the Poor Law Commissioners who themselves prepared their Report on the basis of laborious inductions from a large mass of facts specially examined. It was upon the recommendation of this famous Report that the first real piece of legislation on poor law was enacted, *viz.* the Poor Law Amendment Act, 1834.

[9] C. W. Everett's bibliography to E. Halévy's *The Growth of Philosophic Radicalism*, London (1928), p. 542.
[10] *Works*, Vol. 8, p. 424.
[11] *Works*, Vol. 8, p. 361.

In the ' Essays on the Subject of the Poor Laws ' Bentham formulates the principles of his theory of the poor law. The object of a proper system of poor law, he says, ' is to make provision for the relief not of poverty but of indigence. . . . Poverty is the state of every one who in order to obtain subsistence, is forced to have recourse to labour. Indigence is the state of him who, being destitute of property . . . is at the same time either unable to labour or unable, even for labour, to procure the supply of which he happens to be in want '.[12] He shared with economists of his time the theory that poverty is the natural lot of man and an unavoidable disease in society, opulence being the exception, and further that the preservation of poverty is essential to wealth. ' As labour is the source of wealth, so is poverty of labour. Banish poverty, you banish wealth . . . '.[13] The duty of a government is simply to relieve indigence and not to concern itself with abolishing poverty or maintaining a definite minimum standard of civilised life in the interests of society. And this theory held the field until late in the nineteenth century. Its policy is to be one of *laissez faire;* to let the pauper fend for himself or else go into the workhouse to earn the bare minimum of subsistence. The element of compulsion in the wider interests of the community is absent. Nor, in this period, does legislation on the poor law concern itself with meeting the problem at its source instead of after the effects of destitution are felt. The latter is a recent conception—the result of a collectivist approach to social problems, the successful effect of which can be seen today in the gradual attempt to break up the poor law and ultimately to render it altogether unnecessary.

In return for relief the government may offer, it is entitled to impose conditions of service as to the amount of work to be exacted; submission to rules laid down in relation to the place where relief is to be administered; the place where work is to be performed; and the mode of living in each place.[14] The Report of the Royal Commission uses the same phraseology as Bentham.[15] No relief is to be administered except on condition

---

[12] ' Essays on the Subject of the Poor Laws ', MSS., folio 1.
[13] *Op. cit.,* folio 2.
[14] *Op. cit.,* folios 6, 7.
[15] *Poor Law Commissioners' Report of 1834,* reprinted 1905, Cd. 2728, p. 228.

of work being obtained in return, except that, to utter inability, relief must be given without requiring work. Bentham was strongly opposed to the existing system of out-allowance or out-door relief, that is, relief administered outside the workhouse, particularly to the able-bodied pauper, and whether the relief given be in money or in kind.[16]   At this time it was customary for the indigent to be relieved as of right, in their own home, in money or in kind. Wages were made up to a minimum out of the poor rates on a sliding scale tied up with the cost of bread known as the Speenhamland Scale. Children's allowances were also paid. All these, in the opinion of Bentham, encouraged idleness and mendicity, and gave a status to poverty by making the condition of the poor superior to that of the industrious and independent poor. Indeed in 1797 Pitt went to the extent of introducing a bill to legalise such outdoor reliefs coupled with the curious ' cow money clause ', whereby the poor in possession of a plot of land were to apply to a justice of the peace for a sum of money to buy a cow. Bentham criticised these proposals in the strongest language in his *Observations on the Poor Bill introduced by the Rt. Hon. William Pitt.*[17] This work was not published until 1838, but it appears that Bentham's views were communicated to Pitt and this may have contributed to the abandoning of the measure altogether.[18] The elemental principle to be observed, says Bentham, is that the condition of the non-labouring recipient of poor relief must be less eligible than that of the industrious poor, otherwise the very incentive to work would be removed. This principle of less eligibility found direct expression in the report of the Poor Law Commissioners,[19] and formed the basic principles of the new Poor Law. Consequently the Report recommends the abolition of out-door relief, that is relief otherwise than in a well regulated workhouse, except as to medical attendance.[20]

Although Bentham does not appear to be the inventor of the principle of centralisation in the administration of poor law,[21] nevertheless he was an enthusiastic advocate of it. Hitherto the

---

[16] Essays MSS., folio 23 ; *Works,* Vol. 8, p. 370.
[17] *Works,* Vol. 8, pp. 440 ff.
[18] Webb, *op. cit.,* p. 35 ; *Works,* Vol. 8, p. 440.
[19] Report, *op. cit.,* p. 228.
[20] Report, *op. cit.,* p. 262.
[21] Thomas Mackay, *A History of the English Poor Law,* Vol. 3, pp. 28–29, London (1899).

policy and conditions of relief were a matter for each parish alone, and this independence was jealously guarded by a strict enforcement of the law of settlement. Neither in policy nor in the actual administration of relief was there any uniformity. Each parish relieved its own poor out of the poor rates, which the unpaid parish overseers collected and disbursed haphazardly and in an amateurish fashion. The justices of the peace also had concurrent jurisdiction and ordered relief to the poor at their own discretion, sometimes over the head of the overseers. The evils of such a system, or rather the absence of a system, could only be remedied, in the opinion of Bentham, by vesting the ultimate control of poor law policy in a central body. In his own words, ' The management of the concerns of the poor . . . to be vested in one authority and the expense charged upon one fund. . . . The whole body of the burdensome poor to be maintained and employed in a system of Industry Houses upon a large scale distributed all over the country '.[22] In his ' Essays ' this Central Body is the Government with a Central Office directing the system of Industry Houses [23] and in his ' Pauper Management Improved ' it is a Joint Stock Company with a Board of Directors, who shall lay down the general policy based on the principles Bentham advocated upon which relief is to be administered and who shall have power to purchase land to build the Industry Houses all over the country.[24] But in a letter to Arthur Young, editor of the *Annals of Agriculture,* dated September 1797, which is preserved among his manuscripts, he says ' . . . government understood in an abstract sense—any authority in which the management of the Houses would come to be reposed; *e.g.* Joint Stock Co, magistrates of the counties, committee of the Privy Council, or a Board instituted for the purpose . . . '.[25] It is significant that the Poor Law Commissioners adopted outright this principle of centralisation. Their Report contains the following statement, ' We recommend, therefore, the appointment of a Central Board to control the administration of the Poor Laws . . . and that the Commissioners be empowered and directed to frame and enforce regula-

---

[22] *Works,* Vol. 8, p. 369.
[23] Essays, folio 6 ; Essay, ' Collateral Uses derivable from a System of Industry Houses, Essay the Second ', folio 2.
[24] *Works,* Vol. 8, p. 370.
[25] ' Poor Laws—Observations, letter to A. Young ', folio 55.

tions for the government of workhouses, and as to the nature
and amount of relief to be given and the labour to be exacted in
them, and that such regulations shall . . . be uniform throughout the country '.[26]

Bentham's actual plan of pauper management,[27] which had
been printed more than once in his lifetime and which, besides
anticipating specific nineteenth century reforms, indicates his
inventiveness, love of detail and comprehensive grasp of essentials. It was of course much ahead of its time, and utopian in
many ways. The central control of poor law administration was
to be vested in a joint stock company, with a board of directors
whose qualifications were to be similar to those of the Directors
of the East India Company. The Board were to build about
250 Industry Houses all over the country, each house to contain
about 2,000 poor persons. These Houses should be built on the
Panopticon principle of central inspection, i.e. circular buildings
in which the governed may be inspected from the centre as
explained by a detailed architectural plan. It is to be properly
staffed by salaried officials. The Panopticon idea does not
appear to have impressed the Poor Law Commissioners, but they
realised the necessity for a system of ' well regulated workhouses '.[28] No relief ought to be given except upon the terms of
coming into the house and working out the expense of maintenance. Mendicants and vagrants were to be apprehended and
brought into the workhouse and given employment. The sick
were to be maintained until cured; the children or non-adult
paupers were to be received as apprentices; the insane, dumb,
deaf and blind were to be segregated. The same plan of management was to be observed in all the Industry Houses.

The collateral uses which could be derived from a system
of Industry Houses[29] are indicative of Bentham's genius for invention. Thus temporary indigence caused by unemployment or
sickness could be relieved by a system of loans granted by the
governor of the Industry House on security or upon working out
the loan. The governor of each Industry House should keep a
bank of receipt and deposit to enable the poor to deposit their

[26] Report, op. cit., pp. 297, 314.
[27] Works, Vol. 8, pp. 369ff.
[28] Report, op. cit., p. 262.
[29] Essay on the Subject of the Poor Laws; Essay, ' Collateral Uses derivable
from a System of Industry Houses ', folio 1ff.

savings in proper custody—very much on the lines of the existing Post Office Savings Bank. The Industry Houses could also work out a system of Pecuniary Remittances, whereby a person might remit a sum of money to, say, his dependants in another part of the country through a chain of workhouses, in anticipation, as it were, of the invention of the Telegraph Money Order. Another collateral use to which the Industry Houses might be put is that of serving as frugality inns or inexpensive convenience stages for poor travellers, those in transit seeking temporary employment elsewhere, and as halting places for the conduct of convicts and arrested debtors. The more important item Bentham seems to have thought of is that each Industry House was to keep an Employment Gazette under the co-ordination of a 'Central Office of General Inspection with regard to the demand for work'[30] almost identical with our present technique. In Bentham's own words, '. . . Demand for work may exist in abundance, but its existence is unknown, and while a man should be performing the work that he may eat and live, he must be hunting for it and starving'.[31] He also recommended a system of book-keeping and accounting which he says is indispensable 'to good management . . . and a security for the due discharge of the several obligations'.[32] 'Book-keeping is child's play . . . it is one of the main pillars of my system'.[33] This suggestion was adopted by the Poor Law Commissioners.[34] The Industry Houses were also to provide education for non-adults, midwifery courses, facilities for recreation and physical exercise, and a 'National force' could be formed of the inmates trained by a drill-sergeant in the art of warfare.[35] The significant thing is that Bentham clearly appears to have foreseen the civilising benefits of his reforms by emphasising the need to reform the morale and character of the inmates so as to cultivate in them self-reliant, independent and industrious habits.

To Bentham's teaching is owed the beginning of the reconstruction in English local government first carried out by the new Poor Law Amendment Act, 1834, and by the Municipal

[30] *Op. cit.*, folio 6.
[31] *Op. cit.*, folio 8.
[32] *Works*, Vol. 8, p. 391.
[33] Poor Law Observation; Pauper Population Table, letter to A. Young, folios 33, 34.
[34] Report, *op. cit.*, p. 319.
[35] *Works*, Vol. 8, p. 420.

Reform Act, 1835. Both these measures, which were largely due to the energies of two of Bentham's ardent disciples, Sir Edwin Chadwick and Sir Francis Place, were the outcome of a reformed Parliament elected on a wider franchise introduced by the Reform Act, 1832, the majority of whose members were 'tinctured, if not fully possessed by the scientific ideas of Bentham and the philosophical radicals'.[36] Indeed, Bentham works out in his Constitutional Code the details of an ideal administration—a system of specialised central departments under the general control of the Prime Minister and each headed by a Minister, exercising executive control but itself not administering, with a network of elected local authorities carrying out the powers entrusted to it by Parliament. In this system he would place the department of administration of poor law in the hands of an 'Indigence Relief Minister'.[37] If one looks at the hierarchy of administrative machinery dealing with poor relief at the present time, one is struck by the remarkable resemblance. Today the various local bodies and *ad hoc* authorities, *i.e.* the Public Assistance committees, sub-committees or guardians' committees of the county councils or county borough councils, which are directly concerned with administering poor relief, are all under the central control of the Minister of Health.

Lastly, in appreciating Bentham's contribution to the development of the new Poor Law policy, one must not be unmindful of the obligation due to Sir Edwin Chadwick. It is through his direct agency that many of the reforms advocated by Bentham found expression in the Poor Law Commissioner's Report, whose recommendations were ultimately enacted in the Poor Law Amendment Act, 1834. Appointed at first, in 1832, as assistant commissioner under the Poor Law Inquiry Commission, and in the following year as Commissioner, he played a leading role and was largely instrumental in preparing the Report of 1834. He first met Bentham in 1829 when at the beginning of his long public career. From that time until Bentham's death in 1832, he had ample opportunities of knowing Bentham intimately as well as of studying his doctrines first hand, and of becoming one of his staunchest disciples. We have the authority of Sir Edwin Chadwick's biographer, Maurice Marston, supported

---

[36] Mackay, *op. cit.*, p. 23.
[37] *Works*, Vol. 9, p. 441 *sq.*; Webb, *op. cit.*, p. 30.

by that of reliable historians of the poor law, *e.g.* Sir George
Nicholls,[38] Thomas Mackay,[39] and the Webbs,[40] that Sir Edwin
Chadwick derived the principles and details of his Report from
the teachings of Bentham. ' Many details ', says Marston, ' of
the New Poor Law 1834 were taken from Bentham's unfinished
but amazing Constitutional Code . . . '[41] Chadwick was
Bentham's literary secretary in 1830 when this work was written.
There can be no doubt that Chadwick studied Bentham's manuscripts on poor law carefully before completing his Report.
Indeed, in some instances in his Report, he uses the actual words
of Bentham contained in the ' Essays '. This appears to be
further substantiated by the existence among Bentham's manuscripts of Chadwick's own writings, and glosses written on
Bentham's own paper between the years 1831 and 1838.[42]

---

[38] *A History of English Poor Law,* Vol. 2, p. 117, London (1898).
[39] *A History of English Poor Law,* Vol. 3, p. 40, London (1899).
[40] Webb, *op. cit.,* pp. 30, 53, 82.
[41] *Sir Edwin Chadwick,* by Maurice Marston, London (1925), p. 23.   (Cf.
pp. 37–38, *ibid.*)
[42] See *Catalogue of Manuscripts of Bentham* in the library of University
College, London, p. 54, Contents of box 153 (b).

CHAPTER 4

BENTHAM ON CIVIL PROCEDURE

M. I. Zagday

' . . . the darkness in which the whole system of procedure is involved by the thick cloud of technicalities'. Bentham, *Works*, Vol. 2, p. 171.

THE subject of judicial procedure was a favourite theme with Jeremy Bentham. Of all his versatile writings those on civil and criminal procedure constitute the largest in bulk. Most of these, and fortunately the important works, had been printed either during the latter period of his life or soon after his death in 1832, but there are several tracts more or less connected with procedure which are still unpublished. Although the ' Principles of Judicial Procedure with the Outlines of a Procedure Code ' appear in the second volume of his collected works,[1] suggesting its earlier appearance in print, yet it is the *Scotch Reform* [2] that appears to have been the first important exposure of the existing system of procedure to see the public light. This work appeared in 1808 and went into a second edition in 1811.

After 1820, more works on procedure appeared in print, important among them being the ' Elements of the Art of Packing as supplied to Special Juries ', 1821 [3]; ' Rationale of Judicial Evidence ', 1827,[4] which is a lengthy and exhaustive work occupying two volumes of his collected works and containing valuable material on the existing system of procedure; his ' Constitutional Code ',[5] 1828, which devotes a special place to procedure as it ought to be with the usual contrast with what it is in fact; and ' Justice and Codification Petitions . . . being forms proposed for signature by all persons whose desire it is to see Justice no longer sold, delayed or denied ',[6] 1829. Even in his last years he had the subject of procedure and law reform foremost in his

---

[1] *Works*, Vol. 2, p. 6.
[2] *Scotch Reform*, considered with reference to the plan proposed in the late Parliament for the administration of Justice in Scotland with illustrations from English non-reform. . . '; 2nd ed., London (1811).
[3] *Works*, Vol. 5, p. 61.
[4] *Op. cit.*, Vols. 6 and 7.
[5] *Op. cit.*, Vol. 9.
[6] *Op. cit.*, Vol. 5, p. 438.

mind and as late as 1830 embarked on the Law Reform Association Proposal[7] which unfortunately did not materialise during his lifetime.

As with every part of the system of the law, so with judicial procedure, Bentham subjected its detailed and technical rules to the test of his utilitarian formula. Just as to him the end in view of the substantive law is the maximisation of the happiness of the greatest number of the community, so the ultimate object of the adjective branch of the law ought to be ' the maximisation of the execution and effect given to the substantive branch of the law . . . and minimising the evil, the hardship '.[8] But that was exactly what the law of procedure was not. Of what use is a right when a remedy for its breach is virtually denied? In contrast with the ' natural ' or ' summary ' system, presented by common sense in which the truth of the dispute can be arrived at summarily without delay, useless expense or vexation, he found the then existing system ' technical ', riddled with archaic, corrupt technicalities, whose sole and sinister object is the gathering of fees by the judges and other officers of the courts and productive of nothing but delay, expense and vexation to the parties. In Bentham's own forceful words, ' Our whole Judiciary establishment with the system of procedure, self-styled the regular, by which it works, is one entire mass of corruption; fruits of it depredation and oppression '.[9] Many of these absurd rules of procedure he says were manufactured by the judges themselves by means of systematic and deliberate devices [10] with a sinister view to increase their remuneration which was by a system of fees, by prolonging litigation and increasing the number of occasions on which fees may be extracted from the parties.

In this sinister scheme the judges had the lawyers as accomplices. ' About sixty years ago ', he says, ' I deserted from it [the army of lawyers] and have been carrying on against them a guerilla war ever since '.[11] The two formed an illicit ' law partnership ', ' Judge & Co ', with the judges as managing

---

[7] *Op. cit.,* Vol. 11, p. 30.
[8] ' Principles of Judicial Procedure ', *Works,* Vol. 2, pp. 7–8.
[9] Bentham's letter to the Duke of Wellington enlisting his support for the Law Reform Association, *Works,* Vol. 11, p. 9.
[10] Justice and Codification Petitions, *Works,* Vol. 5, pp. 445–446; *Scotch Reform,* pp. 10–11.
[11] *Works,* Vol. 11, p. 9.

partners and with the object of robbing parties wholesale.[12] He laid at the door of this conservative association the intense opposition to his schemes, most of which he had a vision to see fulfilled in his lifetime. This frustration of his plans produced the most bitter invective from Bentham's pen. He spared no one and often descended to personalities, and picked upon Lord Eldon, whom he typified as the arch conservative and enemy of law reform and bestowed on him the most virulent abuse imaginable.[13] He had patience neither with the conservatism of the common lawyers who turned up their noses at his schemes for codification, nor with the system of the common law itself. Common law in his opinion is nothing but judge-made law and an usurpation of the power of the legislature to make law. According to him, the legislature alone is the repository of law-making power. Legislation and codes were with him an obsession. He was always ready, if asked by Parliament, to draft the codification of the whole of the English law, including a Code of Judicial Procedure and Judiciary establishment.[14] ' No otherwise than by codification can the reforms prayed for . . . be carried into effect '.[15]

Opposition to his schemes from the judges and lawyers was understandable. But why was the legislature and the government apathetic to his law reform? Probing a little deeper he discovered the reason. He found that the government was itself contaminated by these ' ruling classes the sub-ruling few '.[16] In his own words, ' In England the government has for its end not the greatest happiness of the greatest number but the greatest happiness of the few '.[17] And the laws were so framed as to preserve the power of this class. It ultimately dawned on him that the only way to carry out the reforms was to reform the legislature itself. This was therefore the theme of most of his later writings. What Bentham failed to see was that, notwithstanding the passionate conservatism of the legal profession, the

[12] *Scotch Reform,* pp. 6–7 ; Rationale of Judical Evidence, *Works,* Vol. 7, p. 199.
[13] Indications respecting Lord Eldon, *Works,* Vol. 5, p. 348ff.
[14] *Works,* Vol. 11, p. 30. In a letter written in 1811 to the President of the United States, James Madison, he offers to draw up for his country a complete code of law, a ' Pannomion ', statute law. *Works,* Vol. 4, p. 453. This offer was declined as impracticable.
[15] Justice and Codification Petitions, *Works,* Vol. 5, p. 439.
[16] Principles of Judicial Procedure, *Works,* Vol. 2, p. 120.
[17] *Op. cit.*

legal institutions of his time were deeply entrenched in the soil and could not be uprooted overnight by a stroke of the legislative pen.

Possessed of wide knowledge of the continental systems of law with their codes, he could pick holes in the English system of procedure and evidence with the greatest ease. Whatever part of the law he criticised, it was generally accurate and not usually exaggerated. Although he did not engage in active practice, he kept himself sufficiently abreast of the latest developments of the time. In his works he quotes several contemporary writings dealing particularly with the abuses of procedure.[18] He had a passion for classification and tabulation, and used this device most effectively to condemn some of the absurdities of the system of procedure. See for example ' *Scotch Reform* . . . with illustrations from English non-reform in the course of which diverse imperfections, abuses and corruptions in the administration of justice with their causes are now for the first time brought to light with tables in which the principal causes of factitious complication, delay, vexation and expense are distinguished from such as are natural and unavoidable '. In the appendix to this work are added sheets headed ' Delay and Complication Tables '. In the ' Justice and Codification Petitions ' are tabulated fourteen devices by which ' the ends of justice defeated '.[19]

A few of the more pressing reforms which Bentham advocated indeed materialised more or less either during the last few years of his life or soon after his death, because they had the official backing of the Parliamentary Commissions which had been appointed during the years 1818–1832 to inquire into the practice and procedure of the superior courts. These deal, for example, with the improvement in the selection of juries (Jury Act, 1825); the system of writs for initiating an action (Uniformity of Process Act, 1832); the appointment of additional puisne judges and regularising court sittings (1830); improvement in pleadings laid down by the judges under an Act of 1833; and minor enactments. But the main underlying principles of his reforms were considered for the times too visionary and utopian, and his views appear to have been ignored and

---

[18] Elements of the Art of Packing, *Works,* Vol. 5, p. 66 ; p. 102 footnote, p. 163 footnote.
[19] *Works,* Vol. 5, p. 445.

did not find acceptance until a fruitful beginning was made by
the two famous Commissions on the Common Law which sat
round about 1850. This year is significant in English legal
history as it marks the beginning of the era of radical law
reforms and the fruition of Bentham's teachings. Even as late
as 1898, when the testimony of parties in criminal cases was for
the first time made admissible in evidence, one cannot help
recalling the teaching of Bentham, who about eighty years
previously had consistently advocated its acceptance. There are
other schemes of his still to be adopted.

Bentham's complaint was not there were too many courts
at that time—and he himself numbered thirteen of them—but
that they were so hopelessly organised. In the first place, the
jurisdiction of the courts, especially the common law courts,
he says, was 'split and spliced' [20] and almost entirely overlapping.
The choice of a court in which to initiate an action depended
solely on clever drafting of the writ and the form of action.
If a plaintiff failed he could invariably proceed to another court
under the guise of a different form of action. Both in common
law and equity cases were 'bandied from court to court on a
variety of pretences'.[21] In place of 'this entanglement of
jurisdiction' [22] Bentham suggested that each court ought to be
given 'cognisance of causes of one description, to another court
cognisance of causes of another description, each to the exclusion
of the other; with pure intentions, the line of demarcation can
easily be drawn'.[23] Country causes were triable at Nisi Prius
or Assizes, but the rarity of circuits and the short sittings at
Assize as at Westminster, resulted in many causes being left
unheard (remanets) besides the inconvenience and delay attendant upon sending a cause to and fro between the Common
Pleas Division and Nisi Prius.[24] Bentham recommended the
establishment of a system of smaller tribunals, distributed all over
the country and easily accessible, which could administer justice
speedily and cheaply, presided by a single judge generally with-

---

[20] Justice and Codification Petitions, *Works,* Vol. 5, p. 531.
[21] *Scotch Reform, op. cit.;* Justice and Codification Petitions, *Works,*
Vol. 5, p. 516.
[22] Rationale of Judicial Evidence, *Works,* Vol. 7, p. 289.
[23] *Op. cit.*
[24] *Scotch Reform,* p. 16; Justice and Codification Petitions, *Works,* Vol. 5,
p. 469.

out a jury.[25]   In 1846 a system of County Courts was established
which since then have worked most satisfactorily.   Bentham had
also suggested as a temporary measure the establishment of two
courts to dispose of the large number of cases that were still
unheard, to be called The Equity Dispatch Court [26] and The
Court of Lords Delegates.[27]   But nothing was done until 1830,
when additional puisne judges were appointed to each of the
superior courts, and the Terms and return days of each Term
fixed and increased to facilitate early dispatch of the arrears of
work.

Bentham censured in strong language the practice that
prevailed in each of the common law and equity courts as being
so perverse as to defeat the very ends of justice it pretended to
serve.   Each of the common law courts had its own technical
writs and its own variations on the pleadings suited to the
different forms of actions, all of which had to be observed with
scrupulous care on pain of losing the action and were riddled
with fictions, the action of ejectment topping them all with
fiction after fiction in the romantic adventures of John Doe and
Richard Roe.   Bentham contemptuously defines a fiction in law
as a ' wilful falsehood uttered by a judge for the purpose of
giving to injustice the colour of justice '.[28]   What is needed he says,
' is the most common of all, common honesty '.[29]   The technical
rules about motion for adjournment, especially in equity suits at
the instances of plaintiff or defendant; the time taken to cover the
ground of the various stages of the lengthy pleadings, particularly
when the general issue had been pleaded in the common law
suits, and between interrogation and answers in equity suits;
the technical rules relating to joinder of parties whereby the
death of one necessitated a new bill; the very short sittings of
the judge and master, as little as three to four hours a day for
only five months in the year; and lastly the frivolous writs of
error in arrest of judgment and appeals in equity—all these were
glaring instances of the futility of the entire system of procedure.
The delay that resulted from such rules in both the systems of

[25] *Scotch Reform*, p. 15.
[26] Equity Dispatch Court Proposal, *Works*, Vol. 3, pp. 303ff.
[27] Summary View of the Plan of a Judicatory under the name of Court of
Lords Delegates, *Works*, Vol. 5, p. 55 *sq*.
[28] *Scotch Reform*, p. 24.
[29] Indications Respecting Lord Eldon, *Works*, Vol. 5, p. 365.

law and equity was unbelievable. Years would elapse before the suit was finally settled : in equity a period of twenty to thirty years was not unusual, and sometimes the period was so long that the parties, if not already ruined by the heavy expenditure, did not live to know the final decision. Bentham sums up this system in three words, delay, vexation and expense. The root cause of all this, he repeatedly tells us, is the sinister interests of the judges and officers of the courts. ' The cause of factitious complication, intricacy, obscurity, unintelligibility, uncognoscibility, in the system of procedure . . . is the multiplication of the occasions of exacting fees '.[30] ' Hence . . . insincerity hypocrisy, and lawyer craft, become natural '.[31] And hence ' Judge & Co ', the ' virtual partnership—the law partnership—with the judges as managing partners at the head of it '.[32] The general dissatisfaction at the system of remuneration of officers of the courts led to the appointment of several commissions from the year 1816 to examine the duties, salaries and emoluments of such officers of the superior courts. An imposing list of forty-five officials of the King's Bench alone appears at the beginning of the Report of the Commission of 1818. A small beginning was made by an Act of 1837, when about thirty-seven offices of the superior courts were abolished and masters were appointed in each court with fixed salaries for themselves and their clerks. The 1851 Common Law Commission finally recommended that *all* officers of the courts should be paid fixed salaries by the State.

Bentham's own plan of procedure is a considerable improvement on the then existing system. It is a simple plan, shorn of all technicalities and fictions. He calls it the summary, natural or domestic system, in which the parties would appear before the judge for the speedy settlement of the suit in very much like the way quarrelling sons or servants appear before their father or master to have their disputes settled. It is astonishingly on the lines of our modern system.

The process by which all personal actions are to be begun at common law is by a simple writ of summons, stating briefly the nature of the action, instead of by the perplexing mode varying with the equally perplexing forms of actions then

---

[30] *Scotch Reform,* p. 7.
[31] *Scotch Reform,* p. 8.
[32] *Op. cit.,* p. 7.

prevailing in the three Common Law Courts. The defendant is to put in an appearance in person or by proxy, thus doing away with the process of outlawry—a reform wholly accepted by the Uniformity of Process Act, 1832. The parties to the suit must then be brought face to face before the judge in chambers as soon as possible and ought not to be excluded from his presence until the trial as was then the practice.[33] They are then and there to settle with him the future course of the trial. Pleadings are to be short and simple, and he even went to the length of recommending the use of standard printed forms.[34] The pleading of the pernicious general issue, pleading double and special pleas, is to be forbidden as tending to make pleadings uselessly prolix, complicated and tricky, and as he says, ' the ingredients of which are falsehood, nonsense and surplusage '.[35] In equity procedure the written evidence of the witnesses upon interrogation by the Examiners of the Court ought to be taken down subject to the right of counsel, hitherto denied, of cross-examining the witness in the presence of the parties. The Equity Commission of 1826 was in favour of this proposal. Bentham went further and approached our present position (see O. 37, r. 11, of the Supreme Court) in recommending public viva voce testimony in the Court of Chancery in place of the written evidence by commission.[36] The important reform relating to pleading came in 1833 when by the Civil Procedure Act of that year the common law judges were authorised to make alterations in the mode of pleading by general rules and orders. Such rules and orders were in fact made in the following year, although the alterations were not very drastic.

The suit is now ready for trial before a ' single seated judicatory consisting of a judge without a jury '.[37] This is his principle of single-seatedness.[38] Although Bentham admits that a jury can sometimes be an effective safeguard against official interference with personal liberties of the subject, it is in the general case accompanied with additional inconvenience, delay and expense. Nor is it, as it is supposed to be, really a check

---

[33] Justice and Codification Petitions, *Works*, Vol. 5, p. 522.
[34] *Scotch Reform*, p. 20.
[35] *Scotch Reform*, p. 20.
[36] *Op. cit.*, p. 13.
[37] Elements of the Art of Packing, *Works*, Vol. 5, p. 116.
[38] Principles of Judicial Procedure, *Works*, Vol. 2, p. 22.

upon the judge, as jurors are often intimidated and dependent on the judge, in whom they have blind confidence.[39]   He often derisively called them ' guinea-men, guinea corps '.[40]   Moreover, the selection of the special jurors from the panel has of late, he says, become an art, the art of packing, and persons ' behind the curtain ' and ' with connections '[41] are secretly selected and struck by the master of the court instead of by rotation and ballot.   In this respect the several Juries Acts of 1825, 1870 and 1922 have introduced the latter method of selection.   Bentham's view regarding the futility of the jury system appears to have been justified by events when one remembers the drastic curtailment of the use of juries in present-day civil and criminal matters. It is interesting to note that the present-day agitation regarding payment to jurors of an allowance for loss of time and travelling expenses had the support of Bentham, who also suggested that this expense should come out of the county rates.[42]

The same judge ought to have the power to decide questions of both law and equity—principle of omnicompetence.[43] Bentham's views on the fusion of law and equity are remarkably ahead of his time and went a long way to prepare for the fusion that was completed by the Judicature Act, 1873.   This distinction between law and equity which is peculiar to England is, he says, purely arbitrary and absurd.[44]   Nor are the ends of justice served by this distinction.   Familiar with continental codes, in which the dual system does not exist, he has no patience with this peculiar phenomenon of English legal history.

On the subject of evidence he had rather strong views, as is shown by the following essay, ' Bentham's Influence on the Law of Evidence '.   Bentham's views on the subject of imprisonment for debts were farseeing and humane.   He opposed it as being unnecessary and useless as a deterrent, and of benefit to no one except, he says, to the judges themselves.[45]

Whatever may have been Bentham's inspiration for writing on the subject of the office of Public Prosecutor and legal aid to

---

[39] Elements of the Art of Packing, *Works,* Vol. 5, pp. 67, 88.
[40] *Op. cit.,* p. 80.
[41] *Op. cit.,* pp. 80, 81.
[42] Elements of the Art of Packing, *Works,* Vol. 5, p. 168.
[43] Principles of Judicial Procedure, *Works,* Vol. 2, p. 22.
[44] Justice and Codification Petitions, *Works,* Vol. 5, pp. 516ff.; Rationale of Judicial Evidence, *Works,* Vol. 7, pp. 290ff.
[45] Rationale of Judicial Evidence, *Works,* Vol. 6, pp. 176ff.

poor persons,[46] there is no doubt that he has made some valuable and stimulating suggestions. Every court, he says, ought to have attached to it a Government Advocate and an Eleemosynary Advocate in place of the Attorney-General, whose office was defective in many ways, as *e.g.* his right to be paid fees, and the absence of a public duty to prosecute or assist poor litigants in civil and criminal cases.[47] The Government Advocate or Pursuer General is to be a salaried official whose duty it would be to officiate on behalf of the Crown generally in civil matters, and to act as Public Prosecutor in criminal cases, *i.e.* superintend prosecutions initiated by private persons and in other cases to initiate them himself.[48] Here indeed are the germs of the Office of Director of Public Prosecutions set up by the 1879 Act. The duty of the other officer, the Eleemosynary Advocate, the Advocate of the Helpless,[49] was to give free legal advice and to plead in court on behalf of all poor persons who obtained a certificate from the judge. The government ought to set up a fund to defray the expenses of litigation and there ought to be other voluntary additions to this fund, *e.g.* a sound suggestion that every court ' to have an Equal Justice Box for charitable contributions '.[49] In this connection, the Poor Persons Defence Acts of 1903 and 1930, together with the recent recommendations of the Rushcliffe Committee on legal aid to the poor, are indications of the soundness of Bentham's ideas.

Besides the many special instances indicated above in which Bentham's ideas found acceptance, his greatest contribution to the reform of the law of procedure lay rather in this, that he brought to bear upon the system of procedure, as upon the whole existing legal system, a very critical attitude and a questioning frame of mind. Where others had eulogised, especially Blackstone, whom Bentham quotes as having said, ' Everything is as it should be ',[50] or where others had accepted without question the existing rules of law, he criticised without fear or favour. It is this aspect of his contribution to the development and reform of the law that Brougham [51] and Dicey [52] specially praise.

[46] See Draught of a Code for the Organisation of the Judicial Establishment in France, *Works,* Vol. 4, pp. 285ff.
[47] *Works,* Vol. 2, p. 22 ; Vol. 4, p. 405.
[48] *Works,* Vol. 4, p. 384 ; Vol. 9, pp. 570–571.
[49] *Works,* Vol. 9, p. 493.
[50] Elements of the Art of Packing, *Works,* Vol. 5, p. 95.
[51] Speeches of Lord Brougham, *Works,* Vol. 2, pp. 287–288.
[52] *Law and Opinion in England,* 1930, pp. 126ff.

The effect upon public enlightened opinion of his works on the system of procedure which came to be printed in rapid succession in the last ten years of his life cannot be exaggerated. There is no doubt that his teachings, along with other fortunate circumstances, greatly accelerated the movement for law reform. Romilly first, and Brougham and Denman and less notable figures later, were sufficiently inspired not merely to pay tribute to his reforming energies but also more positively to move for Parliamentary Commissions to examine that state of the law and recommend reforms.[53] It is true he was not the only one who pointed out the abuses in the procedural system. Indeed he quotes several tracts by contemporary writers who were equally aware of the position.[54] But, at any rate, it was he who powerfully and methodically brought criticism to bear upon the entire system and pressed home the necessity for reform. He anticipated, as has been pointed out, to a remarkably accurate degree some of the specific reforms in procedure and evidence carried out in later years. Although it is easy, as Stone says,[55] to argue *post hoc propter hoc,* yet the consensus of opinion of authoritative writers of his time and of the middle and latter half of the nineteenth century, is that these reforms are directly traceable to Jeremy Bentham.[56] No tribute could be more fitting than that of his contemporary Brougham, who says, ' All the great improvements in our system of jurisprudence which have been made during the last twenty years . . . may easily be traced to the long and unwearied and enlightened labours of Mr. Bentham and his school '.[57]

[53] In an interesting letter to Bentham, Brougham says that he intends to make a speech in Parliament on the enormities of Common law and Chancery . . . and carry a motion moving for a commission and that he intends to tap Bentham's reservoir of exposition, attack and invective. To this Bentham replied that he was ' delighted and excitably overcome ' and endearingly addressed Brougham as ' My dearest Best Boy ', ' Dear sweet little Poppet '. *Works,* Vol. 10, p. 574. But Bentham appears to have been disappointed at the tameness of the speech.

[54] See Elements of the Art of Packing, *Works,* Vol. 5, p. 66 ; p. 102 footnote ; p. 163 footnote.

[55] *The Province and Function of Law,* 1947, p. 267 *sq.* at p. 270.

[56] Dicey, *Law and Opinion in England,* 1930, p. 127 ; Odgers, *Century of Law Reform,* 1901, p. 40, and Chaps. 7 and 8 ; Holdsworth, *History of English Law,* s.v. Bentham.

[57] *Speeches,* 1838, Vol. 2, p. 301.

CHAPTER 5

BENTHAM'S INFLUENCE ON THE LAW OF EVIDENCE

G. W. Keeton and O. R. Marshall

PRE-BENTHAMITE LAW OF EVIDENCE

BEFORE we can assess the extent of Bentham's influence upon the development of the Law of Evidence, it is first necessary to say something of the development of this branch of the law before Bentham wrote. Although claims have been made from time to time that the rules of evidence are of great antiquity,[1] it would seem to be the case that they are the product of the century which begins with the Restoration. It was at this time that this branch of the law took definite shape, as a body of rules which the judges were compelled to follow, even though the general principles upon which the rules were founded were generally understood at an earlier date. Thus, Chief Baron Gilbert's famous treatise on *Evidence,* which was published in 1756, though it was written a good deal earlier, may be said to sum up the work of this formative period, and to present a first draft of the modern Law of Evidence.

Prior to this period, the principles of evidence had not been regarded as a definite part of English law fettering the judge in his conduct of the case, but as guides to be used or set aside as the circumstances of the trial seemed to indicate. This is particularly apparent, for example, if we study the evolution of such rules as the so-called ' best-evidence rule ', or the growth of the hearsay rule with its various exceptions. So long as the jury combined the functions of the modern jurors with those of witnesses, no general exclusion of hearsay was possible, for the jury could form their own knowledge from documents not submitted in evidence, or from information transmitted to them at second or third hand, whilst even in court they might be permitted to listen to the unsworn narratives of counsel or witnesses. This laxity worked particularly oppressively in criminal trials, especi-

---

[1] *E.g.* by Lord Kenyon, C.J., in *R. v. Inhabitants of Eriswell* (1790), 3 T.R. 707, 721.

ally in State trials. Thus, Raleigh was condemned in 1603 mainly on hearsay,[2] and Archbishop Laud objected to some of the evidence offered against him on the ground that it was hearsay.[3] During the seventeenth century, the idea gained ground that hearsay was an unsatisfactory kind of evidence, and in 1670, Sir Matthew Hale ruled that it was inadmissible as direct evidence, though it might still be used as corroboration.[4] By 1716, however, Hawkins records that hearsay must be excluded, on the grounds (1) that the party was not on oath, and (2) that there had been no opportunity for cross-examination.[5] Thereafter, the main problem for the courts to decide was how far the well-understood exceptions to the hearsay rule, many of them of ancient origin, survived under the stricter system of the eighteenth century.

The exclusion of hearsay at the beginning of the eighteenth century was simply part of a wider movement towards tightening-up the rules of evidence, which was summed up by Gilbert in his famous ' best evidence rule ' in the following terms : ' The first and most signal rule in relation to evidence is this, that a man must have the utmost evidence that the nature of the fact is capable of. The true meaning of which is that no such evidence shall be brought which *ex natura rei* supposes still a greater evidence behind in the party's own possession or power .' By this rule, Gilbert understands that three types of evidence, formerly admissible, were excluded : (1) hearsay, (2) secondary evidence of documents, where the originals were in existence, and (3) proof of attested documents, otherwise than by attesting witnesses.[6] It is true that from the beginning of the nineteenth century, the ' best evidence rule ' was progressively abandoned, but it had served its purpose in putting an end to a number of laxer practices which had characterised earlier phases of the development of the law of evidence. In so far as the ' best evidence rule ' excluded hearsay, then, if Best's view is correct that the judiciary retained their discretionary powers with regard to its exclusion or rejection so as not to fetter the executive in its

---

[2] Jardine's Cr. Tr. 427.
[3] 4. Howe, St. Trials 431.   Hale was one of the counsel for Archbishop Laud.
[4] Phipson, *Evidence,* p. 217.
[5] 2 Pleas of the Crown, 596–597.
[6] Phipson, *Evidence,* p. 45.

prosecution of those accused of political crime,[7] the growth of the stricter rule may be regarded as one of the legal consequences of the ' Glorious Revolution ' of 1688.

In so far as the ' best evidence rule ' required the production of the originals of documents in court, this rule appears to have its origin in the ancient practice of authenticating deeds and other formal documents which in themselves decided actions founded on them. Later, when production of deeds and other formal documents ceased to be a mode of trial, and became simply a method of proof, the practice was established of requiring profert of all documents used in pleading, in order that the court might satisfy itself upon their genuineness. Profert eventually became formal, and was abolished by the Common Law Procedure Act, 1852, s. 55. Finally, independently of profert and about the end of the seventeenth century the court, on the analogy of profert, required production at the trial of all documents relied on, whether subject to the rule of profert or not. The rules governing production reached their maximum strictness in the eighteenth century. From 1800 onwards, the rules were relaxed in the interests of convenience—a development to which Bentham contributed, for in his treatise on *Judicial Evidence,* he argues forcefully for a less rigid rule.[8]

Another great principle of the modern law of evidence was slowly taking shape during the eighteenth century—the principle that a witness speaks from his knowledge of facts, and not from his opinion—a principle to which the admission of the opinions of experts is a notable exception. No such principle is known to Chief Baron Gilbert, writing in the first half of the eighteenth century, but the rule is stated in its modern form in Peake's *Treatise on Evidence,* published in 1801, and again in Starkie's treatise, published in 1824.

One other great characteristic of the law of evidence as it existed in Bentham's day requires brief notice—the strictness of the rules disqualifying witnesses on the ground of interest. Until 1843,[9] any person having an interest, no matter how small, in the proceedings, was excluded from giving evidence in it. The absurdities resulting from this were clearly seen by Bentham, and

[7] *Evidence,* 12th ed., p. 98.
[8] Book 9, and especially Chap. 12.
[9] This disqualification was removed in 1843 by 6 & 7 Vict., c. 85 ; see below.

were repeatedly denounced by him. ' If interest, taking the word
in its most general sense, is a sufficient reason of exclusion, we
must infer that all testimony, proceeding from a human mouth,
ought to be excluded. Were there no interest, that is, no motive,
there would be no testimony. . . .

' When the witness is under an influence which inclines him
to lie, the more evident this interest is, the less dangerous is it for
the judge.

' Is it a pecuniary interest? Its seductive tendency is seen at
once ; its strength may even be estimated by the amount of the
sum, or the rank and character of the witness. Is it to be presumed that a man will sacrifice his conscience, and endanger his
reputation as an honest man, for a gain which is as nothing in
comparison with his fortune? This is the sort of interest which
has been made the reason of almost all the exclusions known in
English law. Love, properly so called, the love of power, friendship, hate, and all the other passions of the human heart, seem
to have been reckoned undeserving of the same precautions. It
might be said that English lawyers, in estimating the danger,
made no account of all these motives. Pecuniary interest is
apparently the only one whose influence they recognise. This is
a fragment of the barbarism of ancient times '.[10]

Bentham then goes on to point out that whilst English law
rejects the testimony of those incompetent on account of pecuniary interest, it admits the evidence of accomplices ' and the
longest experience has furnished no reason to believe that it is
dangerous to admit it. What is the security against it? What
we have just pointed out ; the obviousness of the seductive
interest, and the proportional degree of distrust in the judge '.

Bentham was not a legal historian.[11] Had he probed into
the history of this exclusionary rule he would have found obscurities and inconsistencies. At first relatives or servants of parties
were freely admitted to give evidence, but by the beginning of
the seventeenth century the evidence of the parties, and of all
others with an interest, had been excluded, both in civil and
criminal cases. Professor Wigmore suggests that the reason for
this exclusion was probably the desire to exclude from the

---

[10] *Judicial Evidence,* Book 7, Chap. 13, pp. 248–249.
[11] Stephen writing at the end of the last century attributes the partial
decline of Bentham's influence in his generation to the greater study of
legal history. *Digest of the Law of Evidence,* Introduction, p. xxi.

privilege of testifying on oath those who were likely to perjure themselves, but it is probable that the last word on this important change has not yet been said.   In any event, by the nineteenth century, the rule had become purely arbitrary, often excluding those who alone were in a position to speak with knowledge. Its abolition in 1843 by Lord Denman's Act was a direct result of Bentham's criticism, for Denman and Brougham were the outstanding advocates of Benthamite theories of law reform. In so far as the incapacity of parties and of husbands and wives of parties was concerned, this was removed by the Evidence Act, 1851, and the Evidence Amendment Act, 1853, both being the products of Lord Brougham's reforming zeal.

If we sum up the Law of Evidence as it existed at the beginning of the nineteenth century, we can say that it was practically entirely judge-made law, the product of the decisions of the courts in the first century after the Restoration. Not all its rules were clearly understood, the origins of a number of them were obscure, and the application of others was uncertain. There were, moreover, wide variations between the rules of evidence applied in Common Law Courts and those enforced in Courts of Equity. Some parts of the law of evidence—for example, that which relates to documentary evidence, and especially to public documents—was still primitive and unsystematic. Finally, the rules had grown up in isolation. They were the product of our own peculiar legal history, and they had few points of contact with continental legal thinking on similar topics. By far the most important of Bentham's contributions to the law of evidence was that, for the first time in English legal history, he undertook to test the rules of evidence by reference to general philosophy and logic, and in the light of his knowledge of the rules of continental systems.

The result was that many artificialities and technicalities were swept away; others were modified, and a simple and more coherent system was substituted for the mass of isolated instances and only half-understood particular rules which had existed before, and which had led Bentham to a memorable denunciation of the existing unreformed system of evidence and procedure :

' Were we to go over the history of tribunals, and select all the rules of practice which have been established to the prejudice of truth, to the ruin of innocence and honest right, the picture would be a most melancholy one. In many cases, there had been more error than bad faith; while establishing a course the most opposite to the interests of justice, men believed they were doing her good service. But it must be acknowledged that legislators, timid from their ignorance, have allowed lawyers to assume absolute empire in forms of procedure; and the latter, contemplating every judicial operation as a source of gain, have laboured to multiply unjust suits, unjust defences, delays, incidents, expenses. The greater the complication and obscurity which they contrived to introduce into the system, the more necessary did they render themselves; the courts of justice have been peopled with harpies, who devour the unhappy litigants; legal fictions, nullities, superfluous forms, privileged lies, have covered the field of the law; and the unfortunate individual who is oppressed, when obliged to vindicate his rights, often finds the reparation of an injury more ruinous than the injury itself '.[12]

That is a typical Benthamite reaction to the complexities of the law of his day. Perhaps Wigmore had it in mind when he wrote :[13]

'General denunciations of the system [of evidence] and general denunciations against reform of it will do little service either way. A great national and racial system cannot be easily set aside; and its historic growth indicates that it has at least some right to exist, as it is and where it is. What is needed rather is detailed study and concrete criticism. The specific rules must be tested in their original purpose, their workings, their fitness to survive under present conditions. Complete and long-continued discussion by men of varied experience along the lines here sketched in this Preface would ultimately bring an intelligent consensus as to the parts to be pursued or emphasised and the parts to be modified or cast off. . . . To see poor results around us, and to assume publicly the attitude of reform may signify both intelligence and courage. But it does not signify what is to be the tenor of the proposed reform. And until that tenor is revealed, we cannot say whether it is either desirable or feasible '.

No one can accuse Jeremy Bentham of either lack of intelligence or lack of courage, but whether he bestowed upon the law

[12] *Judicial Evidence,* Book 1, Chap. 13, p. 37.
[13] *Evidence,* 1934 ed., p. 147.

of evidence that detailed study of specific rules which for Wigmore is the prerequisite of concrete criticism is open to doubt.[14] Indeed, Bentham, the universal legislator, preferred not to base his treatise on the English system as it existed in his day : he chose instead the natural model of legal procedure. For him the rules of evidence were most perfectly applied in the domestic tribunal.[15]

Bentham declines to prove the simplicity of the original law of evidence by ' erudite research ' into history : rather he takes as his model the family unit—the domestic tribunal. ' I am like a lapidary who would search for a diamond in a pebble which has been trodden underfoot for ages. The code which I announce combines the merit of antiquity with that of novelty ; it is an universal practice and yet an unexampled innovation '.[16]

In this lies the essential difference between Bentham and FitzJames Stephen. Stephen drafted a code of evidence in 1872 at the request of Lord Coleridge (then Attorney-General). It was based on the practice of law of England as it existed in his day, and such amendments of the existing law as it contained it was possible to recognise with comparative ease. Stephen's code was in the form of an Act of Parliament with precise rules for the guidance of the judge. Bentham's code, on the other hand, in spite of his claim for it, is hardly a code at all. It is written in general terms, and offers little specific aid to the judge. It abounds with general warnings to the judge to be ' suspicious ' of certain evidence, and frequently points out to the legislature certain dangers which will have to be guarded against without specifying what the precautions should be. It is only incidentally that Bentham mentions a specific rule of English law, and the criticisms which he directs against those rules are aimed at their complete abolition, rather than their modification by amendment of existing rules.

GENERAL PRINCIPLES OF BENTHAMITE REFORM

' To find infallible rules for evidence which insure a just decision

---

[14] Cf. Stephen, *Digest of Evidence*, Introduction, p. xxi. ' It is obvious to me that he had not that mastery of the law itself which is unattainable by mere theoretical study, even if the student is as Bentham certainly was, a man of talent approaching closely to genius '.

[15] *Judicial Evidence*, Book I, Chap. 3, pp. 4–8.

[16] *Judicial Evidence*, Book I, Chap. 3, p. 6.

is, from the nature of things, absolutely impossible', says Bentham, ' but the human mind is too apt to establish rules which only increase the probabilities of a bad decision. All the service that an impartial investigator of the truth can perform in this respect is to put legislators and judges on their guard against such hasty rules '.[17]

The clue to Bentham's attitude to the law of evidence is to be found in Book 7, Chapter 15 of his *Judicial Evidence*, where he says :

' Throughout the whole of this work, this practical conclusion is perpetually recurring : Do not exclude any evidence or testimony merely from the fear of being deceived.

' Indisputable, however, as this principle is in itself, it is so new, and so contrary to the prejudices and habits of lawyers, that all I may have to say on the precautions to be employed will appear to them to be but a very weak remedy in comparison with the evil '.[18]

The cogency of Bentham's arguments had such weight, both with writers and courts, that from this time onwards the ' best evidence rule ' was progressively abandoned. Bentham, indeed, would have gone further than statutes or courts have yet done. He would have ended the exclusion of hearsay altogether ; but at the same time, he would have clearly labelled such testimony ' suspicious '. The principle of *suspicion,* in fact, ought to be substituted for the principle of *exclusion,* and in order to deal with suspicious evidence, Bentham suggests the preparation of a code of instructions, bringing under the eye of the judge all those circumstances which, by diminishing the value of a testimony, ought to excite suspicion, and so cause it to be received with caution. It will thus be seen that Bentham's approach to the law of evidence is founded upon the hypothesis that the tribunal (whether judge alone, or judge and jury) possesses the ability and the detachment to weigh the various kinds of evidence. Thus, the changes which he advocates would have brought the English rules of evidence closer to continental systems, and also closer to the methods adopted in a philosophical or historical inquiry. Moreover, running through Bentham's treatise is the idea that the domestic forum, *i.e.* a father inquiring into the wrongdoing

---

[17] *Judicial Evidence,* Book 5, Chap. 16, p. 180.
[18] *Op. cit.,* p. 255.

of a child, is the most nearly perfect tribunal, and on several occasions Bentham argues against the exclusion of some type of evidence on the grounds that it is accepted without ill-effect in domestic proceedings. Sometimes, however, this argument leads him badly astray, as where, in discussing the *onus probandi*, he says: 'The obligation to furnish the evidence ought, in every case, to be laid on the party who can fulfil it with least inconvenience, that is, with least delay, expense and vexation ',[19] a thesis which he unconvincingly attempts to harmonise with the existing rules upon the topic.

In one other respect Bentham's philosophic approach and knowledge of other systems led him astray. Bentham was rightly sceptical of the value of those systems of proof, based ultimately on the Canon Law, which required a mathematical computation for the establishment of a case. Thus, there existed full proof, half-proof, with even subtler gradations. Similarly, the testimony of witnesses was given mathematical value.[20] Nevertheless, the mathematical approach evidently had attractions for Bentham, for he devises his own scale:

' Imagine a scale divided into ten degrees. It has a positive side, inscribed with the degrees of positive belief (that is, affirmative of the fact in question) and a negative side, inscribed with the degrees of negative belief (that is, denying the same fact); at the bottom of the scale is O, denoting the absence of all belief either for or against the fact in question.

' Such is the simplicity of this mode of expression, that it is not even necessary to imagine a material scale. The witness says, my belief is ten or five degrees on the positive side, or ten or five degrees on the negative side ; just as, in speaking of the temperature indicated by the thermometer, we say that the mercury is ten degrees above zero '.[21]

So far the courts have resisted the temptations of a belief-meter, the objections to which are many and weighty. Even the industrious Dumont recoils from the problems it would present, and adds, ' Were this scale adopted, I should be apprehensive that the authority of the testimony would often be inversely, as the wisdom of the witnesses '.[22]

[19] *Judicial Evidence*, Book 7, Chap. 16, p. 257.
[20] These subtleties are well described by Best, *Evidence*, pp. 59–62.
[21] *Judicial Evidence*, Book 1, Chap. 17, pp. 41–42.
[22] *Op. cit.*, p. 46.

On the other hand, Bentham's uncompromising rationality led him to an energetic onslaught upon the oath as a guarantee of veracity in judicial proceedings, and this from two distinct points of view. In the first place, he castigates the absurdity of excluding from the category of witnesses those persons who, for religious reasons, are unable to take the oath in prescribed form. Secondly, he denounces the oath as a form which is ineffective as a deterrent to those who intend to deceive. He regards it, in fact, as a survival of an ancient superstition. Although English law has not yet reached the point where it can dispense with the judicial oath, substituting a penalty for false testimony for the crime of perjury, nevertheless, Bentham's influence was directly responsible for the removal of disabilities due to the form of the oath. Thus, the Oaths Act, 1838, provided that oaths are binding which are administered in such form and with such ceremonies as the witness may declare to be binding, whilst the Evidence Further Amendment Act, 1869, and the Oaths Act, 1888, permitted affirmations in lieu of oath where the judge was satisfied that the taking of an oath would not bind the conscience of the witness.

In one of the less spectacular branches of the law of evidence, Bentham performed an enduring service. Book 4 of his treatise is concerned with Pre-Constituted Evidence, a term which Bentham himself invented, and by which he means ' evidence the creation and preservation of which have been ordained by the law as prerequisite to the existence of certain rights and obligations, so that those rights or obligations shall not be sustained without the production of this evidence '.[23]

He would apply the term to the following :

    1. Facts which have legal effects ; for example, births, deaths and marriages.

    2. Contracts : all settlements and agreements having legal effects.

    3. The proceedings of the judicial department.

    4. The proceedings of the legislative department.

    5. The proceedings of the administrative department.

    6. Written statements of a fact drawn up immediately after it has happened.

    7. The registration of copies.[24]

[23] Book 4, Chap. 1, p. 115.   [24] Book 4, Chap. 2, p. 119.

Here Bentham's knowledge of foreign legal systems was responsible for the formulation of a number of definite rules, many of which have since been embodied in legislation. Writing of the law of evidence in 1849 Best said, ' Sufficient attention was not paid to official pre-appointed evidence. And although some steps have been taken in this direction—*e.g.* by the Births and Deaths Registration Act, 1836, 6 & 7 Will. 4, c. 86, under s. 38 of which a certified copy of an entry in the register of births is evidence of all the contents of the entry, including the date of birth, and subsequent statutes for the registration of births, marriages, and deaths; by the Judgment Act, 1836, 1 & 2 Vict. c. 110, s. 9, and the 32 & 33 Vict. c. 62, s. 24, requiring professional attestation to cognovits and warrants of attorney to confess judgment; and by the Court of Probate Act, 1857, 20 & 21 Vict. c. 77, s. 91, establishing depositions for the wills of living persons, etc.—there is still room for improvement; and the principles adopted in the laws of some foreign countries on the subject might, under due restrictions and with the required caution, be advantageously introduced here '.[25] This is pure Benthamism, as are also Best's further remarks on the desirability of securing some cheap and expeditious means of perpetuating testimony—*desiderata* which were secured by a succession of nineteenth century statutes.

Books 5 and 8 of Bentham's treatise discuss matters which are usually dismissed briefly in works on Evidence, but which are nevertheless of great interest. Book 5 is an extended analysis of circumstantial evidence (in which Bentham includes real evidence). It contains some excellent illustrations of the fallacy of the assumption that ' Circumstances cannot lie ', and also a comparison of the value of direct and circumstantial evidence. Bentham points out that it is essential to compel the party who produces circumstantial facts to connect all the links of the chain in such a manner that the first shall be joined to the principal fact, and the last to the first, without interruption. If this rule is not followed a man may be called on to give an account of every circumstance of his life, for there is no action which may not be connected with any crime by bold conjectures.[26]

In Book 8, Bentham embarks upon a philosophic inquiry

[25] *Evidence,* pp. 104–105.
[26] Book 5, Chap. 17, p. 189.

into the nature of the impossible and the improbable. The force of Bentham's reasoning is emphasised by the fact that many matters which were regarded by Bentham's contemporaries as impossible are now commonplace occurrences.[27] Indeed, there was a certain prophetic cogency about Bentham's remarks [28] concerning such topics as the period of gestation in women [29] (he knew of instances of pregnancy extending over thirteen months) and the duration of the period of childbearing in women [30] (he thought he had seen a case of a woman bearing a child when she was over seventy).

BENTHAM'S INFLUENCE ON SPECIFIC RULES OF THE ENGLISH LAW OF EVIDENCE

Bentham was as fortunate in his editors as he was in his disciples. For while Dumont and John Stuart Mill [31] were polishing the rough diamond of Bentham's work, and making him not merely a genius unto himself, but also an inspiration to legal reformers on both sides of the Atlantic, Denman and Brougham in this country, and Appleton, Chief Justice of Maine, in America, were soon to take practical steps to introduce his suggested reforms into the respective legal systems of both countries. It was in a large measure due to their efforts that Benthamite principles were eventually put on the Statute Book, so that today it is possible to

---

27 *E.g.* aerial navigation. Book 8, Chap. 2, pp. 264–265.
28 Book 8, Chap. 7, p. 274.
29 Cf. *Wood* v. *Wood,* [1947] 2 All E.R. 95 *per Lord Merriman, P.,* at p. 96: 'One can add grains of corn together, and there must come a time when they become a heap. It may be said to be impossible to know where to draw the line, yet it can plainly be seen that one case or another must be on the wrong side of any line that can possibly be drawn. . . . I absolutely decline to hold that this period of 346 days is on the wrong side of any line which can possibly be drawn'.
30 *Ward* v. *Van der Loeff,* [1924] A.C. 653.
31 In this article references have been made to Bentham's *Treatise on Judicial Evidence* which was published in French in 1823 by Dumont, and first appeared in England in 1825. Dillon, *Select Essays in Anglo-American Legal History,* Vol. 1, pp. 492, 509, 510, regards this as in some respects the most important of all his censorial writings on English Law. He says: 'It produced no immediate effect on the professional mind. It was generally regarded as the speculations of a visionary. As I write I have before me Starkie's *Evidence,* the third edition of which appeared in 1842, and the wisdom of the exclusionary rules of evidence is not so much as criticised or questioned'. References have also been given to Bentham's *Rationale of Judicial Evidence* edited by J. S. Mill in 1827, and occupying Vols. 6 and 7 of Bowring's Edition of Bentham's *Works.* This is in some respects more elaborate and mature than Dumont's edition.

say with Wigmore, ' Remembering that in less than three generations nearly every reform which Bentham advocated for the Law
of Evidence has come to pass, we might also regard his condemnation of any rule as presumptively an index of its ultimate
downfall '.[32]

We have already mentioned some of the statutes which
introduced Benthamite principles of law reform.   Thus in 1843,
Lord Denman's Act removed the incompetency of witnesses
from interest or crime ; Lord Brougham's Evidence Act of 1851,
and Evidence Amendment Act of 1853, established the competency of parties and of the husbands and wives of parties; and
the Oaths Act, 1838, permitted Quakers and Moravians to make
an affirmation to the same effect as if they had taken an oath in
the usual form.   The disqualification of Quakers on account of
their religious opinions had drawn from Bentham some of his
most vehement criticism. ' In England the evidence of a Quaker
is admitted in civil, but not in penal matters ; it is received where
the necessity is small, and refused where the necessity is extreme.
If a woman of this society suffers the highest of outrages, to
revenge her virtue she must abjure her religion.   A miscreant set
fire to his house, in the midst of London, to defraud the insurers.
A Quaker, a witness to the fact, appeared on the trial ; but as he
refused to take the oath, it was necessary to let loose an incen-
diary upon society. What absurdity ! Are those who have
scruples about an oath less tenacious of veracity than others ?
On the contrary, their very refusal to take it arises from good
faith.   What occasions the rejection of their testimony is precisely that which ought to secure its admission '.[33]   Criticism
which was both forthright and justified had its effect.

Let us proceed to consider Bentham's views on one of the
most controversial aspects of the Law of Evidence, namely the
question of protection from disclosing evidence on the grounds
of privilege, taking first the privilege of a witness to refuse to
answer criminating questions. This provides what is perhaps the
solitary instance of Bentham's ' erudite research ' into legal
history and at the same time of his failure to convince posterity
of the soundness of his criticisms. The rule in its modern form
may be stated as follows, ' No one is bound to answer any ques-

[32] *Evidence*, 1934 ed., s. 2251.
[33] *Judicial Evidence*, Book 7, Chap. 13, s. 4, p. 252.

tion if the answer thereto would, in the opinion of the judge, have a tendency to expose the witness to any criminal charge or to any penalty or forfeiture which the judge regards as reasonably likely to be preferred or sued for '.[34] Bentham proved that this privilege did not antedate the Restoration. He attributed the origin of the privilege to the abhorrence with which men viewed the proceedings of the Courts of Star Chamber and High Commission, in both of which there was arbitrary power to force men's consciences. ' In a state of things like this what could be more natural than that by a people infants as yet in reason, giants in passion, every distinguishable feature of a system of procedure directed to such ends should be condemned in a lump, should be involved in one undistinguishing mass of odium and abhorrence ; more especially any particular instrument or feature from which the system was seen to operate with a particular degree of efficiency towards such abominable ends? ' [35] Bentham though recognising the origin of the privilege, and sympathising with the necessity for it in the time of High Prerogative Courts, expended some of his most effective criticism on its unsoundness. His criticisms [36] may be summarised as follows :

1. It is, no doubt, a vexation to a man to be examined on facts by which he may inculpate himself. But so is every investigation which tends to inflict punishment.

2. If the danger of subjecting the accused to punishment in consequence of his answers to questions put to him directly is the reason for which they are to be prohibited, it seems to be an equally good reason for not admitting any other evidence against him.

3. The case would be different if accused persons had a natural inclination to subject themselves to punishment, even when they are innocent, but there is no trace of any such self-enmity.

4. The rule does not operate to protect the innocent. ' If all the criminals of every class had assembled, and framed a system after their own wishes, is not this rule the

---

[34] Stephen, *Digest of the Law of Evidence,* 12th ed., 1936, Article 129, p. 152.

[35] *Rationale of Judicial Evidence,* Book 9, Part 4, Chap. 3 (Bowring's ed., Vol. 7, pp. 456–460).

[36] *Judicial Evidence,* Book 7, Chap. 11, pp. 240–245 ; see also *Rationale of Judicial Evidence,* Book 9, Part 4, Chap. 3 (Bowring's ed., Vol. 7, pp. 452ff.).

very first which they would have established for their security? Innocence never takes advantage of it; innocence claims the right of speaking as guilt invokes the privilege of silence '.[37]

5. If the rule has been established with the intention of sparing the accused the chagrin of furnishing evidence against himself, this object is not accomplished since letters written by him and his conversations are received as evidence without scruple.[38]

6. The privilege does not exist in domestic procedure.

7. The common law privilege is inconsistent with 1 & 2 Phil. and Mar. c. 13 ; 2 & 3 Phil. and Mar. c. 10 ; which empowers ' the justices of the peace before whom a person accused of felony is brought to examine the prisoner, and those that bring him ' concerning the fact and circumstances thereof. With what view? In order that the answers thus obtained may contribute to the conviction of the guilty, says the statute; and it is for this reason that it directs that these answers shall be taken down in writing, and be duly certified '.[39]

8. Finally ' the want of this judicial instrument is the more to be regretted, as the evidence drawn from the mouth of the culprit himself is always the most satisfactory, and the best fitted to produce in the public mind an uniform feeling of conviction '.[40]

These criticisms were vigorously promulgated by Bentham's disciples and in particular by Denman [41] in an article in 1824 in the *Edinburgh Review,* and by Appleton, Chief Justice of Maine, in his *Treatise on Evidence.* Dumont,[42] on the other hand, perceived clearly the distinction between the competency of a prisoner to give evidence on his own behalf, and the privilege of a witness not to disclose evidence which might criminate him. He would make the prisoner a competent witness, because in some cases ' If it had not been allowed to examine the accused,

---

[37] *Judicial Evidence,* Book 7, Chap. 11, p. 241.
[38] Cf. *Bradshaw* v. *Murphy* (1836), 7 C. & P. 612, where it was held that an incriminating *public* document in the custody of the witness was not protected.
[39] *Judicial Evidence,* Book 7, Chap. 11, p. 242.
[40] *Op. cit.,* p. 245.
[41] (1824) 40 *Edinburgh Review,* p. 190.
[42] *Judicial Evidence,* Book 7, Chap. 11, p. 245.

it would have been impossible to convict him '; but he would preserve the privilege, because a judge, ' irritated by the resistance,
evasions and denials of the accused, becomes his opponent,
harasses him with questions, strives to intimidate him, or to surprise him by quibbles, subjects him to a species of torture, and
from self-love engages in a contest in which he loses his character
of impartiality '. This is substantially Wigmore's [43] reason for
retaining it. He points out that for the ordinary witness
Bentham's argument seems to fail. ' The witness-stand is today
sufficiently a place of annoyance and dread. The reluctance to
enter it must not be increased '. On the other hand for a
prisoner-witness, assume him to be guilty and Bentham's criticisms are justified; but the rule was designed for the innocent.[44]
' The real objection is that any system of administration which
permits the prosecution to trust habitually to self-disclosure as a
source of proof must itself suffer morally thereby '.

In spite of Bentham's criticisms of the privilege, English law
has retained it and rightly so, it seems, for the reasons pro-
pounded by Dumont and Wigmore. But Bentham's vehemence
has been partly rewarded. Thus, by the Criminal Evidence Act,
1898, a person charged with an offence and the wife or husband
of such person are made competent, and in certain cases, compellable witnesses. By the same Act a prisoner-witness may be
asked any question in cross-examination notwithstanding that it
would tend to criminate him as to the offence charged. Nevertheless the privilege is preserved to this extent that he may not be
asked questions tending to show that he has committed other
offences except under the conditions prescribed by the Act. So
too under s. 15 of the Bankruptcy Act, 1914, debtors cannot
refuse to answer questions put to them on the ground of self-
crimination, and their answers are admissible in evidence against
them in subsequent criminal proceedings with the exception of
offences under ss. 75, 76, 82, 83 and 84 of the Larceny Act, 1861
(relating to frauds by agents, trustees and bankers) or of offences
under ss. 6, 7 (1), 20, 21 and 22 of the Larceny Act, 1916
(relating to larceny of wills, fraudulent conversion, etc.).[45] In
addition to the exclusion of evidence in these excepted cases, the

---

[43] *Evidence,* 1934 ed., s. 2251.
[44] Per Byles, J., in *Bartlett & Lewis,* 12 C.B. (N.S. 5) 249, 265.
[45] Stephen, *Digest of the Law of Evidence,* Art. 129, p. 153.

debtor is given a certain immunity from prosecution.[46]   Again under the Corrupt and Illegal Practices Prevention Act, 1883, a witness before an election court is not excused from answering any question relating to an offence connected with the election on the ground of self-crimination, but he is entitled to a certificate of indemnity, and his answers are not admissible against him in subsequent proceedings, except proceedings for perjury in respect of his evidence.   And under the Explosive Substances Act, 1883, s. 6 (2), where the Attorney-General orders an inquiry to be held by a justice of the peace, witnesses at such an inquiry are not excused from answering questions on the ground of self-crimination.   But these statutes are nothing more than sporadic exceptions.   The privilege itself remains deeply rooted in the English Law of Evidence.

Bentham was of the opinion that the disclosure of communications made to a Catholic priest or any other by way of confession according to the rites and belief of the Church could not be compelled.[47]   His argument was that ' a law which compelled the priest to depose, or admitted his deposition, would operate like a penal law, prohibiting confession. . . . Such a law therefore would be contrary to the law of the state which allows the exercise of the catholic religion.   It would be an act of tyranny over the conscience '.   Wigmore[48] approves of the soundness of Bentham's argument, while recognising that there is no English decision which upholds the privilege, and admitting that the text-writers[49] deny it.   Stephen[50] agrees that English courts are free to decide the question either way; but ' I think that the modern Law of Evidence is not so old as the Reformation, but has grown up by the practice of the courts, and by decisions in the course of the last two centuries.   It came into existence at a time when exceptions in favour of auricular confessions to Roman Catholic priests were not likely to be made. The general rule is that every person must testify to what he knows.   The exception to the general rule has been established

---

[46] By s. 85 of the Larceny Act, 1861, and s. 43 (2) of the Larceny Act, 1916.
[47] *Judicial Evidence*, Book 7, Chap. 9, p. 237. *Rationale of Judicial Evidence*, Book 9, Part 2, Chap. 6 (Bowring's edition, Vol. 7, pp. 367ff.).
[48] *Evidence*, 1934 ed., ss. 2394–2396.
[49] *E.g.* Taylor, ss. 916–917; Roscoe, 176; Roscoe, Cr. Ev. 178. Phipson *Manual*, 6th ed., p. 91.
[50] Stephen, *Digest of the Law of Evidence*, Note 21, pp. 219, 220.

in regard to legal advisers, but there is nothing to show that it extends to clergymen, and it is usually so stated as not to include them '. This merely goes to show that there is probably no privilege for communications to priests in English Law : it does not disprove the desirability of such privilege, and in this we agree with Bentham and Wigmore. All that we can say for certain is that communications made to priests in ordinary conversation, *i.e.* not by way of confession, are not privileged.[51]

Whereas Bentham approved of the privilege of ministers of religion, which English law apparently denies, he disapproved of the privilege of legal advisers, which English law certainly upholds.[52] Bentham, himself a member of the Bar, was not a supporter of its privileges. He was fearful of abuses and suspicious of corruption. He was prone to see a conspiracy between the judge and the advocate for the oppression of the innocent, and the salvation of the guilty. Thus in speaking of the brow-beating of witnesses he says, ' Brow-beating is that sort of offence which never can be committed by any advocate who has not the judge for his accomplice '.[53] He was excessively critical of the privilege of legal advisers not to disclose communications made to them by clients. He says, ' When the lawyer employs his superior knowledge to discover means of escape and subterfuges which may save the guilty from the punishment which he deserves, or to conceal, by his artifices, the dishonesty of his client, and procures it a judicial triumph ; ought he to be considered in any other light than as an accomplice after the fact ; with this difference that accomplices properly so called are blinded by passion and danger ; while on the part of the lawyer, there is an utter indifference to good and evil, dexterity in managing weapons both of offence and defence, and absolute impunity, even when he uses them most injuriously to the community ? '[54] . . . ' Lawyers look on themselves as having a patent to offer their assistance and most solemnly promise secrecy beforehand to every one who will make them confidants of a crime, or associates in a fraud '.[55] Whatever the conduct of

---

[51] *Normanshaw* v. *Normanshaw*, [1893] 69 L.T. 468.
[52] *Judicial Evidence*, Book 7, Chap. 12, pp. 246–247.
[53] *Rationale of Judicial Evidence*, Book 2, Chap. 9 ; Book 3, Chap. 5 (Bowring's ed., Vol. 6, pp. 338 and 406).
[54] *Judicial Evidence*, Book 7, Chap. 12, p. 246.
[55] *Op. cit.,* p. 247.

members of the legal profession may have been in Bentham's time, his censures are now outdated. Bentham assumed that counsel took unfair advantage of their privileged position to ensure the escape from justice of persons whom they knew to be guilty. This is a complete misunderstanding of the position. Thus the Bar Council [56] have ruled that if the prisoner confesses before the trial, the advocate should withdraw from the case and request the prisoner to retain another advocate. If, on the other hand, the confession is made during the trial, or in such circumstances that the advocate cannot withdraw without seriously compromising the position of the accused, the advocate is not released from his duty to do all he honourably can for his client, but such a confession imposes very strict limitations on the conduct of the defence. ' An advocate " may not connive at, much less attempt to substantiate a fraud ". While, therefore, it would be right to take any objection to the competency of the court, to the form of the indictment, to the admissibility of any evidence, or to the sufficiency of the evidence admitted, it would be absolutely wrong to suggest that some other person had committed the offence charged, or to call any evidence which he must know to be false having regard to the confession, such, for instance, as evidence in support of an alibi, which is intended to show that the accused could not have done, or in fact had not done, the act; that is to say an advocate must not (whether by calling the accused or otherwise) set up an affirmative case inconsistent with the confession made to him '. The privilege, however, of not disclosing communications made by the client, is distinct from the privilege of appearing (within the limits above described) for a person who by his own confession is guilty. Bentham, indeed, confused them, as the quotations from his treatise prove. Nevertheless the privilege of non-disclosure has been retained by English law in spite of Bentham, and this, it seems, for two good reasons. First, it is essential that legal advisers should have the fullest knowledge of the facts before they can give competent advice. Lack of frankness on the part of clients would be prejudicial to competence on the part of their counsel. Secondly, it is a cardinal principle of the English Law of Evidence that the prosecution must prove its case, so to speak, ' of its own '. Resort to self-crimination as a method of proof is exceptional,

---

[56] See Lord Macmillan, *Ethics of Advocacy*.

and the exceptions should not be extended. To compel legal advisers to disclose professional confidence will have two results: (1) it will induce clients to refrain from imposing such confidences. This may be detrimental to their cases as we have already demonstrated. (2) If they do impose such confidences, then compelling the legal advisers to disclose them is but an indirect way of compelling the client to criminate himself. It is to be observed that Dumont was not happy about Bentham's views on this subject. He says in a footnote,[57] 'Admit this opinion of Mr. Bentham, it is said, and the accused have no longer counsel; they are surrounded by agents of justice and the police, against whom they ought to be so much the more upon their guard, as no man of a noble or elevated mind would stoop to such an employment. They are so many spies and informers placed round the accused. This is to suppress the defence entirely. The question ought to be examined in this new shape'.

The exclusion of evidence on the ground of marital relationship was also ridiculed by Bentham.[58] One of the earliest results of his derision was the removal of the incompetency of spouses by the Evidence Amendment Act, 1853, in civil cases, and by the Criminal Evidence Act, 1898, in criminal cases. But the incapacity of one spouse to testify for the other is distinct from the privilege not to testify against the other.[59] Bentham would have destroyed this privilege altogether. 'No asylum', he says, 'ought to be opened for criminals; every sort of confidence among them must be destroyed, if possible, even in the interior of their own houses. If they can neither find mercenary protectors among the lawyers, nor concealment at their own firesides, what harm is done? Why they are compelled to obey the laws, and live like honest people!' Bentham then went on to point out that no such privilege existed as between parent and child [60] and cited as an example the following case: 'The Newgate Calendar contains the trial of a shoemaker who, on the evidence of his daughter, was convicted of having hanged his wife. If he had hanged his daughter in the presence of his wife, he could not have been punished'[61] Various reasons have been

---

[57] *Judicial Evidence*, Book 7, Chap. 12, p. 247.
[58] *Judicial Evidence*, Book 7, Chap. 10, pp. 238–239.
[59] See Wigmore, *Evidence*, 1934 ed., s. 601.
[60] Glanville L. Williams, *The Legal Unity of Husband and Wife* (1947), 10 *Modern Law Review*, 15, 20 makes the same point.
[61] *Judicial Evidence*, Book 7, Chap. 10, p. 239, footnote.

advanced for the existence of the privilege.   Blackstone [62] rests it
on the unity of husband and wife.   Coke,[63] on the other hand,
suggested that were the rule otherwise, it would be the cause of
dissensions between husband and wife.   Wigmore [64] explains it
on the ground that it is undesirable to condemn a man on the
evidence of those who share the secrets of his domestic life.   None
of these explanations is entirely satisfactory, and the general
principle that spouses are competent and compellable witnesses
for and against each other has gradually been evolved.   But there
are exceptions :   (1) The spouse of an accused person is only
competent against the other spouse in (a) common law cases
involving personal violence and (b) those within the schedule to
the Criminal Evidence Act, 1898, as amended by later Acts.   In
common law cases and cases under s. 1 of the Married Women's
Property Act, 1884, the spouse is also compellable.   (2) The
spouse is always a competent witness for the accused on his
application, but never compellable.[65]   (3) Neither spouse is compellable to disclose communications made by the other during
the marriage (Evidence Amendment Act, 1853, s. 3 ; Criminal
Evidence Act, 1898, s. 1 (d).   However, Bentham may be
said to have contributed by his writings to the evolution of the
general principle.

CONCLUSIONS

In this article we have attempted to give some account of the
scope of Bentham's voluminous writings on the Law of Evidence ;
but, of necessity, many things which are of interest have had to
be omitted.   We have shown that the removal of the ' interest '
disqualification, the abolition of the incompetency of parties and
their spouses, the permission of all persons, whatever their
religious beliefs, to give evidence, and the adoption of some rules
of ' preconstituted ' evidence were in some measure due to his
efforts.   We have pointed out the great service which he rendered
to lawyers by his systematic treatment of exclusionary rules, and
in particular of ' hearsay '.   We have shown that he would have
substituted the principle of suspicion for the principle of exclusion, which may broadly be said to have formed the basis of

[62] Comm., Vol. 1, p. 443.
[63] Co. Litt. 6b. Cf. *Barker* v. *Dixie* (1735).   Cas. temp. Hard. 264.
[64] *Evidence*, 1934 ed., s. 2227.
[65] Phipson, *Manual*, 6th ed., p. 215.

the Evidence Act, 1938, a statute, however, of very limited application. We have portrayed Bentham as the arch-enemy of the privilege of witnesses. His criticisms of these have been singularly unsuccessful, with the exception that in certain cases a spouse is now a competent witness against the other spouse. But it cannot be maintained that the final word has been said about this controversial matter. We have indicated that though he was generally careless of legal history, he was capable of discovering the original reasons for a rule, when he condescended to delve into that erudite research which he despised. We have shown him to be a fearless and vigorous critic whose ' assault on the system of judicial evidence was like the bursting of a shell in the powder magazine of a fortress, the fragments of the shell being lost in the ruin which it has wrought '.[66] Bentham's works may have gone out of favour, but the system which he set out to destroy has been rebuilt to no mean extent on Benthamite principles.

---

[66] Stephen, *General View of the Criminal Law of England*, p. 206; cited by Dillon, *Influence of Bentham, Select Essays in Anglo-American Legal History*, pp. 492, 510.

CHAPTER 6

THE RESTLESS SPIRIT OF ENGLISH LAW

R. H. *Graveson*

Two hundred years ago Jeremy Bentham was born into a world well pleased with itself. At home the Jacobites had just failed for the last time. Whig and Tory were obstructing each other in trying to make effective an English constitution under a line of foreign kings whom Pitt accused of considering England ' only as a province to a despicable electorate '. With war against France abroad, everything must have appeared traditionally right to the Englishman of 1748. England in that year was a country of contrast and compromise, a place of pleasant fields and growing slums; of political ability and scandalous patronage; of new-found wealth and incoherent poverty; of decadent morals and religious revivals; of poor taste and rich craftsmanship; of colonial expansion and enclosure of commons; of commercial fact and legal fiction; of law in books and law in action. True, there were ripples on the surface of this prosperous complacency. The star that marked the birth of Bentham marked also the publication of Montesquieu's *Esprit des Lois*. The writings of Rousseau could not be confined to France, nor were they utterly condemned in England because of their alien enemy origin. Lord Mansfield himself was refusing to observe the feudal frontiers of the common law when the requirements of commercial progress justified their violation. But the Chief Justice of the Court of King's Bench was a lonely voice crying in a wilderness of legal and political indifference. The reforms he attempted were almost two centuries ahead of their time,[1] and were destined to fail.[2] The eighteenth century is notably conspicuous for its almost complete lack of legal reform and

---

[1] Cf. Dicey's opinion: ' Lord Mansfield lived at least two centuries too late '—*Law and Opinion in England*, 2nd ed., p. 167.
[2] *Pillans* v. *Van Mierop*, [1765] 3 Burr. 1663, overruled in *Rann* v. *Hughes*, [1778] 7 T.R. 350. Cf. recommendations of Law Revision Committee, 6th Interim Report on the Doctrine of Consideration; and most recently the judgment of Denning, J., in *Central London Property Trust Ltd.* v. *High Trees House, Ltd.*, [1947] 1 K.B. 130.

legal development. The common law bench can indeed look for redemption in that period of legal sterility to Lord Mansfield; but few others lived then to save its name. Equity presented a somewhat brighter picture, for its history from the time of the Restoration to that of Lord Eldon was one of gradual development and innovation to fill some of the many gaps in the system. But in general courts of law and equity were alike paralysed by antiquated procedure, inefficient organisation, multiplicity of fee-charging officials and popular disrepute. Those familiar with the system were myopes or cynics; those who in ignorance went to law were optimistic fools. Legal education had touched its nadir, though it was soon to be raised again by the institution of the Vinerian Chair at Oxford. Nevertheless, the main bodies of substantive law and equity, though antiquated, were reasonably sound. If punishment for crime was vicious by modern standards, it was not far behind contemporary thought. If the land law was enchained in the fetters of feudalism, England was still a predominantly agricultural country of large landed estates and small holdings; and the prophetic and premature attempts of the seventeenth century to reform this branch of law had failed.[3] If the common law was still confined within the forms of action, the judicial and judicious use of fictions and the still somewhat free doctrine of precedent had allowed it to keep pace with a slowly changing society. But always between the law and the litigant stood a terrifying barrier of procedure, formalities and officials, which only determination, time and money could hope to surmount. Of such free English air Bentham drew his first breath. How different was the scene when, eighty-four years later, he drew his last, is in part the measure of his work; though he never lived to see the full realisation of success which his reforming zeal achieved, for he died, as he had lived, with the pen in his hand. The exquisite irony of fate decreed that the Reform Bill of 1832, to which Bentham had given so much, should receive the Royal Assent the day after his death.[4]

Sufficient is generally known of Bentham's life and background,[5] his distaste for legal practice and his becoming a recluse

[3] See Holdsworth, 'Reform of the Land Law', in *Essays in Law and History*, pp. 100ff.
[4] Kayser, *The Grand Social Enterprise*, 1932.
[5] For excellent short accounts of Bentham's early life, see Dicey, *Law and Opinion in England*, Lect. 6; Allen, *The Young Bentham*, in Legal Duties.

in the house he significantly called ' The Hermitage ', to arouse immediate suspicion on the part of practising lawyers of his ability either to understand or to help them. He '. . . shrank from the world in which he was easily brow-beaten to the state in which he could reign supreme '.[6] This fact, too, meant that Bentham himself would have exercised far less influence on the outside world if he had stood alone. Fortunately for him, he numbered among his disciples men of standing, not only in England but in many European countries, who could help very substantially in putting his theories into practice. Sir Samuel Romilly, for example, who was greatly impressed by Bentham's ' Fragment on Government ', became his particular mouthpiece in Parliament; while his contacts with political statesmen, including the Prime Minister, at Lord Shelburne's house, kept his theories alive in the minds of public men. He was, moreover, fortunate to be most ably assisted by men like James and John Stuart Mill, who made his cause of utilitarianism their own. Bentham was more than an individual : he became a school of thought.

Bentham discriminated little between common law and equity. Both systems, to the extent of their case-law content, received his biting censure in generous measure. The course of legal history and the centuries of tradition which had dictated the division into the two great branches of English law could not have had so little significance for him had he been a practising lawyer. For him the emphasis lay on the method of making law, not on its content, a fact which coloured most of his theories and made him an iconoclast towards the English system of case law in general and the doctrine of precedent in particular. With that system there could be for him no compromise. He had to destroy before he could rebuild,[7] and the frame of his new edifice of English law was to be legislation in the form of a simple, intelligible code.

Before Bentham's eyes lay the failures of many of Lord Mansfield's attempts to reform the common law by judicial methods. More and more he was persuaded by circumstances

---

[6] Sir Leslie Stephen, *The English Utilitarians,* 1900, p. 175.
[7] Of his *Comment on the Commentaries,* Bentham wrote : ' The business of it is rather to *overthrow* than to *set up;* which latter task can seldom be performed to any great advantage where the former is the principal one '. (*Works,* Vol. 1, p. 239.)

of the need to start from the top rather than from the bottom.
In his opening campaign of demolition his attacks struck at four
things : antiquated and obsolete rules of law ; the judicial technique generally, and particularly the use of fictions; the grossly
inefficient machinery of justice ; and his greatest enemies, apathy
and complacence. In the full measure of his stature he became
' a Trojan horse of reform within the gates of the chaotic,
obsolete law of his time '.[8] But in so doing he sometimes wrote
below the level of fair criticism and resorted to pure abuse. His
first and most famous broadside, which in parts bore this character, was his ' Comment on the Commentaries ', a considered
statement of his revulsion of feeling against the publication of
Blackstone's ' Commentaries on the Laws of England '. If one
may, while conscious of the dangers that await post-Glossators,
comment on this ' Comment on the Commentaries ', one might
properly admit that Blackstone's ' narcotic complacency ',[9]
specious reasoning and justification of every rule of English law
were indeed an inviting target for anybody's criticism ; but what
Bentham refused to admit, and at times may have failed to
perceive, was the accuracy, for the most part, of Blackstone's
statements of law, and the fact that his inaccuracies were limited
to the need he felt to give reasons for rules of law where in truth
no reason need exist. Blackstone, like most of his contemporaries,
saw in English law the embodiment of the law of nature.[10] But
Bentham had not only listened to Blackstone's lectures : he had
discovered a less complacent view of English law in Montesquieu's
two books, the *Lettres Persanes* [11] and *Esprit des Lois*.[12] Nor
was Bentham himself entirely free from the addiction to that
pretentious type of reasoning of which he attempted to give
Blackstone a monopoly. His comments on the Vinerian
Professor's distinction between statute and case law as written
and unwritten [13]; and on the requirement of immemorial user in
custom,[14] make it clear that the two were thinking on different

[8] Stone, *The Province and Function of Law,* 1947, p. 268.
[9] The expression is Dr. C. K. Allen's.
[10] ' In essence the law of Nature was identical in Blackstone's eyes with the
law of England '. Jones, *Historical Introduction to the Theory of Law,*
p. 90.
[11] 1731.
[12] 1748.
[13] *Comment on the Commentaries,* p. 158.
[14] *Op. cit.,* p. 171.

planes and regarding law for different purposes. Law looked at through the eyes of a teacher or a practitioner bears a very different appearance from law looked at through those of a reformer.

How, then, did the common law appear to Jeremy Bentham? His description of it as ' An assemblage of fictitious regulations feigned after the image of those real ones that compose the Statute Law ' [15] is almost as well known as his account of the creation at the hands of judges of what he stigmatised as ' dog law ' [16]; though the connection between this *ex post facto* judicial process and the theory of a rational or natural basis of the common law, which he equally deplored, is not immediately apparent. ' Ask a lawyer ', he wrote,[17] ' What is Common Law? it's more than he can tell. But he is certain that it is the perfection of reason. For Lord Coke has told him so; and a thousand compilers have repeated it after Lord Coke. Blackstone, the author of the Commentaries, has repeated it after a thousand compilers.

' He knows not (very well) what common law is: however, he knows what it is *not*; or rather what is not *it* : which is always something. " Whatever is not reason is not Law ". And this he knows by the same means . . . What reason? What, this man's reason or that man's reason, or my reason? Oh no, nothing like it—a particular sort of reason—a sort made on purpose—a legal reason. The Common Law of Common Lawyers is according to reason : but it is legal reason '. Such writing is far from brilliant, but Bentham ends on an even weaker note when he asks, ' In short would you know precisely what Common Law is? It is Common Law '. He is more precise, if less complimentary, when he identifies the system as,[18] ' That very sort of bastard law I have been describing to you, which they themselves (Coke and Blackstone) call the *unwritten law,* which is no more made than it is written—which has not so much as a shape

---

[15] *Op. cit.,* p. 126.
[16] ' Do you know how they make it? Just as a man makes laws for his dog. When your dog does anything you want to break him of, you wait until he does it and then beat him. This is the way you make laws for your dog, and this is the way judges make laws for you and me '. *Truth v. Ashhurst* (1792), *Works,* Vol. 5, p. 231.
[17] Law Common and Statute (c. 1780); unpublished MS. Cat. No. LXIII, 49–50.
[18] *Works,* Vol. 5, p. 236.

to appear in—not so much as a word which anybody can say belongs to it—which is everywhere and nowhere—which comes from nobody and is addressed to nobody—and which, so long as it is what it is, can never, by any possibility, be either known or settled '. ' The French ', he concludes, ' have had enough of this dog-law '. Here we have the curious spectacle of Jeremy Bentham, legal reformer, the enemy of tradition, decrying the common law because it was unsettled. Perhaps he deliberately ignored the fact that it was this very elasticity of the system which, through the various devices of judicial technique, enabled it to expand and make at least the attempt to keep pace with the needs of changing society, though he gave somewhat grudging recognition to this purpose and use of fiction. For whatever truth there was in Maine's remarks [19] about Bentham's history, none could accuse him of ignorance of law. It is more than doubtful whether his ideal form of statute could have done either so much or so well; for, in the words of Sir Leslie Stephen ',[20] ' The legislative system under which Bentham grew up was a Parliament of country gentlemen who were incompetent ignorant amateurs in the job, without interest in general principles, awesome of tradition, and with a profound veneration for the law. In particular they had no understanding of commercial affairs '. Though today, in a much reformed Parliament, these epithets would be generally inappropriate, the law of England is now less knowable, chiefly because it is infinitely more statutory, than it was in Bentham's day. In his view, one could only hope to understand the common law by imagining some corresponding article of statute law that should represent it. The dangerous and un-English method of trying to fit facts to theory shows up in Bentham's statement that, ' The Common Law is but the Shadow of the Statute Law although it came before it. Before the appearance of the Statute Law even the word Law could hardly have been mentioned '.[21] How far removed in thought and sympathy he stood from the spirit of the common law on questions of the technique of law-making is plain from his view that a rule of law must be predicated of some assemblage of words, and never of a ' bare assemblage of naked ideas '.[22]

[19] Popular Government (below).
[20] *The English Utilitarians*, 1900, p. 22.
[21] *Comment on the Commentaries*, p. 125.
[22] *Op. cit.*, p. 244.

Bentham perceived how the judges had developed English law by means of fiction and analogy. Of these practical methods he despised the one and bemoaned the other. ' In English Law ', he wrote,[23] ' fiction is a syphilis which runs into every vein and carries into every part of the system the principle of rottenness '. His attitude of contempt towards the use of fictions was one which, perhaps, as a legislative reformer and an advocate of the systematic code, he had perforce to adopt. But it is an attitude which does not fit very well into his general theory. He himself acknowledged that it was only through the use of fictions that judges were able to observe the form laid down by time-honoured precedent and yet to achieve the results, albeit very slowly, demanded by the conditions of a changed society. Only by the use of such fictions and by reference to a nebulous and unknown common law could the judges make any progress in bringing law up to date. But judges are not alone guilty in resorting to this device. It is, perhaps, fortunate that Bentham's reactions to the supreme example of a modern statutory fiction, that of summer time and double summer time, are not recorded.[24]

It was only after digesting Priestley's principle, repeated from Beccaria and Helvetius, of the greatest happiness of the greatest number, that Bentham gave serious thought to the extension of the common law by analogy. He realised that ' The Judges cannot make any exceptions to a rule of Law, but what are deducible from some other ',[25] while commenting that, ' It is not always that the line of analogy ordered is that of utility : the former is straight and inflexible : the latter takes on throughout inflexions from the influence of the circumstances it meets within its course '.[26] Maintaining that there was no analogy in legislation, Bentham argued,[27] ' It seems as if it could not be right for a Judge to prefer analogy to utility unless it were more easily agreed about the former than the latter. If they are more easily agreed about the analogy than utility, why is it expedient that the Legislature itself should make any alterations in the law of analogy for the sake of utility? ' It was a question to which he gave no answer. For judicial analogy Bentham gave two

[23] *Works,* Vol. 5, p. 92.
[24] See Jones, *Historical Introduction to the Theory of Law,* p. 165.
[25] Law Common and Statute, MS. Cat. No. LXIII, 49–50.
[26] *Op. cit.*
[27] *Op. cit.*

reasons : (1) ' to keep the Judge from assuming the province of
the legislator, which he would do if he were governed solely by
considerations of convenience ' : (2) ' that those who act in any
new case may be better able to conjecture beforehand what is
likely to be the decision, and to order their conduct accordingly '.[28]   It is impossible to deduce from Bentham's argument
in this manuscript whether, in disapproving of the doctrine of
analogy he also disapproved of the limitation contained in
judicial powers in the first of his two reasons, though there is little
in Bentham's writing to support the granting of legislative powers
to the judge.   Indeed, his chief complaint was against the
exercise of such powers in the creation of ' dog law '.   Within
the rules of analogy Bentham recognised limitations inherent in
the nature of this judicial process.   Thus, in considering the rule
of common law that capital punishment of murderers is by
hanging, he used this example[29] : ' Comes another murderer
and says a Judge, " This is a cruel, desperate villain, I think I'll
burn him ".   His colleague advises against such a course, as it
had never been done.   " You had better not, it will be thought
strange ".   Now ', added Bentham, ' what one can't avoid seeing
is that one time or another there is a vast stride must have been
taken from Liberty (choice) to obligation '.   In other words, the
recognition of precedent as binding had replaced, if it ever
existed in this matter, free judicial discretion.

Sir Henry Maine's accusation[30] that Bentham ' was careless
of remote history ' finds some justification in Bentham's treatment of specific topics in the common law.   For example, in
dealing with criminal libel he was doing no more than echo the
general contemporary feeling of frustration and persecution
when he wrote, in *Truth* v. *Ashhurst*,[31] ' What neither Mr. Justice
Ashhurst, nor Mr. Justice Anybody-else, has ever done, or ever
will do, is to teach us how we are to know what is, from what is
not, a libel.   One thing they are all agreed in . . . that if what
they call a libel is all true, and can be proved to be so, instead
of being the less, it is the more libellous . . . so that the more
wickedly a judge or minister behaves, the surer he is of not
hearing of it '.   It was a shrewd and well-aimed shot, but one

---

[28] *Op. cit.*
[29] *Op. cit.*
[30] *Popular Government*, Preface, p. viii.   See also pp. 84 and 86.
[31] *Works*, Vol. 5, p. 234.

which Lord Mansfield himself had fired years before. 'This we get', Bentham concluded, 'by leaving it to judges to make law, and of all things the law of libels'. Was he aware, one wonders, of the legislative ancestor of criminal libel in the Statute Scandalum Magnatum, or of the very wide development of this offence in the Council and Star Chamber as a quasi-administrative remedy for the suppression of disorder?

Bentham wrote critically, frequently, and at some length on the jury system, and no aspect of that system received more vehement invective than the practice of the Crown in maintaining special panels of jurors to secure convictions in the trial of cases of seditious libel.[32] He had little faith in the ability or independence of twelve fellow-men when subject to the emotional eloquence of an advocate. In an unpublished manuscript [33] of about 1791, Bentham wrote with bitter philosophy, 'Every relative generates its correlative. Slaves breed tyrants: impostors are bred by dupes, Ignorant and prejudiced Judges breed disingenuous, shameless, overbearing advocates. English Jurymen breed Old Bailey and Nisi-prius Lawyers.

'The disease sinks deeper, and prisons the vitals of government. The Bar is a chief nursery for the House. The morals of the Bar become the morals of the House. Learn manly virtue at the Bar, learn female at Drury-Lane . . .

'The recipes for poisoning Juries are as well known as the recipes for poisoning rats, and almost as infallible. The same cause, as will occur, that furnishes one hand ready to administer the poison furnishes another hand equally ready to apply the antidote. But the poisoner and the physician do not contend upon equal terms. The triumphs of reason are sure but they are very slow: the triumphs of eloquence are instantaneous'.

In the eyes of Bentham equity and Lord Eldon were one and he despised it. For under the Chancellorship of Eldon equity had become almost completely obscured by an exuberant overgrowth of procedure, expense and great delay. 'This is a finer sort of law they call equity', wrote Bentham,[34] as though he were a stranger to English law, 'a distinction as unheard of out of England as it is useless here to every purpose but that of

---

[32] In his pamphlet 'The Elements of the Art of Packing'. *Works*, Vol. 5.
[33] 'Juries—poison lawyers', Cat. No. XXXV, folio 10, pp. 93–98.
[34] *Truth v. Ashhurst*, in *Works*, Vol. 5, p. 234. See also *Some Indications concerning Lord Eldon.*

delaying justice, and plundering those who sue for it'. The administration of the Chancellor's court was a notorious scandal, deserving of all the vigour of Bentham's vitriolic pen. But because he failed, not surprisingly, to see the wood for the trees, he brought within his general condemnation the substance of equity, which was not fundamentally unsound, when the real grounds of criticism were those of its administration and its cost. There is little doubt that Charles Dickens, in such novels as *Bleak House,* did more than Bentham for the reform of the administration of equity. In a manuscript entitled ' Equity and Common Law ' [35] Bentham, somewhat on the analogy of his calculus of pains and pleasures, analyses the situation ' Where the Common Law, pretending to give a Right, gives no other remedy than one which is not adequate '; and almost approaches the point of admitting the utility of the equitable remedy of specific performance. He stops short, however, and goes off instead into an exercise of arithmetic in the assessment of what he describes as ' grains of satisfaction '. As this document has not been published, it may be of some interest to give an extract showing Bentham's method of analysis.

' This is the case ', he wrote, ' in Contracts for specific things to be delivered or services to be done. For default of not sending or doing, as the case is, in guise of compensation the Common Law provides this remedy : viz. so much money as 12 indifferent persons shall judge proper to be given in lieu.

' It is plain that the remedy cannot be adequate but upon the supposition that money is a match for anything; that is, that money will be a means to any man of providing to him either any assignable thing or service to be rendered him, for the rendering of which he can have contracted with another or which comes to the same thing, a quantity of satisfaction equal to the quantity which that thing or service would have given him. Now neither of these facts is always true; the first manifestly never can be, when he or more than one man have such desire for the same thing and as between those two or more is equal, tho' greater than that [illegible word] desire of the rest of mankind for it makes what is called its value.

' The 2d. often is not, when it is understood of such a sum of money as one man can be supposed to possess, and as it would

[35] *Circa* 1776. Cat. No. LXX, 57–59.

be deemed proper to take from him for the benefit of another. I use this restriction; because, if it be true what has been the saying of a celebrated Minister, that " every *man* has his price ", wherein under the action of *man* are included all the services he is capable of rendering even at the expense of his honour and his conscience, much more is it, that every *thing* has its price, upon the supposition of an unlimited power to augment that price at pleasure. (I am assuming for that price an unbounded power of augmentation.) However this be, it is often not true of such a sum as has just been mentioned; as may be made accurately manifest by an example '.[36]

But Bentham's genius did not neglect the possibility of improvements and innovations in the body of law and equity. Not the least of his achievements among the matters now assigned to the Chancery Division was his scheme for a system of limited liability companies, which bore fruit in the Companies Acts, 1856–1862.

Through his burning sense of the injustice of judge-made law and the judicial making of law which was unattainable save to the wealthy, persistent and long-lived, Bentham at times allowed his heart to govern his head. Thus he wrote, ' " We will deny justice "—says King John—" we will sell justice to no man ". This was the wicked King John. How does the good King George? He denies it to ninety-nine men out of a hundred, and sells it to the hundredth '.[37] In fighting a system so much in need of reform he rallied its defence by overstating the case against it and by failing to exclude from his usually well-founded reasoning scandalous abuse, which not only did not help in dealing with His Majesty's judges, but went far to destroying the good that his sound arguments might have done. Bentham never went so far as to say that judges were corrupt : their incorruptibility he explained by the fact that it paid them to be honest and to support a radically corrupt system. But this distinction was almost too fine to cloak the allegation of judicial corruption. The hostility he raised among judges and officials to his theories at large by the attribution of corrupt

---

[36] The example he gives concerns an agreement by V to sell to P–1 a house for £1,000. The house is worth £2,000 to P–1. Before conveyance, V sells the house to P–2 for £1,500. Bentham assesses the loss to P–1 by means of a kind of balance sheet.

[37] *Truth* v. *Ashhurst, Works,* Vol. 5, p. 233.

methods to admitted abuses and practices of long standing,
particularly in procedure and the payment of countless official
fees for largely unnecessary steps in bringing an action, created
a strong and influential body of opposition to the realisation of
his reforms.   His influence on the technique of judicial decision
was commensurate with his lack of sympathy with judge-made
law.   But his attitude to abuse and corruption must evoke the
keenest admiration.   It is fortunate for English law that Bentham
had the independence of both mind and means to say such
things.

So far we have been seeing Bentham the critic and destroyer.
Having criticised, if not destroyed, how did he propose to
rebuild?   It is a question of his science of legislation, which may
be answered elsewhere.   At this point one can only mention the
mainsprings of Bentham's theory as the foundation for those
reforms of English civil law,[38] which have, two centuries after
Bentham's birth, borne fruit and become part of our legal
heritage.   'The only object of government', wrote Bentham,[39]
' ought to be the greatest possible happiness of the community ',
an object to be secured by legislation.   The measure of happiness
secured was Bentham's yardstick of utility by which he tested
every rule and every idea of reform, rejecting inexorably those
rules and ideas which fell short of his ideal.   Yet, paradoxically
it seems, individual freedom was to be preserved and, wherever
possible, extended.[40]   This freedom of the individual was no
party creed : it was, as Dicey has shown,[41] the common property
of Whig and Tory, Liberal and Radical alike, in the nineteenth
century.   Bentham accepted the English Puritan tradition,
expressed by the seventeenth century philosophers, that that
government governs best which governs least; but the solution
to his paradox of *laisser faire* and legislative reform must be
sought in the hedonistic theory of sum totals of individual
pleasures and pains.[42]   Pleasure and pain must necessarily be
predicated of individuals capable of emotional feeling; and the

[38] Here it is proposed to deal only with those reforms which do not fall
under those branches of English law, *e.g.,* criminal law, constitutional
law, poor law and evidence, dealt with elsewhere in this volume.
[39] *Theory of Legislation* (Hildreth's translation), 7th ed., p. 95.
[40] Professor Stone finds a clue to the solution of this apparent paradox in
The Province and Function of Law, pp. 279–280.
[41] *Law and Opinion in England,* Lect. 6.
[42] See Stone, *op. cit.,* pp. 278–279.

mathematical, and purely *quantitative,* totalising of the pleasures of many into the greatest possible happiness of the community does not rob the doctrine of its fundamentally individualistic character.

Bentham's influence has been widest in political liberalism, in the technique of legislation (he is the chief English exponent and advocate of codification of law), in theories of penal law, poor law, and their administration, and in the law of evidence, though in many of these fields his influence was greater abroad than in his own country. For the turn of the century represented years of opportunity for Bentham. The legal and political atmosphere on the continent of Europe, for example, was more favourable to codification both in constitutional and private law and the ground more fertile for legal reform. In England itself, it is difficult even by a rough chronological test to determine with any degree of accuracy which of the legal reforms of the nineteenth and twentieth centuries are attributable exclusively to Bentham and which to the school of thinkers generally called the Utilitarians. The attempt to make such a distinction would, in most cases, be as vain as it would be unprofitable; for not only did Bentham habitually discuss his projects for reform with his friends, but after his death his spirit lived on in their work. It is, furthermore, a factor of importance in assessing Bentham's influence that many of his writings were published posthumously, some are only now being published on the bicentenary of his birth, and others have not yet seen the light of day. He would be rash, indeed, who said that Jeremy Bentham, who still sits in his chair at University College, London, had ceased to influence the development of English law. Leaving aside the more important spheres of Bentham's influence on English law mentioned above, one may perhaps indicate shortly a few of the changes in specific rules as well as major principles directly related to his proposals for legal reform in the general field of English law.

In the law of contract Bentham's principle of extending freedom of contract as part of individual liberty became the keynote of the common law during the nineteenth century. It was a principle of the utmost significance in the political, social and economic, as well as in the legal, life of the nineteenth century. Its impact on the law of contract, in particular, had an effect

far wider and deeper than would appear from the particular kinds of contractual relation to which Bentham specifically turned his attention; for, like the corresponding plea for liberty in the disposition of land,[43] it was a far bigger thing than an element of this contract or that: it was a foundation of the whole law of contract. In its aspect of the right of the individual to determine his own actions this doctrine had less influence in the law of torts. The application of the principle, for example, of *volenti non fit injuria* to the increased hazards of nineteenth century industry may have received increased and welcome support from Bentham's doctrines, but it was merely an extension of an ancient principle of the common law.[44] But the perpetuation of the principle in such cases, where indeed there was no more than a fictitious acceptance of risk, until the end of the nineteenth century[45] may owe much to Bentham's individualism. With these considerations in mind, let us look at one or two instances of its application in the law of contract.

By a statement of the relation of master and servant as a matter of contract and by his indictment of Elizabethan legislation, fixing the term of seven years as the period of apprenticeship for all types of craft,[46] Bentham ignored the status relationship which had continued into the eighteenth century and did much to justify Maine's aphorism of the movement of progressive societies up to his day from status to contract.[47] Such theory accorded well with the feelings and interests of a reformed House of Commons consisting of representatives of shopkeepers and manufacturers in an age of commercial and industrial expansion. It was the age of machines, of cheap labour and of the doctrine of common employment.[48] With the same courage of his convictions, Bentham agitated for the repeal of the usury laws; his abhorrence at conditions in debtor's prisons did not deter him from writing his *Defence of Usury*.[49] For not only was usury in accordance with his own creed of individual liberty, but demonstrated in a particular field the economic principles

---

[43] Below.
[44] Bracton states the principle: *De Legibus Angliæ*, 1569 ed., folio 18A.
[45] *Smith* v. *Baker*, [1891] A.C. 325.
[46] *Theory of Legislation*, 7th ed., p. 200.
[47] *Ancient Law*, Pollock's ed., p. 182; see the present writer, *The Movement from Status to Contract*, 4 Modern Law Rev., p. 261.
[48] *Priestley* v. *Fowler* (1837), 3 M. & W. 1.
[49] 1787.

of freedom of trade expounded in Adam Smith's *Wealth of Nations*.[50] Though the usury laws were repealed in 1854, a feeling lingered that Parliament had been betrayed by a high-sounding theory into a course which in practice created hardship disproportionate to the liberty it secured. It realised that economics could deprive a man of real liberty of contracting no less effectively than law itself, and restrictions on moneylenders were again introduced.[51] Bentham's advocacy of the emancipation of slaves is consistent with his demand for increasing individual liberty to its highest point. In view of his general refusal to compromise with circumstances or vested interests, it is surprising to find Bentham favouring gradual emancipation of slaves on the basis of families. The exaggerated dangers which he visualised [52] from a sudden and complete emancipation were never realised when such emancipation took place. It is rare to find Bentham understating a case in which he believed.

Because Bentham regarded marriage in the light of a civil contract, largely ignoring on the one hand the religious character of the ceremony by which it was created and on the other the public character of the status it conferred, he failed to achieve in his proposals for reform in this branch of law the degree of liberty of contracting (and of contracting-out) which his individualistic utilitarianism realised in the broader fields of contract. Ignoring all accepted prohibitions against marriage between persons within certain degrees of consanguinity or affinity, he subjected to the searching test of utility the relationships which should or should not prevent marriage. It is of interest to note his conclusion that a man should be allowed to marry the sister of his deceased wife, and his less strong suggestion that marriage between a man and his deceased brother's widow should be permitted.[53] Both of these reforms have now become law, but only in the twentieth century.[54] Bentham's emphasis on the contractual aspect of marriage assisted substantially in the

---

[50] 1776.
[51] Moneylenders Acts, 1900 and 1927.
[52] 'This operation could not take place suddenly, except by a violent revolution, which, by displacing men, by destroying all property, by putting all persons into situations to which they had not been educated, would produce evils a thousand times greater than all the immediate good which could be expected from it'. *Theory of Legislation*, 7th ed., p. 207.
[53] *Op. cit.*, pp. 218, 219.
[54] Deceased Wife's Sister's Marriage Act, 1907 ; Deceased Brother's Widow's Marriage Act, 1921.

passing of the Marriage Act, 1835, while his views on both marriage and divorce constituted a major influence in the passing of the Matrimonial Causes Act, 1857. While his emphasis on individual freedom dictated that parties who agreed to marry should be capable of agreeing to dissolve their marriage, he did not go so far as to suggest that mutual consent alone should be sufficient for this purpose. 'The dissolution of a marriage', wrote Bentham,[55] 'is an act sufficiently important to be submitted to formalities which would have the effect more or less to counteract the operation of caprice, and to leave the parties time for reflection. The intervention of a magistrate is necessary, not only to establish the fact that there has been no violence on the part of the husband to force the wife's consent, but also to interpose a delay, longer or shorter, between demanding and obtaining the divorce'. The short transition from Bentham's call for some delay between demanding and obtaining a divorce to the statutory interval between decrees *nisi* and absolute, which became law in 1857, refutes the allegation of coincidence. While his influence on the introduction into English law of outright divorce as a judicial remedy is incalculable, some of his incidental recommendations were rejected. Collusion, for instance, was for Bentham a normal and natural manifestation of the contractual exercise of two free wills,[56] the very opposite of an absolute bar to obtaining a decree. The new Divorce Court of 1857 was a secularised version of its ecclesiastical predecessors and unlikely to take kindly to dissolution of marriage on the basis of consent of the parties. In this process of secularisation of jurisdiction the recognition of marriage as an engagement of religious significance passed into a recognition of it as a relation of vital interest to the State and society. In neither stage was the interest of the parties themselves predominant. Marriage could not be dissolved, as Bentham had wished, on demand, but only (and even today) on a prayer. Marriage, in fact, as judges have said from time to time since 1857, is more than a contract: it is a status.[57] Bentham's contractual

---

[55] *Theory of Legislation*, 7th ed., p. 228.
[56] 'He would tempt her, if he had the means, by the offer of an independent provision; or he would find another husband for her as the price of his ransom'. *Op. cit.*, p. 227.
[57] *E.g.*, Judgments of Brett, L.J., in *Niboyet* v. *Niboyet*, [1878] L.R. 4 P.D. 1; and of Lord Dunedin in *Salvesen* v. *Administration of Austrian Property*, [1927] A.C. 641.

theory of divorce was probably suggested by the analogies of similar systems existing in his own day in France and Prussia, and may in its turn have influenced the judicial attitude towards marriage and divorce in many of the United States of America. His rather mechanical proposal that on divorce the custody of children of the marriage should be determined on the principle of boys living with their father and girls with their mother bears the touch of its bachelor authorship. Bentham was obsessed, if we may judge from his writings, by a fairy-tale horror of wicked stepmothers.

In land law Bentham's influence was very considerable, though for the most part it was realised through the patchwork legislative reforms of the 1830s [58] which, bit by bit, increased individual liberty in the ownership and disposition of land. Bentham argued convincingly against the retention of fetters on the alienation of land [59]; but while his arguments found ready acceptance among the new class of industrialists, they met opposition from many of the owners of ancient landed estates. Yet even the latter had to admit the desirability of such proposals as an increase in the powers of mortgage and sale of a tenant for life, and wider general powers of testamentary disposition. Where they stood to lose, as by the abolition of copyholds, they presented a formidable front, so that it was only by gradual degrees that ' the useless formalities and minute vexations ' [60] attendant on the tenure and transfer of copyhold land were mitigated and finally removed in the abolition of the tenure by a series of Acts stretching over a period of eighty-one years.[61] With the final extinction by 1940 of a lord's claim to compensation for loss of manorial rights,[62] Bentham's uneasy spirit may rest at peace on this particular score. Over a period of similar duration [63] the powers of a tenant for life of settled land have been increasingly augmented and widened, reaching in 1926 the point, perhaps undreamed of by Bentham, at which the

---

[58] Prescription Act, 1832 ; Inheritance Act, 1833 ; Wills Act, 1837 ; Real Property Act, 1845. Dicey, *Law and Opinion in England,* 2nd ed., p. 202.

[59] *Theory of Legislation,* 7th ed., pp. 174–176.

[60] *Theory of Legislation,* 7th ed., p. 196.

[61] The Copyhold Act, 1841, is the first chapter in the series and the Law of Property Act, 1922, as amended by the Act of 1924, the last.

[62] Law of Property Act, 1922, ss. 138 and 140.

[63] Settled Estates Act, 1856, to Settled Land Act, 1925.

tenant for life could exercise his powers as an estate owner. Nor, in this sphere, have we seen an end of legal reform; though whether future developments will be based on an increase or a reduction of freedom of alienation is a question which our politicians will have to answer, an answer which may well take the form of a complete abolition of settlements of land.

Bentham's exposure of the defects of tenancy in common of both land and goods was directed particularly against the situation ' that in a country where agriculture is so highly estimated, millions of acres of productive land are still abandoned to the wild state of common tenancy '.[64]   That inclosure of commons was an established practice long before Bentham wrote is an historical fact; but Bentham's support of this policy substantially helped to maintain it in the face of a popular, though incoherent, pastoral and agricultural opposition; and Inclosure Acts continued to be passed with new-found vigour.   Excepting from his declamation of tenancy in common servitudes, partnership property and community of goods between husband and wife, Bentham pointed out the real inequality of this ' source of never-ending discord '.   But his efforts did little to remove joint and common ownership from English law, for though their almost obsolete form of tenancy by entireties was abolished in 1925,[65] the general principle of co-ownership has been sanctified by the halo of a trust for sale.[66]

Insistence on the maximum of personal freedom and security of property did not, however, blind Bentham to the need for their infringement when ' . . . the sacrifice of some portion of security, so far as property is concerned, is necessary, to preserve the greater mass of it '.[67]   In his Principles of the Civil Code [67] he listed six cases in which such a sacrifice was reasonable and necessary.   The first two, general wants of the State against external and internal enemies, provide a philosophical basis (if such be needed) for war-time requisitioning of property and peace-time expenditure on the maintenance of prisons and the administration of justice.   But the last case he mentions, ' the Limitation of the rights of property, or of the use which each

---

[64] *Theory of Legislation,* 7th ed., p. 196.
[65] Law of Property Act, 1925, 1st Schedule, Part 6.
[66] *Ibid.,* ss. 34–36, except in the case of joint tenants of settled land: Settled Land Act, 1925, s. 19.
[67] *Theory of Legislation,* 7th ed., p. 125.

proprietor may make of his own goods, so as to prevent him from employing them to his own injury or that of others ' [68] anticipates a doctrine of the abuse of rights which was completely without influence on the nineteenth century development of English law, however much it may have helped to provide a basis of respectable authority for the development of this doctrine in the United States. For there the frontiers were wide open and a man's garden was not enclosed within a ten-foot wall. But for England Bentham's proposition tramped too heavily on the toes of Mr. Pickles [69] : it seemed like a betrayal of his utilitarian individualism. In one sphere of legislation, however, it is possible to trace the influence of Bentham's sacrifice of security of the individual to that of the community, namely, in the enactment of 1845 of the first Land Clauses Consolidation Act. This statute, nevertheless, preserved to the individual vendor his liberty to make with promoters to whom the Act applied any agreement he pleased, and only on failure to agree would compensation for the land required be determined by an outside body.

Bentham's consuming passion for reform included the operative as well as the substantive aspects of land law. The endless complexity and verbosity of conveyancing in even the simplest cases, leading to uncertainty and insecurity of title, induced him to advocate a system of registration of title which to some extent anticipated, and probably influenced, the reforms of the later nineteenth and of the twentieth centuries.[70] In this matter, however, Bentham had the unusual experience (for him) of swimming with the current of opinion, for the Real Property Commissioners in 1830 had recommended the adoption of a form of registration of title and had the support of the later Commission on the Registration of Title which in 1857 produced a scheme containing many principles embodied in subsequent legislation.[71]

It would be unjust to omit from these examples of Bentham's influence on English law all mention of his model law of succes-

---

[68] *Op. cit.*, pp. 125, 126.
[69] *Mayor of Bradford* v. *Pickles*, [1895] A.C. 587.
[70] Lord Westbury's Act, 1862 ; Land Transfer Act, 1875 ; Land Transfer Act, 1897 ; Land Registration Act, 1925.
[71] See Holdsworth, ' The Reform of the Land Law ', in *Essays in Law and History*, pp. 115–118.

sion.[72] How far removed were the principles of his reform from
those of contemporary primogeniture, heirship, and succession
under the Statutes of Distribution, and how much closer in
essentials are they to the order and shares of succession contained
in the Administration of Estates Act, 1925,[73] is striking evidence
of his influence, even in our own day and age. He would, for
example, for purposes of succession remove all distinction
between the sexes. After a husband's death, his widow should
normally retain half the common property, the other half being
distributed among the children equally: where a child pre-
deceases his father, leaving children of his own, his share should
be divided equally among them. In order to divide the property
among the heirs, while avoiding the inconveniences of community
of goods, Bentham would have it sold by auction, unless the heirs
themselves should come to some other arrangement for its
division. Until the sale and division had taken place the
property was to be entrusted to the keeping of the oldest male
heir of full age. Though many details of Bentham's proposals
differ from the corresponding provisions in the modern law of
succession, certain of the elementary principles which they
embody are not so far removed that one cannot, with justification, see in them the operation of cause and effect.

On the narrow basis of these limited aspects of Bentham as
a critic and a reformer it is impossible to give more than the
roughest assessment of his influence on English law. The late
Professor Dicey in his outstanding lecture on ' The Period of
Benthamism ' [74] rated Bentham's genius as ' of the rarest quality ',
and was prepared to ascribe to his teaching ' that thoroughgoing though gradual amendment of the law of England which
was one of the main results of the Reform Act '.[75] Yet to say
even so much is to understate Bentham's influence, as Lord
Brougham did when, in eloquent if exaggerated praise of ' the
first legal philosopher that had appeared in the world ' he
proclaimed, ' The age of reform and the age of Jeremy Bentham
are one and the same '.[76] For Brougham was an admiring contemporary and Dicey was speaking at the close of the nineteenth

[72] In Theory of Legislation, 7th ed., pp. 178–183.
[73] Ss. 46 and 47.
[74] Law and Opinion in England, 2nd ed., Lect. 6.
[75] Op. cit., p. 126.
[76] Brougham's Speeches, Vol. 2, p. 287.

century. While both had the advantage of living in the period
of Benthamism, to both was denied the advantage of a longer
perspective. We have seen that the influence of Bentham did
not end with the close of his so-called ' period ' The stones he
cast into the stagnant waters of English law caused ripples, and
more than ripples, which spread outwards far beyond his time
and place. When, in his early years, he pricked the radiant
bubble of Blackstone's complacency, he became the first English
lawyer to show England the dirty water of which it was made.
And, having launched his attack, he never withdrew where
injustice or inefficiency held sway. The long and conservative
Chancellorship of Lord Eldon was a constant target for
Bentham's biting criticism ; but if Eldon out-lived most of the
suitors in his court, Bentham was still at work reforming equity
and its administration after the Chancellor had finally resigned
from the Woolsack.[77]

' Argument *post hoc propter hoc* ', warns Professor Stone,[78]
' is always a game of hazard ', pointing out that Bentham may at
times merely have been rationalising incoherent ideas already
accepted in practice by his contemporaries. But even in the
matters to which this sound warning applies one can give to
Bentham the credit for putting before English lawyers and
political philosophers a solid, reasoned system of reform, worked
out on a principle they could understand and in detail they could
usefully employ. In a somewhat different sense the warning is
no less apt. To discover the true hand of Bentham in legislation
of our age calls for a strong suppression of imagination and wish-
ful thinking ; but if what remains is clearly the latest stage in a
development originating in Benthamite thought, one can fairly
say that Bentham's influence has not reached its end. As a
political theory for the present age utilitarianism still has its
champions.[79] It is the fortune of English law to have adapted
Bentham's theories by the compromise of practical requirements.
His call for codification resulted in legislative reform of law, but
not in the manner of his doctrine. His call for individual freedom of contract in place of the traditional relations of English
law was exploited to the point of injustice through the strong

[77] April, 1827.
[78] *The Province and Function of Law,* p. 294.
[79] See Cohen, *Ethical Systems and Legal Ideals,* 1933 ; Jennings, *A Plea
for Utilitarianism,* 2 Modern Law Rev., 22.

hand of economic domination. His call for freedom of alienation of land took effect gradually, and never completely, in a
patchwork variety of statutes. His reforms, in short, have had
to fit into the working machinery of English law, a process which
would have been far slower and far more difficult had not
Bentham had in Parliament friends who believed in him and
who were capable of translating his theories into the realistic
language of everyday life. Of supreme importance was
Bentham's faith in individual freedom, for through the unwaver-
ing constancy of this faith he embodied, consciously or unconsciously, the living spirit of the common law into all his
successful proposals for reform.[80] It was this common factor,
above all else, which enabled those proposals to pass through the
fire of Parliament and to take their place naturally within the
living body of English law.

[80] It was, it is submitted, the untraditional character of his proposals for
statutory codification, and the implicit assault on the judicial function,
which doomed them to failure in England.

CHAPTER 7

BENTHAM AND PARLIAMENTARY REFORM

Richard C. FitzGerald

ON reading Bentham's *Plan of Parliamentary Reform in the form of a Catechism* one is unpleasantly surprised to find that many of the parliamentary problems that caused perturbation to Bentham are still unsolved at the present time.

Bentham wrote his Plan, so he tells us in his Introduction, in 1809, when he offered it ' to one of the time-serving daily prints, in which other papers on the same subject had already found admittance. No name was sent with it : and the weathercock being at that time upon the turn, insertion was declined '. For nine years it was kept upon the shelf, and then, in 1817, the state of things was such that Bentham thought there was a chance of his Plan finding readers, and he consequently published it in London in that year. How true a ring his words have 130 years later. ' Sad condition of human nature ! until the cup of calamity, mixt up by misrule, has been drunk to the very dregs, never has the man a chance of being heard, who would keep it from men's lips '.[1] Is that not the position in the United Kingdom at the present time? Would not Bentham, if he were with us now, experience as much difficulty in getting people to think deeply and honestly of current problems as he did in his own day? And what is true of the United Kingdom is perhaps truer of the rest of the world. Those who think deeply about political matters are usually too partisan to be honest, and those who are honest seem to have come to the conclusion that politics is not a matter worthy of deep consideration on their part. Thus we find intolerance sweeping across the world and discover, to our dismay, that it is blowing through the public life of the United Kingdom.

As in Bentham's time, parliamentary reform must be approached from two broad angles, that of the franchise, and that of the representation of the electorate in Parliament itself.

---

[1] *Plan of Parliamentary Reform in the form of a Catechism,* by Jeremy Bentham, London (1817), Introduction, p. i.

As for the franchise, Bentham enumerated the following four expedients or arrangements as being essentially necessary, *viz.*, (1) virtual universality of suffrage; (2) practical equality of suffrage—*i.e.* practical equality in respect of the quantum of the influence exercised by the several electors in virtue of their respective suffrages; (3) freedom of suffrage; and (4) inviolable secrecy of suffrage.[2]

It must be remembered that in Bentham's time there was no general law regulating the parliamentary franchise in the boroughs. Everything rested on local custom and usage, which, in turn, depended upon the political and personal whims and fancies of the parliamentary committees who decided questions arising on the franchise. In addition to the boroughs there were the county representatives. Also, a small number of powerful and wealthy men controlled all the parliamentary elections, and it has been estimated that for over seventy years before the passing of the Reform Act, 1832, practically one-half of the members of the House of Commons owed their seats to patrons. The easy manner in which a man could be elected a member of that House is shown by the first election of Charles James Fox as a member in March, 1768. His father and uncle were worried at his youthful waywardness (Fox was 19 at that time) and thought that a parliamentary seat would keep him to the right path, or at any rate a better path. They selected Midhurst for him, where the right of election depended on a few uninhabitable smallholdings, the only means of identifying which from the surrounding countryside being the stones placed in the centre of each holding. The sole owner of all these holdings was the then Viscount Montagu, who just before an election was about to take place assigned a few of them to his servants with instructions to nominate the members and then to reassign the holdings back to his lordship, their employer. This was the farce played in March 1768, for Fox's benefit. The returning officer was the steward of his lordship's estate, and he declared that Fox had been chosen as one of the burgesses for Midhurst. To make the situation more ludicrous, Fox was holidaying in Italy at the time of this ceremony. And, as Bentham points out, Fox was under age when he first took his seat as a member of the House of Commons, which legally was not possible.

[2] *Op. cit.,* p. cclxxiv.

The position, then, was that approximately one-half of the members of the House of Commons were nominees of patrons, and each of such members, human nature being what it was and is, was expected to obey the orders of his patron and to protect his interests. Fox himself spoke on this position. He is reported as saying

> ' There is one class of constituents, whose instructions it is considered as the implicit duty of members to obey. When gentlemen represent popular towns and cities, then it is disputable whether they ought to obey their voice, or follow the dictate of their own conscience; but if they happen to represent a noble Lord or a noble Duke, then it becomes no longer a question of doubt; he is not considered as a man of honour who does not implicitly obey the orders of his single constituent. He is to have no conscience, no liberty, no discretion of his own; he is sent here by my Lord this, or the Duke of that, and if he does not obey the instructions that he receives, he is not to be considered as a man of honour and a gentleman; such is the mode of reasoning that prevails in this house. Is this fair? Is there any reciprocity in this conduct? Is a gentleman to be permitted without dishonour, to act in opposition to the sentiments of the city of London, of the city of Westminster, or of Bristol; but if he dares to disagree with the Duke, or Lord, or Baronet, whose representative he is, then he must be considered as unfit for the society of men of honour? This, Sir, is the chicane and tyranny of corruption, and this, at the same time, is called representation. In a very great degree the County members are held in the same sort of thraldom; a number of peers possess an over-weening interest in the country, and a gentleman is no longer permitted to hold his situation, than as he acts agreeably to the dictates of those powerful families. . . '.[3]

If a parliamentary candidate could not find a patron or he wished to be independent, the only way by which he could become a member of the House of Commons was to buy a parliamentary seat. Throughout the eighteenth century and the early part of the nineteenth century parliamentary seats were freely

---

[3] *Woodfall's Debates*, 1797, p. 329, referred to in Bentham, *op. cit.*, pp. cli–clii, footnote.

and openly bought and sold, and were often advertised as being for sale. The price of a seat depended on the place and time, and round about 1809 the average price of a seat purchased for a Parliament was estimated to be about £5,000, a substantial sum at that time. Lord Folkestone in 1809 moved ' A Bill for the more effectually preventing the sale of seats for money, and for promoting the monopoly thereof to the Treasury, by the means of Patronage ' [4]

This being the position, Bentham was moved to use his pen and voice to call attention to the injustices that such a system was bound to create. As regards the purchase of seats, he put the question whether it was upon the whole a pernicious, a beneficial practice, or a matter of indifference, and answered his question by saying that it would ' depend upon the manner in which the universal interest is affected by it '.[5] Bentham's test was that which would also be applied today (assuming that seats could still be sold and purchased)—What is the quality and quantity of the effective influence exercised by the member during his continuance in the seat?—and his criterion also would be the same, *mutatis mutandis*, namely, the consideration of the situation occupied by the member ' with reference to party. Tories, Whigs, People's men, neutrals—taking him during the whole of his career together, with which of all the several classes thus denominated has he acted? ' [6]

Bentham's problem was the nominee member and the purchaser member. Is not the problem still with us? Could not one or other of those labels be attached to most of the present members of the House of Commons? Can it not be contended that most, if not all, of the Socialist members of the present House of Commons are nominee members in the sense that (1) before being adopted as parliamentary candidates by any branch or constituency association they had to be approved by the central organisation of the Party; and (2) having become Members of Parliament they are subject to the ' military ' discipline imposed by the Party Executive, and must vote as directed and not in accordance with their conscience? When one remembers the firm grip the Trade Unions have on Party policy

[4] *Cobbett's Debates,* June 13, 1809, referred to in Bentham, *op. cit.,* p. clxx.
[5] Bentham, *op. cit.,* p. clxvi.
[6] *Op. cit.,* p. clxvii.

and the extent to which the Executive of the Party in Parliament is bound by the programme adopted at the annual Party Conference, one may not be wide of the mark in regarding Socialist Members of Parliament more as nominees of such bodies and organisations than as representatives of their constituents. Party discipline is, of course, not unknown to the Conservative Party and the Liberal Party, and the central organisations of these two Parties also approve candidates, but neither of these Parties exercises such a degree of control over its parliamentary candidates and Party Members of Parliament as does the Socialist Party. But with the Conservative and Liberal Parties the question of purchaser members possibly does arise. Because the branch or constituency associations of those Parties have more independence they are freer to make their own arrangements with candidates, and this fact does lend itself to a wealthy candidate making a more attractive proposition to the local association, as, *e.g.*, by agreeing to pay all his election expenses and to make a handsome annual contribution to the local association funds, than a poorer candidate can, with the result that the wealthy person has a better chance of being adopted as the candidate. The final Report of the Conference on Electoral Reform and the Redistribution of Seats [7] (which Conference will from now on be referred to as ' the Electoral Conference ') records the view that it is to be deprecated that a prospective or adopted candidate or a Member of Parliament should give any substantial donation or contribution to any charitable, social or sporting organisation in the constituency, or to any charitable funds specifically benefiting the constituents. It also disapproved of the direct or indirect payment, or promise of payment, of substantial contributions or annual subscriptions to Party organisations designed to influence the action of such organisations in the selection of a candidate. The Electoral Conference recorded these views in ' the full knowledge that legislation could not deal effectively with these abuses ',[8] but thought that the resolutions passed by the Electoral Conference ' on these subjects should be a definite help to candidates and to Members of Parliament exposed to unreasonable demands, and should also act as a deterrent to those Party organisations inclined to put the financial

[7] Cmd. 6543 (1944).
[8] *Ibid.*

contributions of a candidate or a member before considerations of merit and ability'.[9]   One can picture Bentham vigorously nodding his head in approval of these views, with a possible exception of the view that legislation could not cope with such abuses.   The Conservative Party's Standing Committee on Candidates considered these recommendations of the Electoral Conference and gave further advice to its local associations on the subject of financial arrangements between Party candidates and their constituencies.   This Standing Committee was of the opinion that the annual subscription of a member or candidate to local Party funds should not normally exceed £100 and that the constituency association should provide an election fund from which it should defray at least half of the candidate's election expenses.   If a local association suggested that it could not observe these conditions or either of them, then the Standing Committee intimated that it would give its approval to the candidate only if it is satisfied that conditions in the constituency itself justify a departure from these conditions, and that the onus will be on the association or the candidate to show that there are abnormal circumstances which make it impossible to comply with the conditions.   The Liberal Party, too, has adopted the view that the choice of a candidate must not depend upon his financial capacity to support the local Party funds.   As for the Socialist Party, its political funds are largely derived from the Trade Unions, who, in turn, exact a weekly levy for that purpose from each of their members.   A member of a Trade Union can contract out of the liability to contribute to the political fund, but for one reason or another few take advantage of this right. Bentham's view was that interest is the sole clue to political conduct, no matter whether it be an individual or an aggregate body. He laid down two rules, one positive, the other negative.   To satisfy oneself beforehand what, on a given occasion, will be the course a man will take, ' look to the state of interests : look out for, and take note of, the several interests, to the operation of which the situation he occupies stands exposed '.[10]   This was his positive rule.   His negative rule was that in an endeavour to satisfy oneself ' what, on the occasion in question, is the course he will take, pay no regard whatever to professions or protesta-

---

9 *Ibid.*
10 Bentham, *op. cit.*, p. ccciii.

tions '.[11] These rules may appear cynical, but are they not still sound rules, and are they not rules that the ordinary man applies, even though perhaps unconsciously, when assessing, or attempting to assess, the political situation? In 1809 it was a powerful individual—usually a great landowner—whose instructions the nominee member had to obey, and who did not allow his nominee to have a conscience, liberty or discretion so far as the latter's parliamentary duties were concerned. This it was that moved Bentham to advocate annual elections of members, on the ground that it would diminish, both to purchasers and sellers, the venal value of a seat. For a member of the House of Commons to be so beholden to his chief was bound, from the point of view of the community, to lead to ' mischievous conduct ', and Bentham's idea was to reduce to a minimum the time during which it would be possible for the member to continue such conduct. The two political Parties existing in his time were the Whigs and the Tories, later to become known as the Liberals and the Conservatives respectively. Broadly speaking, the Liberals were in favour of change, whilst the Conservatives were not, but neither Party had any attraction for Bentham, who, looking at the state of the country from the viewpoint of the ordinary man, saw ' the two domineering interests—the monarchical and the aristocratical antagonising with the every now and then struggling, but always vainly and feebly struggling, democratical. . . '.[12] In 1809 the King could personally choose his ministers, but the Whig ministry of Sir Robert Walpole (1721–1742) had created the precedent for one-party ministries, so that even in Bentham's time the King had to recruit the members of his Government from one political party. But the monarchy was undoubtedly a domineering interest, as it had the power, which it exercised, to dismiss the Government at pleasure. Bentham's desire to break the political power of the monarchy was not fulfilled until the passing of the Reform Act, 1832, which brought about the establishment of Party government. How delighted Bentham would have been if he had lived to witness the consequences of the dismissal of Lord Melbourne's ministry by William IV in 1834. Sir Robert Peel, who had agreed to form a ministry and so accepted, *ex poste facto,* respon-

[11] *Ibid.*
[12] *Op. cit.,* Introduction, p. xi.

sibility for the King's action, failed to obtain a majority at the General Election following the dissolution of Parliament. This was the first time that the royal favour had failed to secure a majority for the Prime Minister, and it showed that the extension of the franchise had made the electorate independent of the Crown, and that the Government must rely on a majority in the House of Commons. The Reform Act, 1832, also led to the recognition of the principle that the Prime Minister has a free choice of colleagues, this principle being conceded to Sir Robert Peel when forming his ministry of 1834. What a great pity it is that Bentham died just before the passing of the Reform Act, 1832, and was thus deprived of enjoying the fruits of his leadership of the school of thought that resulted in the passing of that Act.

But though the 1832 Act broke the royal political power and also the power of the landowner, it did not achieve universal suffrage so long contended for by Bentham. That Act extended the county franchise to long leaseholders, certain copyholders, and occupiers of property of £50 annual value, and established a uniform occupation franchise for every male occupier of property of the annual value of £10, but another thirty-five years were to pass before the borough franchise was extended, by the Representation of the People Act, 1867, to every male householder (the class so much in the mind of Bentham) occupying a separate dwelling-house, and to lodgers occupying unfurnished lodgings of the annual value of £10, which Act also made certain changes in the county franchise. Then, in 1884, the Representation of the People Act of that year extended the county franchise to all male householders and lodgers occupying unfurnished premises of the annual value of £10, so that by 1884 the artisan class and most agricultural workers had been given the franchise, and Bentham's desire for the creation of a system under which parliamentary seats were distributed on the principle of equal electoral districts, each returning a single member, was largely achieved by the 1884 Act. Then, at long last, the Representation of the People Act, 1918, was passed, establishing a uniform franchise for county and borough constituencies, and extending the franchise to all males of the age of 21 and over who possessed the qualification either of residence or of the occupation of business premises, and, as though the spirit of Bentham pervaded the legislature at the time, the Act abolished disqualification previously caused by receipt of the poor law. So a century had passed before an almost full harvest was reaped from the labours of Bentham.

The 1918 Act is interesting in that Bentham might have regarded it as recognising his ' legitimate-defalcation principle '. This principle, he stated, is ' that if, in the instance of any class of persons, it be sufficiently clear, that they neither are, nor can be, in such a state of mind as to be, in a sufficient degree, endowed with the appropriate intellectual aptitude—then so it is that, in the instance of such particular class of persons, a defalcation may be made : made, *viz.* without prejudice to anything that is useful in the interest-comprehension principle ',[13] and he cited minors, females, soldiers and sailors as examples of the classes of persons he had in mind. The legislature in 1918 thought that women under the age of 30 years were not, as regards the parliamentary franchise, sufficiently endowed with the appropriate intellectual aptitude, as it refused to give the franchise to women unless they were 30 years of age and they, or their husbands, occupied property of an annual value of at least £5. The Representation of the People Act, 1928, too, is in keeping with the Benthamite outlook. Bentham expressly stated that the duration of the exclusion which the adoption of his legitimate-defalcation principle would cause must only be temporary, and, ' to an indefinite degree, capable of being shortened by the exertions of the individual excluded '.[14] There can be no doubt that women, as a class, had by their exertions earned for themselves the right to political equality with men long before 1928, and the 1928 Act, in making the requirements for the parliamentary franchise the same for men and women, would have secured the approval of Bentham, who would also have approved it on the further ground that it did establish ' universality of suffrage '.

But would the 1918 Act, and the present position as regards the parliamentary franchise, have earned the full approval of Bentham ? The second of his four essential requirements demanded practical equality in respect of the quantum of the influence exercised by the several electors in virtue of their respec-

[13] *Op. cit.*, p. xci.
[14] *Op. cit.*, p. xcvii.

tive suffrages. Bentham wanted to inhibit ' every Elector from
giving his Vote in more places than one ',[15] and it is fairly certain he would not have approved of university graduates having
an additional vote in respect of their university constituencies, or
the husband or wife of any occupier of business premises having
an additional vote by virtue of that relationship. Plural voting
is a medieval anomaly, and is not a matter deserving of much, if
any, support from a person who advocates genuine political
equality, and Bentham would not have viewed with favour the
singling out for special privileges of university graduates and business people, notwithstanding the fact that he was one of those who
inspired the founders of the University of London, University
College. The Representation of the People Act, 1945, has abolished the franchise for the husband or wife of any occupier of
business premises and has put upon the person entitled to the
' business ' vote the onus of claiming the vote, but the university
vote still remains.[o] The Electoral Conference rejected by twenty-
five votes to six a resolution recommending that no person at any
election should vote more than once.[16] Bentham, it is true, had
in mind another aspect when writing of practical equality of
suffrage. He was protesting against the existence of, e.g. ' rotten '
or ' pocket ' boroughs. Before 1832 the ' unreformed ' boroughs
fell into the four main classes of scot and lot and potwalloper;
burgage; corporation, and freemen boroughs, the requirements
for the franchise differing in each. In burgage boroughs, e.g.
the franchise depended on being able to show title to land by
the form of tenure known as burgage tenure, and sometimes
residence, if only for one night, was necessary. But in some
cases residence was impossible. Thus, at Droitwich the qualification of an elector was being ' seised in fee simple of a small
quantity of salt water arising out of a pit ', which pit, it was
proved before a parliamentary committee, had been completely
dried up for at least forty years. Again, at Old Sarum ploughed
fields gave seven votes which returned two members of the
House of Commons. As there was no building on the fields, a
tent had to be erected for the returning officer. At this period,

---

[15] Op. cit., p. cclxxiii.
[o] The Representation of the People Bill, the text of which was issued on
January 30, 1948, proposes to put an end to plural voting by abolishing
the business premises vote and the university constituencies and franchise.
[16] Cmd. 6534 (1944), Appendix, paragraph 2.

Birmingham, *e.g.* did not have a single representative in the House of Commons. Bentham's view was that any progress in the direction of equalisation of suffrage and the elimination of 'snug proprietorship'[17] of parliamentary seats would have to include 'the breaking down of the several Counties, each into two or more less extensive Electoral districts',[17] and he instanced Westminster to support his point. '. . . Look then to Westminster; number of inhabitants, 162,085 :—number of electors, at least 17,000,—Voters, not distributed among Sub-districts, but driven all together—all into one and the same Poll-Booth. . .'.[18] Bentham proposed that arrangements should be made for 'causing the Poll to be taken in Districts of small extent, carved out of the Electoral Districts: say Voting-Districts, or Sub-Districts'[19] and for 'causing the Poll to be taken for all places on one and the same day'.[19] These proposals took root and have grown to maturity. What Bentham desired in these matters the electorate now have. The final Report of the Electoral Conference recommended[20] that increased polling facilities should be provided, particularly in rural areas, these polling stations, if necessary, being of a temporary character, but the Electoral Conference agreed that there were overwhelming objections to the provision of travelling polling booths. The Electoral Conference also recommended[21] that the hours of polling should be the same throughout the United Kingdom and should not be subject to local variation. These recommendations have since received statutory recognition. The Reform Act, 1832, disfranchised many boroughs and transferred the seats to counties and large towns, and introduced the machinery of parliamentary registration of electors, and the 1867, 1884 and 1918 Acts already referred to effected further redistribution of parliamentary seats. But it can fairly be suggested.that it was not until 1945 that what Bentham really desired in the way of distribution of seats came about. On February 2, 1944, the House of Commons passed a resolution welcoming 'the proposal of His Majesty's Government to set up a Conference on Electoral Reform and Redistribution of Seats and to invite Mr. Speaker

---

[17] Bentham, *op. cit.*, p. cclxxiv.
[18] *Op. cit.*, p. ccxcv.
[19] *Op. cit.*, p. cclxxiii.
[20] Cmd. 6543 (1944).
[21] *Ibid.*

to preside '. This Conference was duly set up and consisted of three peers and twenty-nine members of the House of Commons. It met for the first time on February 16, 1944, only a fortnight after the passing of the resolution, and after holding fourteen meetings the Speaker wrote to the Prime Minister reporting the views of the Conference, and this Report is one of the two Reports already referred to, it being Cmd. 6534. The Government had previously to the setting up of the Electoral Conference announced its readiness to adopt the recommendations of the Departmental Committee on Electoral Machinery as to the permanent machinery which should be established for the redistribution of seats. The Report of that Departmental Committee was published in 1942,[22] and the views set out in the Report are closely in line with those that Bentham had published some 125 years previously. Thus, the Departmental Committee stated :

' 64. The fundamental considerations giving rise to a need for the redistribution of seats, though elementary, are so important that we make no apology for recapitulating them. The essential basis of representative Government in this country is that the main representative body of the legislature should consist of persons elected under conditions which confer upon them an *equal representative status*. It is also a fundamental principle of our Parliamentary system that representation should be (with the exception of University constituencies) *territorial*. Both these features appear to us to be of the greatest importance. It follows from them that seats must be assigned to a series of local areas or communities each of which contains as equal as may be a share of the total number of persons to be represented.

' 65. Constituencies created at any time so as to conform to these principles cannot, however, be relied upon to continue to do so. Population is at all times in motion; and even under settled conditions continuous movements over a period of time will transfer population from one constituency to another, either directly or indirectly. If this inevitable process is neglected, the result will naturally be that Members are returned to Parliament in disregard of the principle of equal representative status, and large

[22] Cmd. 6408 (1942).

sections of the people will be grossly over—or under—represented '.[23]

After drawing attention to the fact that since 1917 the question of redistribution of seats had not been any one's business, the Departmental Committee went on :

' 90. Representative Government needs the equipment necessary to enable it to function according to its basic principles. Those principles require, we believe, that the House of Commons should consist of Members holding seats assigned to a series of local areas or communities each of which contains an approximately equal share of the total population or electorate. Our system of representative Government involves, therefore, two requirements : (1) the determination of local areas as suitable constituencies to be represented; and (2) the registration of the electorate of each constituency for the purpose of electing its representative. The adjustment of both constituencies and the corresponding electoral registers is essential for the same reason, *viz.* that population is at all times in motion. The second requirement is the subject of a settled system of registration discharging its important functions completely and precisely. But for the first requirement, which is fundamentally more important and for which it might have been expected that regular provision would have been made, as part of the standing machinery of the system of representative Government, there is a complete hiatus. The two requirements are reciprocal and mutually important; yet only one of them is functioning. From the broad objective of a system of representative Government it is anomalous that the standing machinery should continue to register, for the election, say, of one member, an electorate which on the basic principle of equal representation ought to elect two or three members or is not entitled to separate representation at all ',[24]

and it recommended that there should be a standing administrative body charged with the duty of constantly reviewing the state of constituencies, such administrative body to consist of a separate commission for each part of the United Kingdom, the

[23] Cmd. 6408, p. 14.
[24] *Ibid.*, p. 19.

whole body to be presided over by the Speaker. The forthrightness of these views is worthy of Bentham himself. The Electoral Conference submitted (*inter alia*) that there should be four separate Boundary Commissions—one for each part of the United Kingdom—that the Speaker should be *ex officio* chairman of all four commissions; that each Boundary Commission should be required to undertake, at intervals of not less than three years and not more than seven years, a general review of the representation in the House of Commons of that part of the United Kingdom with which it is concerned; and that the reports of the Boundary Commissions should be submitted to the Secretary of State concerned, he being required to lay every such report before Parliament, together with a draft Order in Council giving effect to any recommendations (with or without modifications) for redistribution, any such draft Order being subject to affirmative resolutions of Parliament. The recommendations of the Electoral Conference were accepted by Parliament and were embodied in the House of Commons (Redistribution of Seats) Act, 1944, and consequently there are now permanent Boundary Commissions and a permanent system of redistribution, which would have gratified Bentham. The Boundary Commission for England has been particularly active, and quickly made recommendations for a redistribution of seats in England, but some of its recommendations caused acute political controversy and were not accepted, and that Commission has had to put forward alternative recommendations.

The difficulty was that the 1944 Act limited the electorate of a constituency to a figure which was to be not more than about 25 per cent above or below the electoral quota for the whole of Great Britain, and when the Boundary Commissioners for England began their task it was soon discovered that adherence to this rule would mean that some of the proposed new constituencies would cut right across local government boundaries and would dismember areas that had been closely linked together for very long periods. Hence the political controversy. An Act amending the 1944 Act was consequently passed, which directs all the Boundary Commissioners to preserve local government areas wherever that can reasonably be done in conjunction with aiming at approximate numerical equality in electorates. Armed with these fresh directions, the Com-

missioners set to work again, and have completed their survey of
the parliamentary constituencies in all four parts of the United
Kingdom. They have considered objections to their proposals,
and have held twenty or so local public inquiries in that connection. If Parliament accepts the proposals of the Boundary Commissioners, then the size of the next House of Commons will be
reduced from 640 to 631, this membership being made up of
500 Members for England (a reduction of 20 in the present
number); 71 Members for Scotland (no change); 12 Members
for Northern Ireland (no change); 36 Members for Wales (an
increase of 1); and the 12 Members representing the universities
in the United Kingdom.[0]

There is one matter which Bentham raised, and which it may
be surmised he would not now allow to remain quiescent in view
of the greatly increased State intervention in every aspect of life,
and that is his suggestion that in the instance of minors, the
acquisition of the franchise should, on proof of possession of
' appropriate intellectual aptitude ', be accelerated. The State
has arrogated to itself the right to conscribe male persons for
military purposes on their attaining the age of 18 years. Surely
on a male person becoming a member of the armed forces, then
whether he is a minor or not he should have the parliamentary
franchise? The State regards him as possessing sufficient intellectual aptitude to be trained as one of its defenders, and should
therefore concede that he is a fit and proper person to have the
right to vote, especially as it can be argued that, the world of
politics being what it is, the ' appropriate ' intellectual aptitude
necessary to cast a vote is not of such a high standard as the
' appropriate ' intellectual aptitude which a man must possess in
order to become a skilled defender of his country. The Electoral
Conference would have aroused the wrath of Bentham in rejecting, as it did by sixteen votes to 3, a resolution recommending
that the franchise be extended to all who have reached the age
of eighteen. It may be noted that thirteen members of the
Electoral Conference abstained from voting on this resolution, as
only nineteen voted out of a total membership of thirty-two.[25]

---

[0] Since this paper was written the text of the Representation of the People
Bill, 1948, has been published : see above. The Bill proposes to reduce
the membership of the House of Commons to 608 (England 489 ; Scotland 71 ; Wales 36 ; and Northern Ireland 12).

[25] Cmd. 6543.

Little need be said of Bentham's third essential, namely, freedom of suffrage. A person entitled to the parliamentary franchise can please himself or herself whether to exercise it or not. No one could write at the present time in the following terms as Major Cartwright was able to in *The Statesman* for February 21, 1817, ' The writer has seen a very numerous troop of tenants, holding under a placeman and sinecurist, conducted to a county election as swine are conducted to market, one steward in the front, and another in the rear, as one hog-driver goes before the herd, and another follows after, to regulate the drift, and prevent straggling ' [26] Some European countries punish, by way of fines, electors who do not vote at elections; at least one of them only allows one list of candidates, all of whom must be members of the same Party, which Party alone has State approval, so that the elector has no real choice. This is in marked contrast with the present position in the United Kingdom, the electorate in which are not likely, deliberately or consciously, to renunciate the political rights which they at present enjoy and which they only acquired through the efforts of such people as Bentham.

There is little, too, to be said of Bentham's fourth essential— inviolable secrecy of suffrage—as that has been achieved, although unfortunately it came about some forty years too late for Bentham to enjoy any personal gratification. The Ballot Act, 1872, introduced the secret ballot as an experimental measure, the Act only remaining in force for one year unless it was renewed. Then, in typical British fashion, it was renewed annually over a period of forty-five years by the Expiring Laws Continuance Act of each year, until it was put on a permanent basis by the Representation of the People Act, 1918. So far as elections in ordinary constituencies are concerned, the ballot is secret, but in at least one university constituency it is believed to be possible for the parliamentary candidates to ascertain, after the election, how the graduates voted. That such an exception should be capable of existing would have been disapproved of by Bentham.

But the two freedoms, the establishment of which Bentham desired so much, and which caused him to advocate the principles of freedom of suffrage and secrecy of suffrage, namely,

[26] Cited by Bentham, *op. cit.*, p. clii.

freedom as against terrorism, and freedom against bribery, are now enjoyed by the electorate.

That Bentham would be writing furiously, were he with us now, chiding the people for their apathy and intolerance, cannot be doubted. Those who are still of this world and who are imbued with the desire to achieve justice for all, and not merely one or two, sections of the community, should regard it as their duty to take all proper steps to make the general public think about the present serious problems arising out of the now defective machinery of government and convince them that, if they are to retain their hard-won freedom, they must not allow the Executive (no matter from which party it is recruited) to use the constitutional machine for furthering its own political objects but must ensure that the constitutional machine is made to work in the interests of the whole community, with the Executive ever and always subject to real and effective parliamentary control. In that way can social reformers and others best honour the debt the community owes to Bentham.

Another wish of Bentham was that changes should be made with a view to ' diminishing the expenses and other inconveniences incident to Elections '.[27] The terms of reference of the Electoral Conference expressly covered ' Conduct and costs of Parliamentary elections, and expenses falling on candidates and Members of Parliament '. The final Report of the Electoral Conference dealt with this topic.[28] At the date of the final Report the maximum expenditure which a candidate was legally permitted to incur was at the rate of 5d. for each elector in a borough, and 6d. for each elector in a county constituency. The Electoral Conference recommended that there should be a basic allowance of £450 in both borough and county constituencies, to which there should be added a supplementary allowance at the rate of 1d. for each elector in boroughs and 1½d. for each elector in county constituencies.[0] Taking a constituency of 54,000 electors—which will be approximately the average quota for a constituency when the full redistribution scheme has been effected—the recommendation meant a saving to the candidate for a borough constituency of £450 (the difference between a

[27] Bentham, op. cit., p. cclxxiii.
[28] Cmd. 6543.
[0] The Representation of the People Bill, 1948, proposes to give effect to this recommendation of the Electoral Conference.

maximum expenditure of £1,125 legally permitted at the date of the final Report and £675, the legal maximum suggested by the Electoral Conference) and a saving of £563 to the candidate for a county constituency (being the difference between the then permitted maximum of £1,350 and £787, the maximum suggested by the Electoral Conference). In the case of double-member constituencies the Electoral Conference recommended no change in the then existing provision whereby, when there are two or more joint candidates the maximum amount of expenses for each of the joint candidates is the amount produced by multiplying a single candidate's maximum by $1\frac{1}{2}$ and dividing the result by the number of joint candidates.[29]

On the whole, it can be said that Bentham would not have too much cause for complaint so far as the present state of the franchise is concerned. His main complaint, it is suggested, would be the length of time that passed before his views were generally accepted. But he would be unhappy about the present position of the electorate's representatives in Parliament, which was his other angle of approach to parliamentary reform.

One of Bentham's suggested reforms was to make the Member of Parliament dependent towards his constituents. Understand dependence to this effect, *viz.* that, in the event of a man's becoming, in the eyes of the acting majority of his constituents, to a certain degree deficient in respect of any of the elements of appropriate aptitude (*viz.* appropriate probity, appropriate intellectual aptitude, or appropriate active talent) it may—before he has had time, by means of such deficiency, to produce in any considerable quantity, any irremediable mischief —be in the power of his constituents, by means of a fresh election, to remove him from his seat '.[30] The proposal is as sound now as it was in 1809, and just as, if not more, desirable to achieve at the present time. As already mentioned, 140 years ago it was a powerful individual whose instructions the nominee Member of Parliament had to obey, and who did not allow his nominee to have a political conscience, liberty or discretion. The nominee Member of Parliament in Bentham's day had most probably acquired that status because he was deficient in one or more of the elements of appropriate aptitude enumerated by

[29] Cmd. 6543.
[30] Bentham, *op. cit.*, p. lxvi.

Bentham and consequently more pliable from his patron's point of view.   Bentham desired above all that a Member of Parliament should have the courage of his convictions and be sufficiently independent of all persons, other than his constituents, to be able to voice his convictions without running any undue risk of being deprived of his parliamentary seat because his views and opinions were not agreeable to such persons.   He wanted to break the political power of the patrons.   Well, *that* patronage has been done away with, but another has taken its place.   And so the battle begun by Bentham is still on, and must be waged until the Executive, the modern ' domineering interest ', is subject to genuine parliamentary control.   It is easy to imagine the great labours that Bentham would have devoted to this modern problem, and the enormous amount of published work that would have resulted.   Or, to be more accurate, the enormous amount of work that would be awaiting publication.   No publisher would have a sufficiently large quota of paper to meet the publishing demands of Bentham's pen.

What was it that Bentham wanted a Member of Parliament to possess in the way of appropriate aptitude?

First, appropriate probity.   ' On each occasion, whether in speaking or delivering his vote—on the part of a Representative of the People, appropriate probity consists in his pursuing that line of conduct, which, in his own sincere opinion, being not inconsistent with the rules of morality or the law of the land, is most conducive to the general good of the whole community for which he serves;   that is to say, of the whole of the British Empire :—forbearing, on each occasion, at the expense either of such general good, or of his duty in any shape, either to accept, or to seek to obtain, or preserve, in any shape whatsoever, for himself, or for any person or persons particularly connected with him, any advantage whatsoever, from whatsoever hands obtainable;   and in particular from those hands, in which, by the very frame of the constitution, the greatest mass of the matter of temptation is necessarily and unavoidably lodged, *viz.* those of the King, and the other members of the executive branch of the government, the King's Ministers '.[31]   So far as political power is concerned, Bentham would, if he were writing that passage in 1947, be compelled to omit all reference to the King.   But apart

[31] Bentham, *op. cit.,* Catechism, Question 4.

from that variation, would any other alteration be necessary? The answer surely is No. In Bentham's time political parties were not elaborately organised, and there was no central Party organisation. A Member of Parliament in those days was not pledged to support a particular Government no matter what it did, or to vote for or against a particular Bill as directed by the Party Whips. It is ironical that the success of Bentham's campaign for universal suffrage should have eventually led to the great power possessed by the twentieth century Cabinet. The extension of the franchise made by the Reform Act, 1867, coincided with the recognition of Gladstone and Disraeli as political party leaders. They were real leaders in that they were strong, dominating, and popular personalities, and it was much simpler for the new electorate to vote for candidates who could be relied upon to support one or other of these leaders than to follow the previous practice of voting for candidates on their personal merits. Each increase in the electorate has brought with it an increase in the exploitation of the personality of each of the leaders of the chief political parties. Each increase in the electorate has increased the amount of work to be done in each constituency, and a Member of Parliament could not, even if he had the requisite administrative ability, be able to find sufficient time to deal with all this work in addition to his strict parliamentary duties. It has been found necessary to employ a full-time paid agent in each constituency, and this expense, plus the expenses of fighting an election, has had the effect of forcing parliamentary candidates to look to the central Party organisation for financial assistance, and this, in the aggregate, has enabled that organisation to obtain and keep control over the political party as a whole. It has meant, too, that a Member of Parliament cannot be too individualistic when passing through the Division Lobbies of the House of Commons. Far too often it is indicated to him beforehand by the Party Whips as to the way in which he should vote on a particular Bill—whether he is to be one of the Ayes or Noes—and for him to disregard or flout such directions will land him in trouble with the Party Whips and, most likely, also with his own local association. The system of free voting in the House of Commons as known in the middle of the nineteenth century has practically disappeared. So strong has Party organisation become that it is to all intents and purposes impossible for a Member of Parliament of the present period to attain the standard of ' appropriate probity ' demanded by Bentham. Were he to insist on doing so, or attempting to do so, he would find himself ostracised by his Party, and that at the next parliamentary election another person had the support—financial and otherwise—of the Party, which would mean the virtual extinction of his career as a politician so far as that Party is concerned, because, although he could stand as an independent candidate, the mode of conducting modern parliamentary elections militates against the election of independent candidates.   The National Liberal Federation, the foundation of which in 1877 was due to Joseph Chamberlain and which was the first national Party organisation to be established in England, in 1891 published the famous Newcastle Programme, which was a list of specific topics, legislation in respect of which the Party pledged itself to pass if returned to power by the electorate.   This had the effect of making the electors assume that every Liberal candidate supported the Programme, unless he openly said he did not, and as this precedent of publishing beforehand the intention of the Party has ever since been followed by all the chief political Parties, it has resulted in an almost total extinction of the possibility of a Member of Parliament ' pursuing that line of conduct, which, in his own sincere opinion, . . . is most conducive to the general good of the whole community for which he serves ; . . .'. Independence is not part of the stock-in-trade of the modern Member of Parliament, and it is the opinion of the Party, not the sincere opinion of the Member of Parliament, that counts.

Secondly, appropriate intellectual aptitude.   This Bentham described as ' Forming a right judgment on the several propositions, which, either in Parliament, or out of Parliament, but if out of Parliament, with a view to Parliament, are liable to come before him :   and, to that end, in Parliament forming a right conception, as well of the nature of each proposition, considered in itself, as of the *evidence,* adduced or capable of being adduced, whether in support of it or in opposition to it, and the observations thereon made, or capable of being made in the way of *argument, for* it or *against* it, above '.[32]   Bentham envisaged

---

[32] *Ibid.,* Question 5.

the electorate's representatives in Parliament being given full information, and proper and adequate opportunities for deliberation, of all aspects of national policy and as having a real say and control in all such matters and things. How sadly disillusioned he would be if he saw the developments of the last forty years or so. Little did he think that delegated legislation would reach the grave proportions that it has reached. Little did he think that it would become the parliamentary fashion to have skeleton legislation—that legislation which contains only the barest general principles, and which leaves all other matters of principle, procedure and details of administration to the Executive—the King's ministers, in whose hands ' the greatest mass of the matter of temptation is necessarily and unavoidably lodged '. There seems to be very little left in respect of which a Member of Parliament can form a right judgment—just a bare general principle, with no free voting power even in respect of that. It is interesting to speculate on what Bentham's reaction would have been to the six reasons given by the Committee of Ministers' Powers in their Report published in 1932 [33] for supporting the system of delegated legislation. Unforeseen contingencies, flexibility and opportunity for experiment may have been reasons acceptable to Bentham, but pressure on parliamentary time and technicality of subject matter would have aroused his ire if they had been put to him as reasons for allowing the Executive to get the upper hand and to control Parliament, as it has for so many years now. Emergency powers, too, would not have been wholly acceptable to him as a proper reason. Was not the nineteenth century one of great industrial progress? Was it not during that period that great strides were made in the use and development of railways, electricity, gas and the like? Did Parliament abdicate its functions to the Executive because of lack of parliamentary time and technicality of subject matter? It may be that everyday life is far more complicated now than it was in Bentham's day. One need have no hesitation in frankly admitting that it is, but it is our own doing and we have only ourselves to blame. More and more have we allowed the experts in every sphere of activity to have the biggest say, and almost the final word. No wonder the Member of Parliament feels far too often that he is out of his depth, and that the

[33] Cmd. 4060 (1932).

subject matter of a particular Bill being too technical for him, it is best to allow the Government to cope with the matter with the aid of the innumerable experts at its disposal. The average Member of Parliament is an ordinary individual (which is what a representative of the electorate should be), but that is no valid reason for depriving him of proper facilities to form a right judgment. And it is no justification for Parliament abdicating its functions to the Executive. What is wanted is a complete overhaul of parliamentary practice and procedure, which is archaic and out of touch with modern conditions. A Select Committee on Procedure was set up by the House of Commons in August 1945, and its Third Report, dated October 31, 1946, was reviewed in the House of Commons on November 6, 1947, when Mr. Herbert Morrison, Lord President of the Council and Leader of the House of Commons, stated (1) that the Government considered the procedure of Committee of Supply was capable of improvement, and proposed that all Supply business should be concentrated in twenty-six allotted days, to be taken any time before August 5; (2) the Government proposed that the Defence Estimates would be issued separately, like the Army, Navy and Air Force Estimates, instead of being included with the Civil Estimates; (3) the Government proposed that the customary debates preceding the motion to go into Committee on the Estimates could arise in future on any allotted day, provided that the motion was moved by a Minister; (4) the Government proposed that the Report stage of the Budget resolutions, on which the Finance Bill is founded, should be formal without debate, thus avoiding a good deal of repetition of debate on the Committee stage of the Bill: and (5) that the Government thought the time was not yet ripe for an inquiry into delegated legislation (thus disagreeing with the Select Committee), and that the Government could not accept the Select Committee's suggestion that the Public Accounts Committee and the Estimates Committee should be amalgamated with a view to strengthening the control of expenditure. He moved a Motion, which was eventually agreed to by the House, that the whole code of Standing Orders of the House, as amended by the results of their debate, should be examined by a technical committee to make suggestions for the improvement of the wording and the removal of ambiguities and absurdities,

Mr. Speaker having agreed to preside over such a committee. As was expected, these proposals evoked considerable discussion and opposition, and the debate on Procedure went on until the early hours of the morning. It is astonishing how conservative the House of Commons is when it comes to reforming its own procedure!

Thirdly, and lastly, appropriate active talent, *i.e.* 'Talents suited to the due performance of the several *operations,* which, in the course of his service, in or out of the House, but more particularly in the House, it may happen to a Member to be duly called upon to perform, or bear a part in : for example, *introducing* or endeavouring to introduce, by way of *motion,* any proposed law or measure which he approves : delivering a *speech* in support of any proposition which he altogether approves; or in opposition to one which he altogether disapproves : proposing an *amendment* to any proposed law or measure which he approves in part only : drawing up, or helping to draw up, a *Report,* concerning such or such matters of fact, for the inquiring into which it has happened to him to have been appointed to act as Chairman, or other Member, of a Committee; putting relevant *questions,* concerning matters of fact, to persons examined before the House, or any Committee of the House, in the character of *witnesses* '.[34]　It will have been gathered from what has already been said under the heads of appropriate probity and appropriate intellectual aptitude, that appropriate active talent is something which, for a long time past, has not been encouraged. Since the outbreak of World War II in September 1939 the Government of the day has had a complete monopoly of parliamentary time. An individual Member of Parliament has had no opportunity to introduce Motions, and in spite of strong protests against the Government's continued monopoly of parliamentary time, all efforts to restore to Members of Parliament the privileges they enjoyed up to 1939 (*e.g.* of introducing private Bills on specified Fridays) have been unsuccessful. As Sir William Young said over 150 years ago, 'A delegation of Members to that House [House of Commons] ought ever to be . . . of persons having one common interest with those who sent them there '.[35]　Likewise,

[34] Bentham, *op. cit., Catechism,* Question 6.
[35] See *Parl. Reg.,* 1793, p. 417. Cited by Bentham, *op. cit.,* p. xlix, footnote.

Mr. Whitbread, ' Sir, I maintain that there ought to be a community of interest between the people and their representatives '.[36] These statements of Young and Whitbread were quoted with approval by Bentham, as obviously they support his advocacy of a House of Commons truly representative of the electorate in the sense that the Members really represented and gave effect to the wishes of their constituents. This ambition of Bentham has still to be achieved. In fact, a far sterner battle has now to be fought and won than ever Bentham could have visualised. But with the passing of time the realisation of the ambition seems to become more and more improbable. Parliament has become a rubber stamp, kept in the custody of the Executive and only used when constitutional formalities and proprieties make it necessary or desirable to do so. Should the Executive experience difficulties with its own supporters it can always threaten resignation, and the possibility of this threat is very effective in making truculent Members bow to the will of the Executive. We still have to translate into terms of reality the statement of Edmund Burke, ' The virtue, spirit, and essence, of a House of Commons consists in its being the express image of the feelings of the nation. It was not instituted to be a control *upon* the people, as of late it has been taught by a doctrine of the most pernicious tendency, but as a control *for* the people '.[37] In order to get within measurable distance of bringing the Executive under the control of the House of Commons, it will be necessary to have freedom of debate in that House in such circumstances that the House is a genuinely free deliberative assembly; to ensure that the Executive must submit to proper demands and criticisms of the House, particularly as regards amendments to Government-sponsored legislation (the only legislation now emanating from the House); and to reduce to proper dimensions the power obtained by the Executive by being able to threaten a dissolution of Parliament. All this is closely bound up with the independence of the Member of Parliament, the extent of such independence depending on the strength of party discipline. Reduce party discipline to a proper maximum and there will then be proper independence of the Member of Parliament.

---

[36] *Ibid.*, p. 465, and cited by Bentham in the same footnote.
[37] Per Mr. Erskine (later Lord Erskine), *Parl. Reg.*, 1793, p. 407, and cited by Bentham in the same footnote.

Party discipline can be so reduced by (1) making parliamentary candidates financially independent of the party organisation. This could be achieved by, *e.g.*, the State refunding to each parliamentary candidate who did not forfeit his £150 deposit the amount of his election expenses legally incurred; and (2) introducing an adequate system of proportional representation. With few exceptions, most parliamentary constituencies are single-member constituencies, in which political activity is directed at depriving the sitting Member of his parliamentary seat. Proportional representation permits of different political parties being represented in the same constituency, and it would mean that the vote of every elector had some value instead of, as under the present electoral system, the votes given to the unsuccessful candidate being completely lost. Bentham would have regretted the attitude of the Electoral Conference to these problems. The following comprehensive resolution on the subject of Proportional Representation (the terms of the resolution would have earned Bentham's approbation) was rejected by 25 votes to 4, *viz.*

' 1. That the Conference reaffirming the Resolution of the Speaker's Conference of 1917, accepts as governing any scheme of redistribution the principle that each vote recorded shall, as far as possible, command an equal share of representation in the House of Commons.

' 2. That the Conference considers that this principle should apply to methods of elections equally with schemes of redistribution.

' 3. That the present method of election fails to produce results fully and truly representative of the views of the voters.

' 4. That the principle reason for this failure is the distribution of the country into single-member constituencies (or double-member constituencies in which each elector has two votes), under which it may be observed.

' (1) there can be and has in fact been in the years 1922–1923, 1924–1929, and 1935 to date [May, 1944] a majority in the House of Commons of one party based on a minority of votes for that party in the country;

' (2) coalition government has prevailed during the
years 1918–1922 and 1931 to date, and government by a single party, having no majority in
the House of Commons, during the years 1923–
1924 and 1929–31 ;

' (3) there has not been at any time since the Speaker's
Conference of 1917 a government formed by
any one party supported by a majority of the
voters.

' 5. That the best remedy for the shortcomings of the
present method of election is the adoption of some system
of Proportional Representations whereunder each elector
has a single transferable vote and constituencies return
several members, a method which in the words of the
present Prime Minister, [Mr. Winston Churchill] " is in-
comparably the fairest, the most scientific, and on the whole
the best in the public interest ".

' 6. That the Conference accepts the principle of Proportional Representation with the single transferable vote
and recommends that it be applied to all constituencies save
those affected by special geographical considerations '.[38]

The Electoral Conference also rejected, by 24 votes to 5, a
resolution recommending that some measure of Proportional
Representation should be applied to the election of the next
House of Commons by way of experiment.[39]

The resolution which the Electoral Conference *did pass,* by
24 votes to 5, was ' The system of election known as Proportional
Representation shall not be adopted in respect of any constituencies where it does not apply at present ' ! [40]

The Electoral Conference rejected by 20 votes to 5 a resolution recommending that at any election in a single-member
constituency where there are more than two candidates (other
than university constituencies) the election should be held on the
method of voting known as the Alternative Vote.[41]

The Electoral Conference agreed not to accept a proposal
that the State should afford direct financial assistance to candidates.[42]

[38] Cmd. 6534, Appendix, § 4.
[39] *Ibid.*, Appendix, § 5.
[40] *Ibid.*, p. 7, § 28.

[41] *Ibid.*, Appendix, § 6.
[42] Cmd. 6543.

It is thought that enough has been said to support the statement that Bentham would not be at all happy about the position of the Member of Parliament from the point of view of the electorate.

Bentham appears to have cherished the fond hope that universal suffrage would put governmental power on a proper basis. But just as the aristocrats of his day wielded power, and derived great pleasure from exercising their power, so the Cabinet, largely composed of Members of the House of Commons, wields power, and derives great pleasure from doing so. The difference between the two periods is that the power of the twentieth century Cabinet is more despotic. ' The arrival of unmitigated despotism ' [43] which Bentham predicted the country would experience unless his ideas for parliamentary reform were adopted is still a long way off, but Parliament, because of the present abnormal conditions, has given the Government unlimited powers by passing the Supplies and Services (Extended Purposes) Act, 1947. Should it ever come to pass that the spirit of compromise no longer governed the relations between the Executive, Parliament, and the country, such kind of legislation could have the effect, to use Bentham's words, ' of driving the country down headlong in the descent that terminates in the gulf of pure despotism . . .'.[44] Would not Bentham, if he were writing of the Reports of the Electoral Conference, have reiterated the following view expressed by him in 1809, ' Ah! When will the yoke of Custom—Custom, the blind tyrant, of which all other tyrants make their slave—Ah! when will that misery-perpetuating yoke be shaken off? When, when will *Reason* be seated on her throne?' [45]   Surely reason, on behalf of the electorate, demands, not a veto on experimenting with some measure of Proportional Representation, but the application to the election of the next House of Commons of some measure of Proportional Representation by way of experiment? If the experiment should be a failure, then the electorate would know from actual experience that the system of Proportional Representation so applied was not the right lubricant for the creaking constitutional machine, and that another solution of the problem of how to

---

[43] Bentham, *op. cit.*, p. clxviii.
[44] *Op. cit.*, p. clxvii.
[45] *Op. cit.*, p. cxcvii.

ensure that the House of Commons is truly representative of the electorate must be sought.   The refusal of the Electoral Conference is stranger still when one remembers that the Speaker's Conference of 1917 was in favour of trying the experiment in certain constituencies.   Is it possible that the clock is being put back so far as parliamentary reform (which is greatly needed) is concerned?

PART THREE—INTERNATIONAL LAW

CHAPTER 8

BENTHAM'S CONTRIBUTION TO INTERNATIONAL LAW AND ORGANISATION

Georg Schwarzenberger

POWER and vested interests, irrationalism and emotionalism, official secretiveness and timidity on the part of scholars are nowhere more strongly entrenched than in the field of international affairs. It is, therefore, not surprising that Bentham's rationalist and uncompromising approach to the problem should either be punished by being ignored or subjected to scathing criticism. In the words of one of the foremost authorities on Bentham in our own time, ' no part of Bentham's teaching has had a reception at the hands of his critics more pathetic than his efforts to aid the cause of Peace '.[1]

It is not the purpose of this Paper to fall into the opposite error and to present an apologia for Bentham. What appears to be required is to assess Bentham's place in the evolution of the doctrine of international law and the theory of international organisation and, in the light of experience gathered since Bentham's days and of the needs of our own time, to separate the wheat from the chaff in Bentham's constructive suggestions.

I. BENTHAM AND INTERNATIONAL LAW

1. *Name.* Bentham's objection to the term ' Law of Nations ' was due to the fact that it appeared to refer to law within the State rather than between nations, and thus was not sufficiently characteristic of the law as applied between nations.[2] In his

---

[1] C. K. Ogden, *Bentham's Theory of Legislation*, 1931, p. xxi. Notable exceptions are C. Colombos' Introduction to Bentham's *Plan for an Universal Peace*, 1927, and L. Ledermann, *Les Précurseurs de l'Organisation Internationale*, 1945.

[2] *Bentham's Collected Works* (1843), (subsequently abbreviated to *Bentham*), pp. 1–2. See also his *Scheme of Series of Contemplated Publications* (drafted between 1776 and 1782), *ibid.*, p. x.

Principles of Morals and Legislation (1780), Bentham refers to the suggestion made by Chancellor d'Aguesseau to term *droit entre les gens* what was then commonly called *droit des gens*,[3] and he might have added that this tradition went back as far as Victoria, the founder of the Spanish school of International Law.[4] The name recommended by Bentham—*International Law*—appears to give expression more clearly than any other term to the basic principle of the equality in status of all subjects of international law. It found ready and general acceptance on the Continent.[5] In Anglo-Saxon countries the term owes its widespread acceptance to Wheaton,[6] Reddie,[7] Wildman,[8] and Sir Robert Phillimore.[9]

2. *Relation to other Subjects and Definition.* As becomes clear from Bentham's *Chrestomathia* (1816), Bentham kept international law sharply separated from what we would call today international relations. The science of international politics— defined by Bentham a century before it made its rather belated appearance—' has for its subject the conduct of Government . . . as towards the members, whether rulers or subjects, of other . . . communities'.[10] International law, however, was recognised by Bentham as one of the two basic divisions of law, the other being internal or national law.[11] Bentham's logical mind refused to accept the customary description of national law as municipal law if used in contrast to international law; for municipal law ' only concerns the inhabitants of a town, of a

---

3 *Ibid.*, p. 149, footnote. Referring to d'Aguesseau's *Œuvres*, 1773, tom. 2, p. 337.

4 Cf. J. B. Scott, *The Spanish Origin of International Law*, 1934, p. 163. Thus the statement in Oppenheim's *International Law* (ed. Lauterpacht), Vol. 1, 1947, p. 90—to be found already, in the 1st edition, Vol. 1, 1905, p. 81—that Zouche was the first who used this term, appears to require correction.

5 The introduction of the term ' *droit international* ' into the legal litera- ture in French-speaking countries owes much to Etienne Dumont, Bentham's populariser on the Continent. Cf. E. von. Ullmann, *Völker- recht*, 1908, pp. 11–12.

6 Already before the publication of his *Elements of International Law* in 1836, Wheaton had used this term in his Address on Kent (1820).

7 *Researches Historical and Critical in Maritime International Law*, 1844– 1845.

8 *Institutes of International Law*, 1829.

9 *Commentaries upon International Law*, 1854–1861.

10 8 *Bentham*, p. 94. This science forms part of Ethics as defined by Bentham (*ibid.*, p. 90, note and p. 93) and more specifically of Polio- scopic (State-regarding) Ethics (see the table facing p. 128).

11 *A General View of a Complete Code of Laws* (1802), 3 *ibid.*, p. 157.

district or of a parish '.[12]   Yet in spite of his gibes at Pufendorf's
and Blackstone's abuse of language in this matter,[13] international
lawyers have remained impervious to this criticism and still
insist on the distinction between international and municipal law.
As this term appears to emphasise the parochial aspects of
national law as distinct from the universal character of international law, such mitigating circumstances may be pleaded for
the survival of this heresy.

Two instances may serve to illustrate Bentham's awareness
of the practical significance of a clear distinction between international and municipal law.

Bentham referred to the famous case of the outlawry of
Philip III of Spain in the court of King's Bench at the instigation
of some London merchants who, on Selden's advice, had recourse
to this measure : ' This was internal jurisprudence ; if the
dispute had been betwixt Philip and James himself, it would
have been international '.[14]

The other example may be taken from the fields of conflict
of laws and State contracts which, owing to the foreign elements
inherent in these transactions, were not always distinguished
from international law by subsequent writers with the lucidity
of a Bentham : ' As to any transactions which may take place
between individuals who are subjects of different states, these
are regulated by the internal laws, and decided upon by the
internal tribunals of the one or the other of those states ; the case
is the same where the sovereign of the one has any immediate
transactions with a private member of the other ; the sovereign
reducing himself, *pro re natû,* to the condition of a private
person, as often as he submits his cause to either tribunal ;
whether by claiming a benefit, or defending himself against a
burden.   There remains then the mutual transactions between
sovereigns as such, for the subject of that branch of jurisprudence
which may be properly and exclusively termed *international* '.[15]

---

[12] *Ibid.* Blackstone, whom Bentham attacked on this point, was not unaware
of the ambiguity of the term (cf. *Commentaries on the Laws of England*
(1765–1769), Introduction, § 2).

[13] *Logical Arrangements* (1811–1831), 3 *ibid.,* p. 292.

[14] *Principles of Morals and Legislation* (1780), *ibid.,* pp. 149–150, footnote.
See also John Selden's *Table Talk* (ed. Sir Frederick Pollock), 1927,
pp. 68–69 ; *De Haber* v. *Queen of Portugal* (1851), 17 Q.B. 171, at
p. 211 ; 15 B.Y.I.L., 1934, pp. 145–146 and 16 *ibid.,* 1935, p. 181.

[15] *L.c.* above in note 14, p. 149.

As long as the term *sovereigns* is merely used to signify the highest organs or groups which are the typical international persons—and without any claim to exclusiveness—the last sentence of this quotation still offers a workable definition of international law.[16]

3. *Sources and Law-Determining Agencies.* In accordance with a hierarchy of sources which equally recommended itself to the draftsmen of the statutes of the two world courts, Bentham gave pride of place to treaties.[17] While he was well aware of the difficulties which may arise from the non-fulfilment of engagements undertaken by States towards each other,[18] Bentham emphasised the reality of international treaty law by reference to confederations such as the Germanic body [19] and dealt in anticipation with such pseudo-sociological arguments as are periodically advanced against the binding character of international treaties : ' It is a trite and idle observation that the engagements of sovereigns are kept no longer than suits their convenience. This is in no other sense true than in that in which it is also true of the engagements of private men.[20] If it means that the engagements of sovereigns have never any effect, and that, after an engagement of that sort entered into, things are in precisely the same situation as if no such event had taken place, it is notoriously false : if it means anything else than this it is nugatory. No man asks without a motive : no man acts against a preponderant mass of motives : but, to the sum of motives which may tend to withhold a sovereign from pursuing a certain line of conduct, does a solemn engagement not to pursue it make no addition? Let experience decide '.[21]

---

[16] In his *General View of a Complete Code of Laws* (1802), Bentham defined international law as the branch of law which ' regulates the mutual transactions between sovereigns and nations ' (3 *Bentham,* p. 157). As States, nations, or other entities have to be recognised as subjects of international law in order to partake of rights under this legal system, it might appear preferable today to replace these instances by the term international persons. Yet even the Permanent Court of International Justice was content to define international law as ' meaning the principles which are in force between all independent nations '. (The *Lotus* Case, 1927, Series A, No. 10, p. 17.)

[17] Letter to J. Henry, January 15, 1830 (11 *Bentham,* p. 34).

[18] See below under 4.

[19] *The Limits of Jurisprudence Defined* (1782–ed. Ch. W. Everett, 1945), p. 154.

[20] See, however, for a more sceptical view expressed twenty years later *A General View of a Complete Code of Laws* (1802), 3 *Bentham,* p. 162, and below under 4.

[21] *L.c.* in note 19 above, p. 154.

Bentham did not limit himself to refuting what he called 'levelling notions', but exposed their social—or anti-social—function : 'the tendency of them being constantly, and the design frequently, to cover and to cherish the very immorality which they represent as being already at the extreme : the existence of which they maintain and pretend perhaps to deplore '.[22]

Bentham's sympathetic attitude to treaties as a source of international law may have been coloured by his hope [23] that they might—as in fact they did—form an important vehicle for the development and improvement of international law. The view which he took was, however, no less due to the certainty which they provide in comparison with customary international law and—worse still—natural law as applied to inter-State relations by seventeenth and eighteenth century writers.

Bentham attacked Grotius, Pufendorf and Vattel. It would, however, be unwise to assume that such criticism may be dismissed as irrelevant today for applying only to the naturalist school of international lawyers.

A priori reasoning and '*ipse-dixitisms*' of these writers formed a favourite target for Bentham's unsparing pen : 'Behold the professors of natural law, of which they have dreamed—the legislating Grotii—the legislators of the human race : that which the Alexanders and the Tamerlanes endeavoured to accomplish by traversing a part of the globe, the Grotii and the Pufendorf's would accomplish, each one sitting in his armchair '.[24] While in any generation there are to be found such ' oracles ' of international law—to use another of Bentham's telling invectives—in historical perspective, Bentham's criticism of the naturalist school of international law in this respect appears unduly severe. Bentham does not allow for the unconscious character of such legislation in disguise nor for the inevitability down to the eighteenth century of the use of the deductive method in the field of international law.[25] Nevertheless, whatever justification

---

[22] *Ibid.*
[23] See below under 7.
[24] *Panomial Fragments* (up to 1831), 3 *Bentham*, p. 220. Cf. also Bentham's *Comment on the Commentaries* (1775), ed. by Ch. W. Everett, 1928, p. 44, and *The Theory of Legislation*, ed. by C. K. Ogden, 1931, p. 7.
[25] See also Sir Thomas E. Holland, *Lectures on International Law*, 1933, p. 23.

existed in the past for this approach [26] sufficient material is now
available in the decisions of international and national courts and
in the diplomatic correspondence of States to discard such
subjectivism and to live up to Bentham's standards.

Bentham's other criticism is still more important. It is
directed against a habit which, though inherent in the naturalist
treatment of international law, is certainly not limited to this
school : the lack of distinction between *is* and *ought*, between
the exposition of existing international law and proposals *de lege
ferenda* : 'Of what stamps are the works of Grotius, Pufendorf,
and Burlamaqui? Are they political or ethical, historical or
juridical, expository or censorial? Sometimes one thing, sometimes another : they seem hardly to have settled the matter with
themselves. A defect this to which all books must almost
unavoidably be liable, which take for their subject the pretended
law of nature; an obscure phantom which, in the imaginations
of those who go in chase of it, points sometimes to *manners,*
sometimes to *laws*; sometimes to what law *is,* sometimes to what
it *ought* to be '.[27]

At least since the publication of Hume's *Treatise on Human
Understanding,* there can no longer be any excuse for such major
methodological errors, and Bentham generously acknowledged
his indebtedness to Hume in this respect.[28]

4. *Binding Force and Sanctions.* In any jurisprudential
approach to the subject of international law the problem of the
binding force of this legal system is bound to loom large. Though
Bentham equated treaties in their legal effects with contracts,[29]
he was fully aware of the relative weakness of international, as
compared with municipal, law. In anticipation of Austin [30] and
modern sociology of international law,[31] Bentham explained the
difference by reference to the contrast in the social backgrounds

---

[26] See further the present writer's *The Inductive Approach to International
Law* (60 *Harvard Law Review,* 1947, p. 540 *et seq.*).

[27] *Principles of Morals and Legislation* (1780), 1 *Bentham,* p. 150, note. Cf.
also *The Limits of Jurisprudence Defined* (1782), ed. by Ch. W. Everett,
1945, p. 19.

[28] *Chrestomathia* (1816), 8 *Bentham,* p. 128, note.

[29] See above text to note 20.

[30] *Lectures on Jurisprudence,* 1869, Lecture 6. See further J. Stone, *The
Province and Function of Law,* 1947, p. 58 *et seq.*

[31] On the relevance of the distinction between Society and Community
Laws see further the present writer's *The Three Types of Law* (53
Ethics, 1943, p. 89 *et seq.*) and *International Law and Society* (1 *Year
Book of World Affairs,* 1947, p. 159 *et seq.*).

of municipal and international law. In the former case men live in a political society, or what we would call now a community : ' When a number of persons (whom we may style *subjects*) are supposed to be in the *habit* of paying *obedience* to a person, or an assembly of persons, of a known and certain description (whom we may call *governor* or *governors*), such persons altogether (*subjects* and *governors*) are said to be in a state of political Society '.[32]   International society, however, is primarily a negative conception of—what Bentham would call a natural—society. Rightly, Bentham warned against the danger of treating such ' pure ' types of classification as incompatibles and as an absolute antimony and emphasised the simultaneity of society and community relations.[33]

In a community the complete, that is to say coercive, type of law prevails, but even here the problem of incomplete law arises in certain fields of political or constitutional law : *Quis custodiet custodes?*   In so far as any laws, by which it is attempted to restrain the sovereign power within the State, are concerned, ' all that human wisdom has been able to devise is reduced to a system of precautions and indirect means '.[34]

International law is in the same position, and this is the reason why, in case of breach, there are differences between treaties and contracts. The position is still more uncertain in the sphere of international customary law : ' The customs which constitute what is called the law of nations, can only be called laws by extending the meaning of the term, and by metaphor. These are laws, the organisation of which is still more defective and incomplete than that of political law. The happiness of the human race would be fixed if it were possible to raise these two classes of law [35] to the rank of complete and organised law '.[36]

Even in the stage of incompleteness international law may hope to be observed to the extent to which it is self-executing,

[32] *A Fragment on Government* (1775), 1 *Bentham*, p. 263.
[33] See *ibid.*, pp. 263–266.
[34] *A General View of a Complete Code of Laws* (1802), 3 *Bentham*, p. 162. See also *Principles of Morals and Legislation* (addition made in 1789), 1 *Bentham*, p. 151.
[35] International treaties and customary law.   Bentham's identification of international law with international customary law in contrast to treaties is still current in the United States of America. Cf. Ph. C. Jessup, *Modernisation of the Law of International Contractual Agreements* (41 *American Journal of International Law*, 1947, pp. 379–380).
[36] *A General View of a Complete Code of Laws* (1802), 3 *Bentham*, p. 162.

that is to say, achieves the union between interest and legal duty by the beneficial character to the law-abiding State of the performance of its legal obligations.[37] Thus the reasonableness of international law which for Bentham is identical with its utility [38] becomes of prime importance and, in order to make the utility of such legal rules apparent it is essential that they should be of a clearly reciprocal character.[39] Then international law may expect to draw added strength from municipal law; for it becomes the interest of States, which have undertaken obligations under international law, to transform such commitments into municipal law and to put behind such obligations the sanctions of municipal law.[40]

Bentham's emphasis on the sanctions inherent in any Law of Reciprocity reduces the problem of the sanctions of international law to its proper proportions. Bentham was, however, convinced that one of the most urgent constructive tasks in the field consisted in strengthening the force behind international law.

In accordance with his general theory of the four sources of pleasure and pain, Bentham distinguished between physical, political (including legal), moral and religious sanctions.[41] In a letter to Dumont,[42] this distinction was refined by grouping sanctions under the two main headings of human and super-

[37] *The Rationale of Reward* (1825), 2 *Bentham*, pp. 199–200.
[38] 'Power gives existence to a law for the moment, but it is upon reason that it must depend for its stability'. *Draught for the Organisation of Judicial Establishments* (1790), 4 *Bentham*, p. 310.
   In Bentham's view, the widespread acceptance of the rules of neutrality which were upheld by Russia and led to the First Armed Neutrality of 1780, was not due to fear of the initiating Power, but to their equitable character, 'that is to say' their 'common utility' (*Principles of International Law* (1786–1789), 2 *Bentham*, p. 537). See also *Anti-Machiavel*, Third Letter (1789), 10 *Bentham*, pp. 209–210. How justified Bentham was, from a long-range point of view, becomes apparent if it is remembered that these principles provided the basis for the Declaration of Paris of 1856. See further W. S. Carpenter, *The United States and the League of Neutrals* (15 A.J.I.L., 1921, p. 511 et seq.), C. J. Kulsrud, *Armed Neutralities to 1780* (29 A.J.I.L., 1935, p. 423 et seq.), and below text to note 61.
   On utility as the yardstick of reforms in international law, see below under 7.
[39] See, for instance, *Principles of International Law* (1786–1789), 2 *Bentham*, pp. 538, 545 and 550, or *A General View of a Complete Code of Laws* (1802), p. 200.
[40] *Principles of Morals and Legislation* (1780), 1 *Bentham*, p. 132, note, or *A General View of a Complete Code of Law* (1802), 3 *Bentham*, p. 200.
[41] *Principles of Morals and Legislation* (1780), 1 *Bentham*, p. 14.
[42] Letter of October 28, 1821 (ibid., note). See further Stone, *l.c.* in note 30 above, p. 281 et seq.

human or religious sanctions, and the former under the sub-headings of physical, retributive, sympathetic, antipathetic, popular or moral and political, including legal and administrative, sanctions.

Applying this theory to international relations, Bentham held that international law might be indebted to all or any of these ' forces by which the human will is influenced '.[43] The clearest instance of an external sanction of international law was for Bentham a treaty of guarantee by which the guarantor is bound to intervene in the contingencies provided for in the treaty.[44] One of the instances chosen by Bentham himself—the guarantee undertaken by France in the Peace Treaties of Westphalia regarding the *status quo* in the Holy Roman Empire—shows, however, the limitations and unreliability of this sanction.

Bentham conceded that there were circumstances in which war could not be avoided and in which self-defence was the only alternative to meek submission to an aggressor.[45] He did not, however, fall into the mistake, not always avoided in the pre-1914 period, of cloaking any kind of war in the respectable garment of a sanction of international law. Awareness of one of the essential features of a true sanction, that is to say, that it must be ' directed by design ',[46] whereas war in its nature is uncontrollable, saved him from this fallacy. As Bentham himself pointed out, the analogy between the laws of peace and the substantive parts of municipal law as compared with the laws of war and procedural law may have a limited value. It is likely to assist in restraining belligerents and in humanising warfare by keeping before the eyes of belligerents the attainment of their substantial claims as the object of the struggle. This distinction also serves as a reminder that, at the most, war is a means to an end, but not an end in itself.[47] Yet his analysis of the causes of war convinced Bentham that, apart from *bona fide*

---

[43] *The Limits of Jurisprudence Defined* (1782), ed. by Ch. W. Everett, 1945, p. 152.

[44] *Ibid.*, p. 152.

[45] Bentham's answer to pacifist objections to defensive war applies as much to our time as it did then: ' What a fine thing it would have been for Buonaparte to have had to do with Quaker nations! ' (10 *Bentham,* p. 581). See also *Principles of International Law* (1786–1789), 2 *Bentham,* p. 545.

[46] *L.c.* in note 43 above.

[47] *Principles of International Law* (1786–1789), 2 *Bentham,* pp. 538–539, and *A General View of a Complete Code of Laws* (1802), 3 *ibid.*, p. 201.

wars which may be likened to ordeal by battle, there are wars of passion, ambition and outright *mala fide* wars.[48]   Bentham perceived that, in a system of power politics, war fulfils a multitude of social—and anti-social—functions, that, in such an environment, peace merely signifies the absence of war,[49] and that to find substitutes for, and effective means of preventing, war is the answer to the riddle of the incompleteness of international law.[50]

5. *Laws of Warfare.* Bentham had no illusions that war, this ' complication of all other evils ' [51] and ' mischief upon the largest scale ' [52] would be dispensed with in the immediate future. He, therefore, coupled his plans for the elimination of war with practical suggestions for the humanisation of the rules of warfare, which would ' soften the evils of war '.[53]   The purpose of war being to overcome the resistance of the enemy State, any interference with non-combatants which is not justified by this major object of warfare must be avoided.   In Bentham's opinion the most efficacious means of protecting the civilian population is to grant a great latitude of powers to the authorities, but to ' render the chiefs responsible in case of excessive oppression '.[54] There is in Bentham's attitude to the problem a certain affinity to the emphasis placed by Rousseau on war as an exclusive relation between States.[55]   Yet Bentham did not challenge the view that a state of war also affected the status of enemy subjects. The power of making war involves the right—classified by Bentham like that of making peace as a branch of the power of specification—to ' transfer a class of foreign friends into the class of foreign enemies '.[56]   Bentham's most constructive suggestion in this field, the ' appointment of war-residents, to provide for

---

[48] *Principles of International Law* (1786–1789), 2 *Bentham*, p. 545, and *Marginal Projects* (1789), Bentham MSS., University College, London, Portfolio 25, f. 11, p. 127.

[49] Letter to J. Henry, June 11, 1827 (in E. Nys, *Études de Droit International et de Droit Politique*, 1901, p. 311). Cf. also 1 L.Q.R. (1885), p. 227.

[50] See below under II.

[51] *Principles of International Law* (1786–1789), 2 *Bentham*, p. 538.

[52] *Ibid.*, p. 544.

[53] *A General View of a Complete Code of Laws* (1802), 3 *Bentham*, p. 201.

[54] *Ibid.*, p. 202.

[55] *Contrat Social*, Book 1, Chap. 4 (1762), ed. Sir Ernest Barker, 1947, pp. 249–251. See further G. Lassudrie-Duchêne, *Jean-Jacques Rousseau et le Droit des Gens*, 1906.

[56] *L.c.* in note 53 above, p. 199. See also *The Limits of Jurisprudence Defined* (1782), ed. Ch. W. Everett, 1945, pp. 96 and 172.

prisoners and to prevent violations of the laws of war',[57] was realised to a certain extent by *ad hoc* arrangements made between the belligerents of the First World War [58] and by the right of inspection granted to neutral protecting powers in the Geneva Convention regarding Prisoners of War of 1929.[59]

'Injustice invites fresh injustice'.[60] Atrocities in warfare, therefore, are likely only to acerbate the struggle between belligerents and to make it more difficult for them to conclude peace. Equally, it is to the interest of belligerents to keep neutrals out of the enemy's camp, and by their treatment of neutrals to contribute to this end.[61] From this point of view Bentham thoroughly examined British prize law as applied during the Napoleonic wars and arrived at the conclusion that it was wanting. His notes—which would be well worth publishing [62]—do not do justice to the compelling reasons which forced Britain to retaliate as best as she could against Napoleon, but they furnish proof of Bentham's acquaintance with the technicalities of British prize law and the major cases decided by Sir William Scott.[63] Bentham was certainly not impressed by the rules of evidence then practised in English prize courts: the 'mode of collecting evidence in these as well as Equity Courts, the worst except perhaps the affidavit mode—the mode which he who wishes to maximise perjury would choose'.[64] In order to counteract the practice of unnecessary destruction of neutral prize, Bentham recommended that the reward for capture should be twice as much as for the destruction of prize.[65] The reliance

---

57 *Principles of International Law* (1786–1789), 2 *Bentham*, p. 545 and *Marginal Projects* (1789), Bentham MSS., University College, London, Portfolio 25, f. 11, p. 127.

58 Cf. Cd. Misc., No. 7, 1915 on Sir Edward Grey's initiative taken in the matter in December 1914, and further J. W. Garner, *International Law and the World War*, 1920, Vol. 1, p. 5 *et seq.*

59 Articles 86–88.

60 *Principles of International Law* (1786–1789), 2 *Bentham*, p. 552. See also *ibid.*, p. 538.

61 This aspect of the matter appears to have influenced Bentham's opinion in favour of the principles of the Armed Neutrality of 1788. See note 38 above.

62 Bentham MSS., University College, London, Portfolio 129b, f. 8, pp. 647–674.

63 For his notes which appear to have been written in November 1810, Bentham used the six volumes of Christopher Robinson's Admiralty Reports, covering the period from 1799 to 1808.

64 *L.c.* in note 62 above, p. 661.

65 *Ibid.*, p. 664.

of prize courts on the ' course of admiralty and the (unwritten) law of nations' was for Bentham due to the desire on the part of all concerned to ' keep up uncertainty, the mother of fees '.[66] In several cases Bentham worked out the amount of fees which, in the case of the condemnation of a prize, every one from Sir William Scott downwards obtained.   Though acknowledging Scott's unrivalled competence in the field, his ' sinister interest ' in the existing state of affairs as a ' fee-fed Judge ' disqualified him to Bentham as a possible draftsman of a prize code.[67]

In a world on the threshold of another post-war period, Bentham's thoughts on peace-making are of special interest.   He was no friend of the concept of collective criminal responsibility of nations—as distinct from their leaders—even in the case of undoubted wars of aggression.   It is in this context—in discussing whether nations have a personality of their own—that Bentham made one of his celebrated diatribes on the abuse of fictions by jurists.   According to Bentham, ' among nations there is no punishment.   In general there is nothing but restitution, to the effect of causing the evil to cease : rarely indemnification for the past; because among them there can scarcely be any *mauvaise foi*.   There is but too much of it too often among their chiefs; so that there would be no great evil if, at the close of his career, every conqueror were to end his days upon the rack ! . . . But however dishonest the intention of their chiefs may be, the subjects are always honest.   The nation once bound—and it is the chief which binds it—however criminal the aggression may be, there is properly no other criminal than the chief—individuals are only his innocent and unfortunate instruments.   The extenuation which is drawn from the weight of authority, rises here to the level of an entire exemption '.[68]   Having witnessed the horrors perpetrated by the totalitarian aggressors in the course of the Second World War, it appears impossible to subscribe to the doctrine—not postulated by positive international law—of the total exemption from responsibility of war criminals acting

---

[66] *Ibid.*, p. 660.
[67] *Ibid.*, p. 658.   How widespread at the time the suspicion of ' vested interests ' in this field was becomes evident from the Preface to the first edition of J. Stephen's *War in Disguise; or, The Frauds of the Neutral Flags*, 1805.
[68] *Principles of International Law* (1786–1789), 2 Bentham, p. 539.   See further C. K. Ogden, *Bentham's Theory of Fictions*, 1932, p. 141 *et seq.*

under superior orders.[69]   Nevertheless, Bentham's warning is salutary as a reminder of the need of individual guilt as a prerequisite of criminal responsibility and as a refutation in anticipation of hazy notions of international criminal responsibility ' additional to and not exclusive of the international criminal liability of the individuals guilty of crimes committed in violation of International Law '.[70]

6. *Sovereignty and State Jurisdiction.*   Sovereignty in the international sphere signifies the absence of a common superior to States [71] or, as Bentham put it elsewhere, a relationship within a state of natural society.[72]   Like the fathers of the American Constitution—and in contrast to Austin [73]—Bentham had no difficulties in conceiving the possibility of a division of sovereign power : ' Every distribution as well as every limitation of power is possible that is conceivable . . . Many are the commonplace phrases in use which would seem to assert the contrary : that an *imperium in imperio* is a monster in politics : that no man can serve two masters : that a house divided against itself cannot stand : and the phrases are made to pass for arguments. . . . Thus much is indeed true, that the same individual branch of power cannot be possessed, and that exclusively, by two persons at the same time.   But any two branches may that are distinguishable : and any one branch of power may be shared among ever so many '.[74]   The various federal experiments made

---

[69] See further the present writer's *International Law and Totalitarian Lawlessness*, 1943, p. 62 *et seq.*, and *The Judgment of Nuremberg*, 21 *Tulane Law Review* (1947), p. 329 *et seq.*
    To a good many of the ' denazification ' and ' defascistisation ' trials carried out by the nations defeated in the Second World War Bentham's judgment on the value of punishing the authors of aggressive wars applies : ' If punishment had been ever applied on such an occasion it would be not for the mischief done to the foreign nation, but purely for the mischief brought upon their own—not for the injustice, but purely for the imprudence '. *Principles of International Law* (1786–1789), 2 *Bentham*, p. 555.

[70] Oppenheim's *International Law* (ed. H. Lauterpacht), Vol. I, 1947, pp. 322–323.   In the present state of international organisation, the answer to the challenge of the gangster State is the outlawry of such an entity if endowed with international personality.   See further Oppenheim's *International Law*, Vol. I, 1906, p. 204 and *l.c.* in note 69 above, 1943, p. 82 *et seq.*

[71] *Principles of International Law* (1786–1789), 2 *Bentham*, p. 544.

[72] See notes 32 and 33 above.

[73] Lectures on Jurisprudence, 1869, Lecture 6.   Cf. for criticism of this view, R. A. Eastwood and G. W. Keeton, *The Austinian Theories of Law and Sovereignty*, 1929, or Sir John Salmond, *Jurisprudence*, ed. G. L. Williams, 1947, pp. 491–492.

[74] *The Limits of Jurisprudence Defined* (1782), ed. Ch. W. Everett, 1945, p. 153.

since Bentham's days and instances of *condominium* between
sovereign States over certain territories such as the British-French
Treaty of 1914 regarding the New Hebrides, the British-United
States Agreement of 1939 regarding Canton and Endenbury
Islands or the Allied *condominium* assumed over Germany after
her unconditional surrender in 1945 bear witness to the soundness
of Bentham's view.

Following in Locke's footsteps and three years before Burke's
celebrated speech on December 1, 1783, on Fox's India Bill,
Bentham attempted to limit the noxious concept of sovereignty
by subjecting it to his all-purposes-test of utility and emphasising
its necessarily fiduciary character.[75] He judged in this light uses
—and abuses—of the exercise of national jurisdiction.   Thus,
in reply to Chauvelin's letter, offering to Bentham the citizenship
of the French Republic, Bentham addressed himself to the French
Minister of the Interior on the question of the proscription of
the French refugees. He pointed out that there were too few of
such refugees to justify the measure as one of precaution and too
many to justify it as one of punishment. As in his view, the
French Republic had firmly established itself,[76] the proscription
of opponents of the regime abroad amounted to unnecessary, and
therefore, lawless punishment.[77]

7. *Codification.* More important than any other contributions made by Bentham to the development of international law
is his advocacy of the codification of international law.   The
private codes put forward in increasing number since the second
half of the nineteenth century, the work of the *Institut de Droit
International,* the codifications of the Hague Peace Conferences
in the fields of the laws of warfare and neutrality, and the work
carried on within the framework of the League of Nations and
of the Pan-American Union, are a tribute to Bentham's vision.
Mainly owing to the interest in the matter shown by the Chinese
Delegation during the Dumbarton Oaks conversations,[78] it has
come to pass that the Charter of the United Nations expressly

[75] *Principles of Morals and Legislation* (1780), 1 *Bentham,* p. 134.
[76] This correspondence took place in October 1792.
[77] 10 *Bentham,* p. 282. See below under 7 for a further instance of the
application of the test of utility to acts of national jurisdiction.
[78] Yuen-li Liang, *The Progressive Development of International Law and
its Codification under the United Nations,* pp. 8–9 (Paper read before the
41st Annual Meeting of the American Society of International Law,
1947).

enjoins the General Assembly to concern itself with the encouragement of the ' progressive development of international law and its
codification '. It is, therefore, of more than historical interest
to examine Bentham's views on this topic. In order to bring out
their full significance, it is essential to distinguish between the
techniques and contents of his proposals.

Bentham recognised that legislation was a subject which, like
any other aspect of law, is capable of scientific treatment.
Already the *Scheme of Series of Contemplated Publications,*
which Bentham drafted between 1776 and 1782, contains a part
which was to deal with ' principles of legislation in matters
betwixt nation and nation, or, to use a new, though not
inexpressive appellation, in matters of international law '.[79] At
various periods of his life Bentham returned to the subject, and
his letters in the British Museum, which he wrote in the period
between 1827 and 1830 to J. Henry, a legal officer in the Ionian
Islands and subsequently a practitioner in London,[80] show the
importance which Bentham attached to the question in the
closing phase of his life.

Until States consented to incorporate such an international
code into treaties and until they established international
tribunals competent to interpret it, the rights and duties embodied
in the code would only have the character of morally binding
rules.[81] Yet even so, an international code would have its value
as it would serve as a directive to public opinion,[82] and remove
international law from the sphere of merely conjectural law.[83]
After the experience of codification under the auspices of the
League of Nations, there is perhaps a tendency today to lean

[79] 1 *Bentham,* p. x. See further *The Theory of Legislation* (ed. C. K.
Ogden), 1931, p. 472.
[80] Henry's pamphlets on *Report on the Criminal Law of Demerara,* 1821,
and the *Judgment of the Court of Demerara in the case of Odwin* v.
Forbes, 1823, suggested him to Bentham as a possible writer who might
deal adequately with the subject in the light of the greatest-happiness
principle : ' No small satisfaction would be to see this subject treated of
by the light of this same principle before I die '. (Letter to J. Henry,
January 15, 1830. 11 *Bentham,* p. 34.) See also *Memoranda from
Bentham's Conversations in 1827–1828 :* ' Few things are more wanting
than a code of international law ' (10 *Bentham,* p. 584).
[81] *A General View of a Complete Code of Laws* (1802), 3 *Bentham,* p. 200.
See further below under II.
[82] Cf. J. H. Burton's Introduction to Bentham's *Collected Works* (1
Bentham, p. 75).
[83] *L.c.* in note 81 above, pp. 205–206. See also Stone, *l.c.* in note 30 above,
pp. 287–288.

more towards the development of international law by means of unofficial rather than official agencies.

If the results achieved by either of these agencies are compared with the unostentatious but so much more effective development of international law by means of international judicial institutions, especially the Permanent Court of International Justice, it becomes evident that the issue of codification has been reopened on a level at which it could not be discussed in Bentham's time. The reluctance shown by members of the United Nations to make use of the International Court of Justice serves, however, as a warning against any exclusive approach to the problem, and there is no reason why the development of international law should not proceed by the simultaneous use of quasi-legislative and common law techniques.[84]

The guiding principle that Bentham wished to see applied to the international—as to any other—code is that of utility, the greatest-happiness principle.[85] In the international field this must mean the ' greatest and common utility of all nations taken together '.[86] In Bentham's view there is both a common and equal utility of all nations, but the difficulty with this notion is that even if States could be expected to agree on the denominator as such, they may have very different views on the application of this principle or hold that diverging national interests of a short-range character should have preference over the ultimate common good.[87] Ultimately these issues depend on the degree of integration which international society has achieved, and on the relative strength of vertical and horizontal loyalties and not on any rational calculation of interests. Where there is a common purpose acknowledged as overriding by all concerned, self-interest will be subordinated to the common task. Where this is lacking, the most persuasive exposition of the requirements of common utility will not have much effect. Yet to the extent to which

---

[84] See further Sir Cecil Hurst, *A Plan for the Codification of International Law on New Lines* (Paper read before the Grotius Society in 1946); Yuen-li Liang, *Methods for the Encouragement of the Progressive Development of International Law* (2 *Year Book of World Affairs*, 1948) and the present writer's *Manual of International Law*, 1947, p. 130 *et seq.*

[85] See above note 80, and *The Dream* (c. 1780), Bentham MSS., University College, London, Portfolio 169, f. 13, p. 79.

[86] *Principles of International Law* (1786–1789), 2 *Bentham*, p. 538.

[87] Cf. E. H. Carr, *The Twenty Years' Crisis*, 1946, p. 166 *et seq.*, and H. Kantorowicz, *The Spirit of British Policy*, 1931, p. 140.

nations are willing to co-operate in the development of international law, the utility principle, whatever its theoretical weakness, offers as good a pragmatic guide of international action as any that have as yet been recommended to take its place.[88] As it was put by Dicey,[89] the saving virtue of utilitarianism in the field of legal planning is that it directs a legislator's attention to the consequences of any proposed change in existing law.

The categorical imperative which forms the basis of Bentham's proposals would have met with the approval of naturalist writers on international law, not excluding Blackstone.[90] Utility, as applied on a footing of reciprocity to inter-State relations, demands, positively, that a nation should do the greatest possible good to other nations, and in this is implied the negative duty not to inflict any injury on other nations. Both duties, however, are qualified by an all-important proviso : ' saving the regard which is proper to its (the nation's) own wellbeing '.[91] If nations adopted these principles as guides to action, peace would be transformed from a negative state of mere absence of war into a state of ' mutual good will '. Such an international community would have to be based on the twin pillars of the equality of its members—Bentham does not make it clear whether he means by this more than equality of status—and on the principle of toleration of one another's forms of government, religions, customs and opinions. In this respect each government merely desires to be ' regarded as persuaded that its own form of government is in its nature, in a higher degree than any

---

[88] See, for instance, H. J. Morgenthau, *Scientific Man* versus *Power Politics*, 1946, and compare his critical onslaught on utilitarianism (p. 168 *et seq.*) with his own ' tragic ' approach to international affairs, an attempt at the revival of the aristocratic-conservative tradition in political theory. Cf. Karl Mannheim, *Das Konservative Denken* (57 *Archiv für Sozialwissenschaft und Sozialpolitik*).

An objection which is frequently raised against the principle of utility is that it is merely natural law in disguise. Bentham himself was fully aware of this connection, but accused naturalists of the ' oblique and roundabout ' way in which they used the principle of utility. See *The Theory of Legislation* (ed. C. K. Ogden), 1931, p. 194 and *The Limits of Jurisprudence Defined* (1782), (ed. Ch. W. Everett), 1945, pp. 117–118. Cf., however, A. Cobban, *The Crisis of Civilisation*, 1941, p. 93.

[89] *Law and Public Opinion in England*, 1930, p. 144. See also W. I. Jennings, *A Plea for Utilitarianism* (2 *Modern Law Review*, 1938, p. 22 *et seq.*).

[90] See Blackstone, *Commentaries on the Laws of England* (1765–1769), Book 4, Chap. 5, Introduction, or Vattel, *Le Droit des Gens* (1758), *Prélim.*, § 13 and Book 2, Chap. 1, § 218.

[91] *Principles of International Law* (1786–1789), 2 *Bentham*, p. 538.

other, conducive to the greatest happiness of the whole number of the members of the community of which it is the government : and by this declaration it means not to contest the fitness of any other for governing in the community in which it bears rule '.[92]

Provided that the premises were accepted, the drafting of the international code should not present any undue difficulties. It should comprise the ' adjustment and pre-appointed definition of all rights and obligations that present themselves as liable and likely to come into question '. In Bentham's view, this would be so much easier if it were done at a time when no concrete disputes were involved than when the subject was complicated by the likely effect of such agreed principles on concrete issues at stake.[93] As became evident in the *Alabama* Case between Great Britain and the United States of America, there may be overriding considerations of achieving concord which may cause a State even to accept the weighing of the scales against it in advance. If, however, such a major inducement is lacking, Bentham appears to have underestimated two difficulties. States never start from a *tabula rasa*. There are always a number of unsettled disputes on the shelves the position in which might be adversely affected by a codification. In addition, Foreign Offices are the guardians of permanent national interests, and in this respect the interests of, for instance, land and sea powers are not always easily harmonised. The Hague Peace Conventions are an example of codifications which were achieved at the price of leaving unsettled really controversial issues in sea warfare such as the scope of contraband goods, the legality of naval bombardments, the use of mines or the place of conversion of a merchant vessel into a man-of-war.

The spirit in which Bentham hoped to see international codification achieved may be illustrated by a few examples.

Territorial disputes were often due to uncertainties regarding the right of succession or the limits of territorial rights in newly discovered areas. Codification could provide criteria which would be conducive to the pacific settlement of such disputes.[94] This suggestion, far from being revolutionary, appears today to be concerned with a very minor problem. One and a half

---

[92] *L.c.* in note 49 above, Article 8. See also below text to note 121.
[93] *Ibid.* Article 7.
[94] *Principles of International Law* (1786–1789), 2 *Bentham*, pp. 539–540.

centuries of international arbitration in this field have shown that
international law does not lack the necessary rules, provided that
States are willing to settle such disputes on the basis of the *lex
lata*.

If the principle of utility is applied to nationality questions,
the test should be the comparatively highest afflictive power of
one sovereign as compared with another.   Birth forms as a rule
such a criterion, being ' not a situation, which at any time may
change, but an event which is past, necessary and unicurrent '.[95]
Bentham realised that in some cases, as for instance in that of
emigration, birth loses its normal significance, and this applies
still more so to the case of the birth of a child in the country of
merely temporary sojourn of the parents.   The case posed by
Bentham of a child born in a country, the nationality laws of
which incorporate the principle of *jus soli*, of parents, whose
nationality is based on the principle of *jus sanguinis*, is a tribute
to Bentham's calibre as a draftsman ; for the question which he
raises regarding the position of such a child in a subsequent war
between the two countries was the issue in the notorious case of
Schwarz, who was born of German parents during a visit in
Corsica and, when captured by the French in the course of the
First World War, sentenced to death as a traitor.   According to
Bentham, any criteria with reference to which nationality may
be determined should be applied elastically, and birth should be
regarded merely as a presumption of nationality.   In the last
mentioned case the option should be with the parents or guardian
provisionally, and with the child when it comes of age.   It was
not until the *Canevaro* Case between Italy and Peru (1912) that
the principle of overriding or effective nationality made its
appearance in international arbitration, and it took until 1930
for the Convention on Certain Questions relating to the Conflict
of Nationality Laws to attack the more specific problem set by
Bentham.   The Convention and the Protocol relating to Military
Obligations of Persons of Dual Nationality came into force only
in 1937, and so far they have been accepted by only ten States.
The solution which was adopted was in line with Bentham's
suggestions.   It will, therefore, become clear that the slow motion
picture of the codification of international law in matters of such

[95] *Ibid.,* p. 542.   See also *Of Subjects* (1786–1789), Bentham MSS.,
University College, London, Portfolio 25, f. 7, p. 65.

trivial importance cannot be explained on the grounds of deficiencies inherent in the utility principle.

Bentham's proposals for international rules regarding ' damages done by vessels to each other and police of ports '[96] were not taken up until a Convention on the Unification of Certain Rules of Law with respect to Collisions was adopted by the Brussels Conference of 1910 and until the Convention on the International Regime of Maritime Ports was signed in 1923. Yet his most constructive suggestions in the field of international maritime law are those regarding the improvement of inter-oceanic communications.   Apart from the forerunner of the Suez Canal in the time of the Pharaohs, schemes for canals linking the Mediterranean with the Red Sea and the Atlantic with the Pacific can be traced back right to the sixteenth century. But to Bentham—like Saint Simon—canals and the improvement of international communications in general meant much more.   They were vehicles of international peace and understanding.[97]   It required the advent of air power to drive home to liberal optimists the lesson that technological progress is neutral from the point of view of the integration of international society, and that modern inventions bring the world together for evil as well as good.

Bentham rightly felt that the time was ripe for the materialisation of such plans, and the legal form which he gave to his *Junctiana Proposal* was eminently practicable.   Both in the interest of peace and the security of the countries bordering the canal, the States most directly concerned—Colombia, Mexico and the United States of America—should exercise a system of trusteeship over the canal zone in the interest of the world at large.   The project should be carried out and operated by a joint-stock company, to be styled the Junctiana Company, and in matters of transit dues, land purchase and leasing of land in the canal zone the principle of equality of treatment should apply : ' The company to admit vessels of all states, at the outset and forever, on exactly the same footing—the state or states with which the agreement is made, not excepted : no favour, direct or indirect, to be given to any one at the expense of any other State '.[98]

[96] *A General View of a Complete Code of Laws* (1802), 3 *Bentham*, p. 201.
[97] See further Morgenthau, *l.c.* in note 88 above, p. 81 *et seq.*, and the present writer's *Power Politics*, 1941, p. 174.
[98] *Junctiana Proposal* (1822), 2 *Bentham*, p. 563.

Four years later Clay, Secretary of State, took up the subject in this spirit in his instructions to the United States representatives to the Panama Congress of 1826. In 1835 the United States Senate passed a Resolution to this effect. In 1849, the United States opened negotiations with Great Britain regarding the neutralisation of the Panama Canal, and on April 19, 1850, the famous Clayton-Bulwer Treaty was concluded between the two countries to settle in a convention the views and intentions of Britain and the United States ' with reference to any means of communication by ship canal which may be constructed between the Atlantic and Pacific Oceans '.[99]   It is also worth mentioning that the tolls controversy of 1912 between the United States and Great Britain over the interpretation of the Hay-Pauncefote Treaty of 1901 arose over an interpretation by the United States of the equality of treatment clause of the Treaty which fell short of the standards expected by Bentham.[100]

Bentham's correspondence in 1828 with Mehemet Ali on the Suez Canal to be established on lines corresponding to the Junctiana Proposal bore fruit in the concession granted to Ferdinand de Lesseps in 1854 by the Viceroy of Egypt.

While Bentham's proposals in this—as in other fields—were in advance of their times, they were conceived in a spirit which was in line with the general trend of international law in the relatively stable period between the Napoleonic wars and the First World War.   In his suggestions for the development and codification of international law Bentham combined acute criticism with a constructive vision which hardly deserves to be described as ' utopian '.[101]

---

[99] See further J. B. Moore, *A Digest of International Law*, 1906, Vol. 3, § 336 *et seq.*

[100] See further G. H. Hackworth, *Digest of International Law*, 1941, Vol. 2, § 217 and L. Oppenheim, *The Panama Canal Conflict*, 1913.

[101] Oppenheim's *International Law* (ed. H. Lauterpacht), Vol. 1, 1947, p. 54.   The chief authority for this opinion is 8 *Bentham*, p. 537.   This reference does not make sense, as it relates to one of Bentham's letters to Count Toréno on the proposed Spanish Penal Code, and the other reference to Nys's article (see note 49 above) is not much more illuminating.   In all likelihood, the first reference was meant by Oppenheim to relate to 2 *Bentham*, p. 537 and the second reference should be to Vol. 1 (not 11) of the *Law Quarterly Review*.   Cf. also note 70 above on the subjective element inherent in views on the ' realistic ' or ' utopian ' character of suggested developments in this field.

II. BENTHAM AND INTERNATIONAL ORGANISATION

(1) *Power Politics.* In spite of Bentham's basically unhistorical approach to social phenomena, he appears to have obtained a true enough picture of the essentials of international affairs, both in so far as the motive powers and forms of power politics are concerned.

Self-interest, and not justice, is the guiding principle of ' national morality '.[102] The test of motives in the international sphere—as elsewhere—is simple : ' Acts are the tests of words '.[103] It did not escape Bentham that the practice of power politics has a vocabulary of its own : ' Justice and humanity have no place in cabinets. It is for weak states to suffer injuries : it is for strong ones to inflict them. Do as you would be done by, a rule of gold for individuals, is a rule of glass for nations. The duty of a king to his subjects and the world, is to compass war, by any means, and at any price ; and the less the profit or pretence, the greater the glory. To do mischief is *honour* : to do it slyly, darkly, and secretly, is *policy.* The number of troops a nation is able to bring into the field, gives the measure of its power : the number of unprovoked and unrequited injuries it has been able to inflict, gives the measure of its virtue. The true contest among kings is, who with least smart to himself shall give the hardest blow '.[104] Or, ' in the nomenclature of politics there are certain established phrases, by which innocence and wisdom are branded with contempt, guilt and folly recommended for admiration and practice. In this dictionary, peace and tranquillity are represented by sloth, obscurity, and insignificance : bloodshed and destruction by vigour, spirit, activity, a sense of national glory, and so on. In the faculty of ringing the changes upon these phrases, consists the skill by which writers of the complexion of this ministerial advocate [105] prove their title to the appellation of adepts in politics '.[106]

---

[102] *Principles of International Law* (1786–1789), 2 *Bentham,* pp. 539 and 552.

[103] *Anti-Machiavel,* First Letter (1789), 10 *Bentham,* p. 205.

[104] Second Letter, *ibid.,* p. 206. See also *The Science of Legislation,* ed. C. K. Ogden, 1931, p. 472.

[105] Bentham's Letters to *The Public Advertiser,* under the pseudonym of ' Anti-Machiavel ' were a reply to letters in the *Gazette de Leyde,* probably wrongly attributed to King George III. Bentham also aimed at Elliott, who was then British Minister at Copenhagen. See further W. E. H. Lecky, *A History of England in the Eighteenth Century,* Vol. 10, p. 210 *et seq.,* and Bentham MSS., University College, London, Portfolio 25, f. 7, pp. 59–67.

The occasion for these strictures was the intention attributed by Bentham in 1789 to British policy to break up the alliance between Russia and Denmark in the interest of the balance of power. It may be argued that any such generalisation—even if justified in the concrete case—overlooks the ordinary behaviour of most powers in most cases. It is, however, probably more correct to hold that, in any age, at least one—if not more—of the greater powers conducts its foreign policy on the level arraigned by Bentham, and this has a tendency to reduce the standards of international affairs to the lowest denominator.

In such a system of international relations secret diplomacy flourishes. Bentham does not mince his words regarding the effect of such practices on the victims most to be pitied, that is to say, foreign ministers and diplomats. It is ' that the prerogatives of place may furnish an aliment to petty vanity; that the members of the *circulation* may have, as it were, a newspaper to themselves; that under favour of the monopoly, ignorance and incapacity may put on airs of wisdom '. In the end, secrecy becomes ' part of the *douceurs* of office—a perquisite which will be valued in proportion to the insignificance of their characters and the narrowness of their views. It serves to pamper them up with notions of their own importance, and to teach the servants of the people to look down upon their masters '.[106]

' Schoolboy notions' of prestige sway adults who should know better; for injury to a nation's prestige is a reflection on the esteem in which a nation is held by others, and this in its turn is determined by its power of retaliation.[107]

Armaments, alliances, counter-alliances and balance of power systems are the customary patterns of power politics. Yet the uneasy and ever shifting equilibrium within such an inter-State system does not really deserve to be called a balance. This term should be appropriately reserved to situations in which there is a really harmonious relationship between nations.[108] Pressure politics finds its culmination in war, and to inquire into its causes might appear to be the same thing as to inquire into the causes

[106] *Principles of International Law* (1786–1789), 2 *Bentham*, p. 558.
[107] Cf. MS. on *Pacification and Emancipation. A Protest against Machiavellianism* (1789), Bentham MSS., University College, London, Portfolio 25, f. 10, p. 121.
[108] Cf. MS. on *Protest International* (1789), Bentham MSS., University College, London, Portfolio 25, f. 9, pp. 106–118 and *The Book of Fallacies* (1824), 2 *Bentham*, p. 447.

of criminality. The only difference consists in the 'magnitude of the scale'.[109]

(2) *Bentham's Approach to Planning.* Bentham, like Kant, scorned the fallacy that what is good in theory can be bad in practice, and conversely—what is more important—that what is bad in practice can be good in theory. The erroneousness of this view is based on a misunderstanding of the meaning and functions of theoretical thinking. Rightly, therefore, Bentham denied that ' a plan, which is essentially incapable of proving good in practice can with propriety be said to be good in theory'.[110]

The Book of Fallacies (1824) contains a delightful catalogue of the typical arguments put forward by the opponents of planning on national and international scales. There is the usual appeal to authority for the maintenance of the existing state of affairs and the corresponding lack of authority for innovation. There is the danger inherent in change as such and the wisdom attributed to delay for whatever reason. Milder forms of the latter are the favourite arguments of the ' procrastinator' for ' snail's-pace' development if change there must be : ' For more effectual recommendation of this course, to the epithet *gradual* are commonly added such eulogistic epithets as *moderate* and *temperate*; whereby it is implied that in proportion as the pace recommended by the word *gradual* is quickened, such increased pace will justly incur the censure expressed by the opposite epithets, immoderate, violent, precipitate, extravagant, intemperate'.[111] Arguments of this type are ably seconded by stratagems of artful diversion and of confusing the issue by the use of ' eulogistic' and ' dyslogistic' terms, of ' passion-kindling appellatives' like honour, glory and dignity.[112] The last ditch of passive resistance, the perpetual argument of the age not being ' ripe' for any reform was jumped by Bentham without hesitation : ' The more it wants of being ripe the sooner we should begin to do what can be done to ripen it; the more we should

---

[109] *Principles of International Law* (1786–1789), 2 *Bentham*, p. 544. See also notes 45–50 above and further *Marginal Projects* (1789), Bentham MSS., University College, London, Portfolio 25, f. 11, p. 127.

[110] *The Book of Fallacies* (1824), 2 *Bentham*, pp. 459–460. See also E. Kant, *Ueber den Gemeinspruch : Das mag in der Theorie richtig sein, taugt aber nicht für die Praxis* (1793).

[111] 2 *Bentham*, p. 433.

[112] *Ibid.*, pp. 435–438. See also *The Theory of Legislation*, ed. C. K. Ogden, 1931, p. 68, above text to notes 104–106 and G. L. Williams, *Language and the Law* (62 *Law Quarterly Review*, 1946, p. 387 *et seq.*).

do to ripen it '[113] Nor was Bentham impressed by the possibility that proposals for reform might be described as utopian.
He only insisted that the term should be used in a rationally
convincing manner and limited to cases in which ' in the event of
the adoption of the proposed plan, felicitous effects are represented as about to take place, no causes adequate to the
production of such effects being found in it '.[114] In modern
sociological terminology it has been found helpful to widen the
notion so as to include ideas which appear unrealisable within
the framework of an existing political, social and economic
order.[115] Though Bentham had a tendency to oversimplify the
reasons for the persistency of these fallacies, he was not so naïve
as to believe that such defective reasoning was merely due to
lack of brain power, but rightly put his finger on social factors
which are likely to cause such intellectual short circuits :
prejudices and vested interests of a personal and group character.[116] It may, however, be added that Bentham did not impugn
the good faith of any opponents of reform, but merely drew
attention to primarily external and irrational circumstances
which condition reasoning.[117]

(3) *Bentham's Postulates of International Order.* Bentham's
proposals for the establishment of a true international order are
based on assumptions which he made articulate at one or other
time, but which have to be elaborated in order to see his plan
in its proper perspective.

International society was to be raised from a mere society
level to a state of community relations in which peace was transformed from mere absence of war to a positive relationship of
' mutual good will and consequent mutual good offices between
all the several members of this confederation '.[118]

---

[113] *Principles of International Law* (1786–1789), 2 *Bentham*, p. 546.
[114] *The Book of Fallacies* (1824), 2 *Bentham*, p. 459. See also note 101
above.
[115] See further K. Mannheim, *Ideology and Utopia*, 1936, p. 111 and *l.c.*
in note 97 above, 1941, p. 353 *et seq.*
[116] *L.c.* in note 114 above, p. 475. See also *The Limits of Jurisprudence*
(1782), ed. Ch. W Everett, 1945, p. 154, note 16.
[117] Modern criticism of Bentham's ' rationalism ' appears to underestimate
the degree of Bentham's awareness of such determinants of reason. This
appears to apply to Morgenthau (*l.c.* in note 88 above, p. 153 *et seq.*).
[118] Letter to J. Henry, June 11, 1827, Article 6 (*l.c.* in note 49 above,
p. 311). See also *Principles of International Law* (1786–1789), 2
Bentham, p. 559 and above under I.
It does not matter very much whether such a relationship on a com-

If nations adopted such an attitude towards one another, they might be expected to put the common good before their individual interest.[119] Wartime co-operation between allies has proved that if there is a common purpose like the defeat of the enemy such self-denial on the part of nations and individuals is not out of the ordinary. In time of peace, experiments like UNRRA or the International Refugee Organisation are so far rather the exceptions which prove the opposite rule.

It will be readily granted that such a community cannot be established on any other footing than that of the complete equality in status of its members and on the basis of freely given consent to whatever limitation of national sovereignty might be required.[120]

Finally, an international community must be based on the principle of mutual respect for, and toleration of, the internal systems of government of the member States and the political and religious views prevailing in them. In Bentham's view all States have one feature in common, that is to say, that ' the general good is everywhere the true object of all political action '.[121] Until the end of the Napoleonic wars it was not so much Czarist despotism [122] as revolutionary France which occupied in the minds of Bentham's contemporaries the place taken in present-day Western political thought by the Soviet Union. The tolerance shown during the inter-war period to Fascist States shows the dangers inherent in any merely opportunist liberalism of thought and in formalist thinking.[123] There

munity basis is considered as ' natural ' or as ' artificial '. Today, we rather tend to doubt the natural harmony of the free-playing interests of individuals or groups. But the creative task remains and becomes only more difficult if it is realised that our effort is not supported by some automatic principle of pre-established harmony or that any synthesis at which we may aim contains already the seeds of new antinomies. See further Stone, *l.c.* in note 30 above, p. 270, and *l.c.* in note 31 above.

[119] *The Theory of Legislation*, ed. C. K. Ogden, 1931, p. 472. See also above under I.

[120] *L.c.* in note 118 above, Articles 1 and 2.

[121] Letter to the French Minister of the Interior in reply to Chauvelin's letter of October 16, 1792 (10 *Bentham*, p. 282). See also *Principles of International Law* (1786–1789), 2 *Bentham*, p. 545 and above note 92.

[122] It has been suggested that Bentham's attitude to ' enlightened ' despotism was more than mere tolerance, and that he expected rulers like Catherine II to carry out his reforms more quickly than the more slowly moving democracies. Cf. Stone, *l.c.* in note 30 above, pp. 268–269.

[123] Kelsen's formulation that ' every State is a government of laws ' comes to mind (*Der soziologische und juristische Staatsbegriff*, 1928, p. 191).

can be no community without a modicum of common values. Yet such reflections affect only the scope of the international community that, in any age, may be feasible. They do not impair Bentham's basic thesis that, within any international community, the principle of toleration must apply to all matters but those which are absolutely vital from the point of view of the community.

(4) *Bentham's Proposals on International Organisation.* Bentham has often been likened to Continental reformers whether by way of compliment or otherwise. Whatever truth there may be in this assertion, in one respect he did not deny the environment in which he grew up and lived. His proposals had always a definiteness and concreteness which may be regarded as typical of Anglo-Saxon thinking.

An illustration may be chosen which, in view of current proposals for an international bill of human rights, has some topical interest. Bentham never made any secret of it that he viewed such charters and declarations with the deepest distrust.[124] He contrasted the Declaration of Rights adopted in 1791 by the French National Assembly with British constitutional experience : ' In the British House of Parliament, more especially in the most efficient house for business, there prevails a well-known jealousy of, and repugnance to, the voting of abstract propositions. This jealousy is not less general than reasonable. A jealousy of abstract propositions is an aversion to whatever is beside the purpose—an aversion to impertinence '.[125]

Bentham attacked such declarations on the grounds of their likely uncertainty and obscurity. If, as it regularly happens,[126] most of these fundamental rights are guaranteed subject to saving clauses, they can formally be ' received, and without making any alteration, into the constitutional codes of Prussia, Den-

---

124 On the French Constitutional Charter of 1830, Bentham observed : ' Charter?—I do not like—I never liked the sound ' (11 *Bentham,* p. 57).
125 *The Book of Fallacies* (1824), 2 *Bentham,* p. 497. See, however, for a very different interpretation of British constitutional law and theory in this field H. Lauterpacht, *An International Bill of the Rights of Man,* 1945, p. 54 *et seq.* Bentham was not more kindly disposed towards the American Declaration of Independence which he called a ' hodge-podge of confusion and absurdity '. (Letter to I. Bowring, January 30, 1827, 10 *Bentham,* p. 63.)
126 See, for instance, the *United Kingdom Draft of an International Bill of Human Rights,* 1947, Articles 4, 10, 11, 13, 14, 15 and 16, or Article 16 of Lauterpacht's *Draft Declaration (l.c.* above, p. 73).

mark, Russia, or Morocco '.[127]   It is apparently a minor blemish of such fundamental rights that they may mean one thing in Denmark and something very different in Russia.

The contents vary not only between State and State, but if such rights are granted only within the framework of existing law, they may be reduced to complete meaninglessness by means of legislation.   Bentham, therefore, arrives at the conclusion that such declarations should be recognised as fallacies; for ' nothing can be more fallacious than a declaration which gives me with one hand what it authorises the taking from me with the other '.[128]   Bentham classified this brand of fallacies amongst the anarchical fallacies,[129] and if he could have observed the use to which declarations and charters of this kind have been put since his time, he might have been tempted to put them also into the category of diversionary pastimes.[130]

Both by nature and in reaction to the futility of merely abstract or irrelevant proposals, Bentham was driven to consider in concrete terms what could be done to establish a true international order.

Bentham shares with Wilson the distinction of having mistaken secret diplomacy for a cause rather than as a symptom of the evil which they both had set out to overcome.   Bentham had enough common sense to realise that the confidential character of preliminary diplomatic negotiations must be respected, but held that ' such secrecy ought never to be maintained with regard to treaties actually concluded '.[131]   Both in the Covenant of the League of Nations and in the Charter of the United Nations his proposal has found a response in the provisions for the obligatory registration and publication of all treaties concluded by members of these organisations.   The real problem is, however, presented by the more informal arrangements between the military, naval and air staffs of States which are closely aligned with each other.   Such understandings do not necessarily bind the governments concerned and are not as

---

[127] *The Book of Fallacies* (1824), 2 *Bentham*, p. 510.
[128] *Ibid.*, p. 534.
[129] *Ibid.*, p. 524.
[130] See further *l.c.* in note 97 above, 1941, p. 380 *et seq.*, and 1 *Year Book of World Affairs*, 1947, p. 320 *et seq.*
[131] *Principles of International Law* (1786–1789), 2 *Bentham*, p. 554.   See also *Can no Secrecy be Dangerous?* (1786–1789), Bentham MSS., University College, London, Portfolio 25, f. 7, p. 60.

a rule legally binding commitments. They merely embody exchanges of views regarding possible joint action in hypothetical contingencies in which such schemes may mature into full dress wartime alliances.

Similarly, the experience of the inter-war period has taught the lesson that disarmament is the fruit of a harmonious balance in a collective system which equally provides for collective security and peaceful change, but that it is hardly the key to the elimination of war. Bentham was, however, fully conscious of the fact that, to any extent to which disarmament is feasible amongst independent States, it must be carried out on a basis of reciprocity: ' There might be some difficulty in persuading *one* lion to cut his claws; but if the lion, or rather the enormous condor which holds him fast by the head, should agree to cut his talons also, there would be no disgrace in the stipulation : the advantage or inconvenience would be reciprocal '.[132] Thus the unilateral limitation of the strength of the Cartagenian fleet after the First Punic War ' placed all the security on one side '. Such a treaty could only be defended on one ground : ' the law of the strongest. None but a conqueror could have dictated it; none but the conquered would have accepted it '.[133] The experiences made with the unilateral disarmament imposed on the former Central Powers bear out the realism of Bentham's judgment.

Apart from reasons of internal policy,[134] Bentham consistently advocated the emancipation of colonial possessions because he considered colonies a main cause of international friction and

---

[132] *Ibid.,* p. 545.

[133] *Ibid.,* pp. 550–551.

[134] The strongest argument that still applies is the danger resulting to democracy at home from the practice of authoritarianism and methods of a police State in colonial possessions (*Emancipate Your Colonies* (1793), 4 *Bentham,* pp. 408–410.

The economic arguments may be summed up in the charge already to be found in a treatise by Sir Robert Cotton ' that our Forraigne Dominions have been to us alwayes a Chardge, noe Beneffitt ' (British Museum, Harl. MSS. 1323, Part 3). See further R. L. Schuyler, *The Fall of the Old Colonial System. A Study in British Free Trade, 1770–1870,* 1945.

It may be thought that Bentham's views on this topic were merely those of an eccentric. Attention may, therefore, be drawn to Sir George Cornewall Lewis's *Government of Dependencies,* 1841, or to the remark made by Disraeli in a letter which he wrote in 1852 to Lord Malmesbury: ' These wretched colonies will all be independent in a few years, and are a millstone round our necks '. (*Memoirs of an Ex-Minister,* 1885, p. 260.)

war.[135]   The alternative posed by Bentham, however, over-simplifies the issue : ' The real interests of the colony must be sacrificed to the imaginary interests of the mother country.   It is for the purpose of governing it badly and for no other, that you can wish to get or to keep a colony.   Govern it well, it is of no use to you.   Govern it as well as the inhabitants would govern it themselves—you must choose those to govern it whom they themselves would choose.   You must sacrifice none of its interests to your own—you must bestow as much time and attention to their interests as they would themselves ;- in a word, you must take those very measures, and none others, which they themselves would take.   But would this be governing?   And what would it be worth to you if it were ? ' [136]

Bentham was clear-headed and frank enough to see that powers acquire colonies because they expect to derive some kind of advantage—not necessarily of an economic character [137] —from such possessions.   He equally had learned from the history of the secession of the American colonies that to rule a colony contrary to the real interests of the colonial population was to ask for trouble and, in the long run, was an impossible undertaking.   He did not, however, appreciate—what is so much easier to see today—the political and economic trends which might make it desirable both for the colonial powers and their dependencies to solve the dilemma on a footing of partnership instead of separation.   In an age of conglomerations of world powers on an unprecedented scale, nominal sovereignty of a former dependency means very little in terms of political independence and national security.   Correspondingly, today a world power must either be a compact continental block or if the empire is primarily based on sea power, it must spread its tentacles all over the world and maintain its foothold on potential naval bases and sources of war materials.   Even in time of peace, economic considerations work in an age of neo-mercantilism and

---

[135] *Principles of International Law* (1786–1789), 2 *Bentham*, p. 547.   See also *Emancipate Your Colonies!* (addressed to the National Convention of France—1793), 4 *Bentham*, p. 407 *et seq.*, and *Canada, Emancipate Your Colonies!* 1838.

[136] *L.c.* above, 2 *Bentham*, p. 548.   Bentham suggested that, until completion of the emancipation of their colonies, colonial powers should invite colonial administrators from other nations to share in the work of colonial government.   ' They will be pledges and evidence, to you and to the world, of the probity of their colleagues ' (4 *Bentham*, p. 410).

[137] See further *l.c.* in note 97 above, 1941, p. 85 *et seq.*

State planning in the industrial and financial fields in favour of the greatest possible areas of production and markets within any of the tariff walls. As the ideas of free trade are bound to remain chimerical in a world of power politics and deep-seated cleavages on social planning, a harmonious balance between agriculture and industry and the requirements of people in moderate, sub-tropical and tropical zones can be more easily achieved within relatively big units as compared with the alternative of independent small powers.

In such a situation, there is a community of interests which binds together colonial powers and their dependencies and which, on a footing of equality, leads to a new conception : the commonwealth of free nations who, on their own accord, prefer to be united in strength to being atomised in isolation. Though there are common material interests which explain to a certain extent on utilitarian grounds the cohesion of any such common-wealth, associations of this kind engender loyalties beyond the limits of utilitarian philosophy. They create what Dicey called ' public spirit touched with emotion '.[138]

Bentham's peace system was to be crowned by a Common Court of Judicature, also called by him a Diet or Congress.[139] As becomes evident from the descriptions used by Bentham, he did not think of a strictly judicial international institution but rather of a conciliation commission of the type represented by the Council of the League of Nations.

Each power was to send one principal delegate and a substitute. The proceedings of the institution were to be public and it was to be empowered to have its reports made public in all the States participating in the scheme. This was to be assured by an

---

[138] *Law and Opinion in England during the Nineteenth Century*, 1930, p. 457. See also J. Lorimer, *The Institutes of the Law of Nations*, 1884, Vol. 2, p. 229, and G. W. Keeton, *Federation and India* in M. Chaning-Pearce (ed.) *Federal Union*, 1940, p. 187 *et seq.*

[139] The view is expressed by Dr. Colombos (*l.c.* in note 1 above, p. 7) that Bentham contemplated both a Common Judicature and Legislature. A comparison between Proposition 13· as formulated in 2 *Bentham* on p. 547 of the *Principles of International Law* and the explanation offered subsequently (pp. 552–554) will show that the proposed Common Court of Judicature and the Diet or Congress are one and the same organ. So also J. B. Scott, Introduction to W. Ladd, *An Essay on a Congress of Nations* (1840), 1916, p. xxxv. Ladd considered that his own original contribution to the perennial discussion on blue prints of international order consisted in the separation of his proposed Court of Nations from the Congress, which figured in his scheme, too. See further the present writer's *William Ladd*, 1935, p. 18 *et seq.*

international guarantee of the liberty of the Press, which would enable the Congress to exercise its influence on public opinion in the States concerned.[140]

Bentham contemplated the possibility of an international police force for the enforcement of the decrees of the court. He, however, considered this only as a last resort and recommended as a more practical means of coercion putting the refractory State ' under the ban of Europe '.[141]

Objections to his—as to any other—scheme for replacing international anarchy by order under law are many. Bentham himself confessed that ' it were an endless task to fill more pages with the shadows that might be conjured up in order to be knocked down. I leave this task to any that will undertake it '.[142]

To a mind as unprejudiced as that of Bentham even the idea of a world State did not present an *a priori* impossibility. His *Comment on the Commentaries* (1775) contains the following pertinent criticism of Blackstone [143]—and others who long after him achieved intellectual comfort from the argument that what is not cannot be : ' His argument is that it is *impossible* the world should be all in one state. Improbable enough indeed I should suppose it, but I pretend not to understand like him what is impossible, nor should I much want to know that one thing (if it be so) is impossible, for the sake of knowing that another thing [144] *is*, which I see with my own eyes '.[145]

Compared with earlier and contemporary schemes for international organisation, Bentham may claim that his *Plan for a Universal and Perpetual Peace* is free from the imperialist *arrière pensées* of Dubois or Sully. Tolerance towards heterogeneity in religion and political structure of States distinguishes his proposals from the rigidity of Campanella and Kant. Broad rationalism and universalism link him with Erasmus,

---

[140] *Principles of International Law* (1786–1789), 2 *Bentham*, p. 554.
[141] *Ibid.* On outlawry in international law, see further *l.c.* in note 69 above, 1943, p. 82 *et seq.*
[142] *L.c.* in note 140, p. 558.
[143] *Commentaries on the Laws of England* (1765–1769), Introduction, § 2.
[144] *I.e.* States.
[145] Bentham's *Comment on the Commentaries* (1775), ed. Ch. W. Everett, 1928, p. 57. On contemporary French thought on the world State, as expressed by Mirabeau, Volney, Pétion de Villeneuve and Cloots, see A. H. Fried, *Handbuch der Friedensbewegung*, 1913, p. 37 *et seq.*

Penn and de la Croix. Relative indifference to the details of constitution-making are evidence of Bentham's belief in the convincing force of the principles of utility, of economic *laissez faire,* and of the identity of national and international interests.

The *Pax Britannica* which followed the upheaval of the Napoleonic Wars only tended to confirm Bentham in the correctness of his interpretation. The First World War, however, put an end to this phase of international relations, and the question mark which confronts another post-war generation is the antagonism between two major power agglomerations.

'Our age has become more sceptical regarding the power of reason and, therefore, takes refuge in the reason of power. The intellectual reflection of this situation is the revival of the pre-liberal conception of policy as an art, the disdain of reason on account of necessarily being conditioned by time and place, and resignation to the inevitability of power politics. If there is one hopeful feature in this rather gloomy picture it is the inarticulate Benthamism of the man in the street everywhere. The overwhelming number of human beings appear to be content with a minimum of happiness and security, and all they ask is that those responsible for their welfare should apply themselves to the achievement of the Four Freedoms. Should this assumption be another self-delusion, then it would be as well that Bentham's utilitarianism—together with the whole tradition of European humanism and rationalism—be thrown to the winds. The study of inter-State relations might then be limited to Chapter 13 of Hobbes's *Leviathan,* describing the ' natural condition of mankind, as concerning their felicity, and misery '

PART FOUR—COMPARATIVE AND FOREIGN LAW

CHAPTER 9

BENTHAM IN THE UNITED STATES OF AMERICA

C. W. Everett

BENTHAM acknowledged that he found his 'greatest happiness principle' in Carneades, in Horace, in Beccaria, in Hutcheson, and in Priestley. Since he took the whole of the activities of man for his province—ethics, legislation, economics, and education marking out only the major fields—to discuss the topic adequately would be to write the intellectual history of the western world in the nineteenth century. Fifty years ago the late Professor Dicey attempted to do as much for law and opinion. His conclusion as to England was that 'the history of legal reform in England in the nineteenth century is the story of the shadow cast by one man—Bentham'. There must have been something to cast a shadow, and the shadow probably reached across the Atlantic. Emerson, for instance, spoke of utilitarianism with contempt, but he classed Bentham with Locke as a system-maker. 'Every new mind is a new classification', he said. 'If it prove a mind of uncommon activity and power, a Locke, a Lavoisier, a Hutton, a Bentham, a Fourier, it imposes its classification on other men, and lo! a new system'.[1]

Bentham certainly meant his work to form a system, and a complete one, extending the scientific principle into law and morals. He was to be, in his own phrase, the 'Newton of legislation'. One can scarcely deal with such large matters as law and morals, and deal with them scientifically, without breaking them up into their component parts. This led Bentham first into an analysis of the nature of law and of sovereignty, then into a study of the human mind, how it operates and why it so operates, and lastly, to the nature of the just State.

Since Bentham's early critics complained that he was too

[1] Emerson, *Essay on Self Reliance*, 1841.

185

radical, and his later ones have charged him with being too obvious, it may be worth while to state briefly his major definitions and conclusions. A sovereign, then, is a person or a group to whom certain people are in the habit of paying obedience. A law is an order by a sovereign creating an offence, for all law is penal in its nature. If the sovereign issues a command, the not obeying it is the offence. If he issues a prohibition, performing the act prohibited is the offence. A testament is valid because the sovereign adopts the testator's will as his own, and forbids the contravening of the desires of the testator. Since man is governed by pain and pleasure, no man performs an act without an expectation that the act will bring him an overplus of pleasure, though it be only a pleasure of malevolence. To do otherwise would be to act without a motive. When a law creates an offence, therefore, to be complete it must annex to the offence an artificial pain, outweighing the expected pleasure to be gained by the offence. This is the *sanction* on which the law relies for its force.

But what are these pleasures and pains? We need not examine in detail the fourteen simple pleasures and the twelve simple pains, which in more or less complex relationship to each other, produce *motives*. These motives, in the clockwork analogy dear to the eighteenth century, are the *springs of action*.

So far, we have described the pattern of law and of behaviour in *any* State, good or bad. Is there anything that can be done to produce, not a painless, but a just State? The vast tomes on evidence and on judicial procedure show that in Bentham's view the first and most pressing question was that of judicial organisation, because it was the judge who measured out pains. The technical system Bentham found in actual existence was so full of anomalies and contradictions that it was tempting to expand the criticism of it beyond measure.

To supplant the traditional system, Bentham divided all law into two branches, substantive law, stating the will of the sovereign, and adjective law, making the proper secondary arrangements to be sure that the sovereign's will should be carried out.

Constitutional law, which is concerned with the organisation of the just State, rested in Bentham's view on three principles: the greatest happiness principle, the self-preference principle, and the principle of the union of interests.   The first of these tells us what ought to be, the second tells us what *is,* and the third is that artificial contrivance, political government, which reconciles the two.   Governors and governed are always two classes whose interests do *not* coincide unless the constitution of government makes them do so.   Individual interests conflict; a good government at least reduces the area of conflict.   In this reconciliation, realities must be faced.   Talk about liberty and natural rights dodges the problem with sentimental phrases.   Bluntly put, ' natural rights is nonsense; inalienable and imprescriptible rights merely nonsense on stilts'.   Montesquieu, in Bentham's view, never thought clearly.   ' Of happiness, he says nothing : instead of security for the people against their rulers, he talks of liberty, and assumes without saying so, that to establish perfect liberty is the proper object of all government : whereas government cannot operate but at the expense of liberty, and then and there only is liberty perfect, where no government has place '.[2]

When Thomas Jefferson made the Declaration of Independence he followed in the track of Montesquieu and the natural rights school; but when the Articles of Confederation broke down from internal weakness, the men who made the Constitution followed another pattern.

In the *Federalist Papers,* for example, the exact language occurs that we find in Bentham's *Introduction to the Principles of Morals and Legislation.*   But Bentham's work was not published until two years *after* the *Federalist Papers.*

The *Federalist Papers* appeared in the New York newspapers during the winter of 1787–1788 in the successful attempt to bring about the ratification of the new federal Constitution by the State of New York.   Time and again, Alexander Hamilton, in the papers we know him to have written, stresses the artificial identification of interests through the coercion by the sovereign of individuals capable of feeling pain and pleasure : ' The great and radical vice in the construction of the existing confederation is in the principle of legislation for states or governments, in their corporate or collective capacities, and contradistinguished from the *Individuals* of which they consist . . . we must incorporate into our plan those ingredients which may be considered as forming the characteristic difference between a league and a govern-

[2] Bentham, *Works,* Vol. 9, p. 123.

ment; we must extend the authority of the Union to the persons of the citizens—the only proper objects of government. . . . It must carry its agency to the persons of the citizens. . . . The government of the Union . . . must be able to address itself immediately to the hopes and fears of individuals; . . . government implies the power of making laws. It is essential to the idea of a law that it be attended with a sanction; or, in other words, a penalty or punishment for disobedience. . . . This penalty, whatever it may be, can only be inflicted in two ways: . . . by the *coercion* of the magistracy or by the *coercion* of arms'. As to the argument of the opponents of the new constitution, ' It at all times betrayed an ignorance of the true springs by which human conduct is actuated. . . . Why has government been instituted at all? Because the passions of men will not conform to the dictates of reason and justice, without constraint '.[3] It was not until 1815 that Bentham's *Table of the Springs of Action* was published.

There was, then, to a very considerable extent, a climate of opinion in America favourable to the growth of Benthamism, a climate in which there were already flourishing almost identical views as to the nature of sovereignty, as to the hopes and fears of individuals, or the psychology which underlay motive and actions, and lastly as to the nature of law as the will of the sovereign. This last doctrine was by no means in control of the field in America, however, for the ' rights of man ' were still important in legal thinking, as they had been at the time of the Declaration of Independence. Jefferson, who had been a strong proponent of that view in his early period, had, it is true, shifted to a more Hobbesian outlook when he found himself in power for eight years, and with a position as official philosopher during the succeeding eight years of Madison's administration, though the ' rights of man ' was to have a rebirth in the 1850's with the extreme Abolitionists' advocacy of the ' higher law '

It is a curious fact that the first American to read Bentham's *Introduction to the Principles of Morals and Legislation* was that stormy petrel, Aaron Burr, and that he read it less than a year after it was published in 1789. From 1791 to 1797, Burr was a conspicuous Democratic leader in the United States

---

[3] *The Federalist,* Essays 15 and 16, *The Insufficiency of the Present Confederation to Save the Union.*

Senate; and in the Presidential election in 1800 he and Thomas Jefferson had an equal number of votes in the electoral college, throwing the election into the House of Representatives. It was not until the thirty-sixth ballot that the House decided in favour of Jefferson, and Burr became Vice-President. In July, 1804, he killed Alexander Hamilton in a duel; and the next year he undertook the mad and mysterious enterprise in the West, which resulted in his trial for treason. Burr arrived in England in 1808, having been acquitted after a trial. He still hoped to engage England or some European government in his project for revolutionising Mexico. He met Dumont in London, and Dumont sent him on to Bentham, reporting of him, ' He has read Principles and Usury; and as soon as he saw the announcement at Paris [of the publication of the *Traités* in 1802] had sent for sundry copies. He spoke of them with the highest admiration—said they were the only works on legislation where there was philosophical method: that compared to these, Montesquieu's writings were trifling, etc. He added, that, in spite of his recommendations, they were little read in America, where anything requiring studious application is neglected. Nobody but Gallatin had felt all their merit, and Gallatin was the best head in America '.[4]

Burr was in financial difficulties, but shortly after his first meeting with Bentham he was established as a guest in Bentham's London house, and Bentham had advanced him £200, which was later repaid. On August 22, 1808, he wrote to Bentham, ' At nine p.m. possession was taken, by depositing the " rattraps " and entry of their owner. Having before been only in the two rooms on the left, and barely looked into the garden, no idea had been formed of the extent and beauty of the premises '.[5]

Bentham was spending the summer at Barrow Green, but the two men saw much of each other, and corresponded occasionally. Burr was deeply impressed by Bentham's generosity. On September 9, 1808, he wrote to his daughter Theodosia, wife of Governor Allston of South Carolina, ' I hasten to make you acquainted with Jeremy Bentham, author of a work entitled *Principles of Morals and Legislation* (edited in French by Dumont) and of many other works of less labour and research.

[4] Bentham, *Works,* Vol. 10, p. 433.
[5] *Private Journal of Aaron Burr,* Vol. 1, p. 33.

You will well recollect to have heard me place this man second to no one, ancient or modern, in profound thinking, in logical and analytical reasoning. . . . In a letter of the third instant he writes, " Make up, if you can find room, for *my* dear little Theodosia, a packet of all my combustibles that you can find, *viz.* Pantopticon; Hard-labour Bill; Pelham's Letters and Plea for the Constitution; Poor Management; Judicial Establishment; Political Tactics and Emancipation. Hard Labour, Tactics, Emancipation, and Hard-labour Bill not being otherwise than in sheets, unsorted and unsewed; but there is not any one on whom the labour can be shifted off ". Thus you see you are to possess his works by his own special gift '.[6]

Learning from Bentham's secretary, Koe, that great quantities of unpublished Bentham manuscripts reposed in the attic, some of them in printed form, Burr tried to examine them, but was baffled by the disorderly accumulation of the work of forty years. He wrote to Bentham, September 12, 1808, ' I mounted to the house top to see the state of the combustibles. . . . Not knowing but there might be some mystical and hidden method, intelligible only to you and to Koe, in that which appeared to me horrid confusion, I replaced the parcel as nearly as possible in the spot where it was found, but the precious antique dust I could not replace, a great portion of it being transferred to my person. I shall now, before leaving town, make Dumont, by a letter, a proposition for expediting the publication '.[7]

Lacking new materials, for the moment, Burr sent Theodosia Dumont's *Traités*. She replied promptly, December 5, 1808, ' I have read a small part of the *Traites de Legislation*. The work is really original. It is truly calculated to make readers think profoundly, and gives a new direction to their reflections. . . . Does J.B. mean to publish the " T. de L. " in English, written by himself? If he does not, and there is no good translation of them, I should like to have the honour of becoming his translator. . . . What a transformation his vehement, comprehensive style would undergo; first, by being beat out into a French style, and then, by a kind of synthesis, being recomposed *by me,* and presented in a resemblance of itself, deprived of all its fire, like the statue of Pandora without the heavenly spark '.[8]

[6] *Op. cit.,* Vol. 1, pp. 47–48.
[7] *Op. cit.,* Vol. 1, p. 50.
[8] *Op. cit.,* Vol. 1, p. 114.

Burr himself, in the meantime, had proposed that he should edit the essay on *Political Tactics,* published in quarto in 1791, with the addition of the manuscript material which later was actually incorporated in the *Book of Fallacies,* published in 1824. Bentham wrote him, March 6, 1809, ' Dumont has been applied to, and has brought himself, though not without some reluctance, to part with *Tactique* out of his hands. The burden which the shoulders of Étienne Dumont sunk under, and those of Jeremy Bentham shrunk from, is now waiting for those of Hercules Burr, on which it will sit as lightly as little Jesus on those of the great St. Christopher in the Cathedral of Notre Dame '.[9]

Burr's fate, however, led to other things than editing Bentham. He was deported from England under suspicion of being a French agent, and, reduced to poverty, he wandered about Europe, hatching vain empires, while Bentham industriously piled new manuscripts upon the old ones. Theodosia was lost at sea when she attempted to rejoin her father on his return to the United States in 1812. Four years later, Bentham wrote to Burr a long letter about the prospect for codification in Pennsylvania. ' You saw everything ', Bentham concluded, ' small or imperfect, stopped by some incident or other, some coincidence or another, for I have always unless it be for my own amusement, too many irons in the fire '.[10]

Burr had spoken of Gallatin, and in 1814 Bentham met Albert Gallatin, who was in London as one of the commissioners to negotiate the peace. Bentham found Gallatin familiar not only with the *Traités,* but with the *Théorie des peines et des récompenses,* published in two volumes by Dumont in 1811. Gallatin knew the *Introduction to the Principles of Morals and Legislation,* too. ' About five-and-twenty years ago (he said) it was put into his hands by Colonel Burr : and from that time (he was pleased to say) he considered himself my pupil '.[11] Gallatin had been Secretary of the Treasury from 1801 to 1813, and Bentham urged Dumont to make use of him as an avenue of approach to President Madison. Dumont saw that the scheme could come to nothing, and begged off. ' I have not forgotten

[9] *Op. cit.,* Vol. 1, p. 180.
[10] *Op. cit.,* Vol. 1, p. 447 (Feb. 23, 1816).
[11] Bentham to Gov. Snyder of Pennsylvania, July 1814. *Works,* Vol. 4, p. 469.

the letter to Gallatin ', he said. ' I wanted to write it. I began it—I applied myself to it two or three times—I could not succeed to my liking. . . . What *can* the President do? . . . His personal invitation is nothing. There must be a decree of the Senate or the Congress and how can this be obtained? Will the Senate read your writings? Will they be able to judge of the aptitude of the author? Burr said he knew not four persons in America who had read the *Principles*. What then can be hoped for, as the author is an unknown being—an Englishman—an English lawyer? Every motive of jealousy and national distrust will operate upon the Americans, among whom presumption and conceit of themselves are the most remarkable characteristics '.[12]

Dumont was certainly right in thinking that Bentham's influence must operate in some other way than by the prescription of the executive, but Bentham persisted in trying that method. His next point of attack was John Quincy Adams. After helping to negotiate the treaty of peace at Ghent in 1814, Adams stayed on as Minister to England until 1817. He met Bentham, and the two men were soon on a friendly footing. Both were early risers and liked walking. It became their custom on any fine morning to follow a seven-mile-long route through the London parks, getting back to breakfast at a time which most people would have considered still early in the morning. What influences sprang from this association it is hard to say, but one can be sure that, given the characters of the two men, the time was not spent in small talk or gossip Adams went back to America to become Secretary of State and President, taking with him a fairly heavy consignment of the works of Bentham. He noted in his journal (Vol. 3, p. 355), ' Bentham sent me this morning a large package, containing twenty-five copies of almost all his works, to be distributed, one copy to the Governor of every state in the Union, and the rest to some other persons '.

Bentham continued to send his books to various American presidents and governors, with no perceptible result except polite letters in return.[13]   He had written to President Madison in 1811. After the War of 1812, Madison replied and thanked Bentham

---

[12] Dumont to Bentham, September 4, 1811. *Works,* Vol. 10, p. 462.
[13] For an account of one such ineffective attempt, in relation to Andrew Jackson, see Everett, *Anti-Senatica, an attack on the U.S. Senate, sent by Jeremy Bentham to Andrew Jackson, President of the United States.* Smith College Studies in History, Vol. 11, No. 4.

for his codification proposal, but pointed out his own lack of power to do anything about it. (*Works*, Vol. 4, pp. 453, 467.) At Bentham's request, Gallatin wrote to Governor Snyder of Pennsylvania. Snyder ordered the statute and case law of the State to be sent to Bentham for study, and he presented Bentham's proposal for codification to the legislature in his message. Nothing was done.[14]

A year later Bentham sent a circular letter to the governor of each State in the Union. This brought him a complimentary correspondence from Governor William Plumer of New Hampshire, but no legislative action.[15] William Plumer, junior, became Governor of New Hampshire in time, as his father had been before him, and he wrote to Bentham in 1826 that legal reform was going ahead in America. ' In many of these inquiries your labors have been noticed, your principles to a certain extent adopted. . . . They rest for their foundations upon the deep and broad foundations of public utility; their end is the happiness of mankind. . . . I am glad to learn that you are not unacquainted with the labors of Mr. Livingston of New Orleans in the field of legislation. He is a man of real talents, of great industry and perseverance, of high standing and influence in his country. He has often spoken of you to me in terms of the highest veneration and respect, and informed me, more than once, that his attempts at codification grew out of what he learned of your views in the works published by Dumont. . . . You could hardly desire a more zealous or more enlightened disciple '.[16]

It was, in fact, through Edward Livingston, apparently that the chief Benthamic influence in the United States was exerted. As a member of Congress in 1795, Livingston had tried unsuccessfully to soften the rigours of penal law. He then served as Mayor of New York City, and through the misconduct of a clerk, became a public defaulter. He went to New Orleans, had great success there as a lawyer, and paid off the sum in default. His reading of Dumont's *Traités* convinced him that only by the adoption of a comprehensive code could the anomalies of the

[14] Gallatin to Snyder, June 18, 1814. *Works*, Vol. 4, p. 468. See also Bentham to Snyder, July 1814. *Works*, Vol. 4, p. 968. See also Snyder to D. M. Randolph, May 31, 1816. *Works*, Vol. 4, p. 475, and the Governor's message, *Works*, Vol. 4, p. 476.
[15] Plumer to Bentham, October 2, 1817, *Works*, Vol. 4, p. 577; also *ibid.*, Vol. 10, p. 504.
[16] September 15, 1826, *Works*, Vol. 10, p. 556.

law be remedied, and he prepared a code of judicial procedure for the State of Louisiana. He sent Bentham a copy of the code, with a long letter recounting its history and Bentham's part in it. ' It is more than thirty years ago ', he wrote,[17] ' that then representing this city in the House of Representatives of the United States, I made an ineffectual attempt to mitigate the severity of our penal laws. The perusal of your works, edited by Dumont, fortified me in a design to prosecute the subject whenever a fit occasion should offer : it occurred about twenty years after by my election to the Legislature of Louisiana, whither I had removed, and I used the confidence of that State, by offering them the system you will find in the accompanying package. . . . In laying before you this work, I offer you little that you have not a legitimate title to : for hereafter, no one can in criminal jurisprudence, propose any favourable change that you have not recommended, or make any wise improvement that your superior sagacity has not suggested '.

The stimulus given to codification by Livingston's activities followed a somewhat curious pattern. For the most part, it was the new States formed on the frontier which were to adopt codes more or less on the Benthamic model, and most of those States came into being in the last half of the century. As early as 1818, however, a Virginia lawyer had pointed out to Bentham that this would probably happen. ' Would it not be a more glorious distinction ', wrote Francis Gilmer to Bentham,[18] ' for a philosopher from his closet in London, to control the principles of legislation and jurisprudence on the banks of the Missouri, or the shores of the Chesapeake, than to leave his researches to the casual, capricious, and ineffectual patronage of an executive officer? New territories and states are every year forming in America. They imbibe in their origin, the principles most approved at the crisis of the foundation '.

How correct Mr. Gilmer's forecast was he would never live to see. It was not until seventy years later, on the admission to statehood of the two Dakotas in 1889, that States with complete codes came into being. Both North and South Dakota operated under a Political Code, a Civil Code, a Code of Civil Procedure, a Justice's Code, a Penal Code, and a Code of Criminal Procedure.

[17] August 10, 1829 ; *Works,* Vol. 11, p. 23, gives the whole letter.
[18] March 22, 1818 ; *Works,* Vol. 10, p. 498.

Before that could happen, however, Bentham's ideas must have permeated the thinking of jurists and of executives, and in fact they did find expression in the messages of governors and in decisions of the Supreme Court long before that time. Interestingly enough, popular journalism played only a small part in the spread of Bentham's ideas, and the writings of American political scientists were mainly hostile. Professor Paul A. Palmer has pointed out this lack of influence,[19] and attributes it partly to Bentham's difficult style, and partly to the reputation he had of atheistic bias. The works of Bentham were not even reviewed in America until 1861, according to Palmer, and then the review was unfriendly.

Traces of Bentham can be found, however, in the first half of the century, apart from legal reform, though they should not be over-stressed. John Neal, Thomas Cooper, William Leggett, Willis Hall, and Richard Hildreth all show the influence of Bentham, and may be considered briefly.

John Neal (1793–1876) of Maine, translated part of Dumont's *Traités* in 1830, and prefaced to the translation an entertaining character sketch of Bentham, with whom he had lived for eighteen months. On seeing the sketch, Bentham commented that he might better have had a rattlesnake in his house. Certainly Bentham's enemies made good use of the picture of the good-humoured but half-mad philosopher.

Thomas Cooper (1759–1839), political economist and president of the University of South Carolina, in his *Introductory Lecture to a Course of Law,* 1832, says, ' The polar star of morals and law is the greatest happiness of the greatest number '.[20]

William Leggett (1801–1839), editor of the *New York Evening Post,* an important Democratic newspaper, in an article on ' The Morals of Politics ', June 3, 1837, says, ' The object of all politicians, in the strict sense of the expression, is happiness— the happiness of a state—the greatest possible sum of happiness '.[21]

Willis Hall (1801–1868), once Attorney-General of New York

---

[19] Benthamism in England and America (*American Political Science Review,* XXXV, 1941).

[20] Dumas Malone, *Public Life of Thomas Cooper,* p. 370. Cited by Palmer.

[21] *Political Writings of William Leggett,* New York 1840, Vol. 2, p. 323.

State, in his Phi Beta Kappa address at Yale in 1844 speaks of
utility as the central principle of the modern age. Dr. Joseph
Blau includes the address in his *American Philosophic Addresses,
1700–1900,* New York, 1947, as characteristic of a somewhat
modified utilitarianism.

Richard Hildreth (1807–1865), the historian and journalist,
translated Dumont's *Traités* in 1864 as *Bentham's Theory of
Legislation,* and several editions of his translation have appeared
since, sometimes without credit to the translator. In his *Theory
of Morals,* published in 1844, Hildreth developed a strain of
Benthamism into a system of his own. Professor Schneider
comments on it, ' Hildreth's system is unique in the American
tradition and deserves to be revived both for its historical unique-
ness, America's only Bentham, and for its intrinsic merit as a
system of philosophy '.[22]

As has been said, none of these publicists and theorists seems
to have had any profound influence on the general current of
opinion, and we must turn rather to the story of law reform to
see the major effects of Bentham's work. As early as 1821,
Justice Joseph Story, engaged then in a digest of Massachusetts
law, objected to the ' theoretical extravagances of some well-
meaning philosophic jurists ',[23] and Chancellor Kent of New
York was no less opposed to theoretical extravagances, though it
is interesting to note that in 1826 he felt himself to be on the
losing side. ' I admit the spirit of the age is against me ', he
wrote to Edward Livingston at that time.[24]

Edward Livingston and David Dudley Field, the other great
' codifier ' of the century, were to have a long struggle, but they
were in the ' spirit of the age ', and they won out, at least as far
as a rationalised and simple procedure was concerned.

A Whig Governor of Massachusetts in the year 1836 might
have been expected to be conservative if any one was, but such
a governor in fact stated the utilitarian creed as a thing taken
for granted. ' Our system ', said Edward Everett in his inaugural
address, ' looks to the People not merely as a whole, but as a
society composed of individual men, whose happiness is the great

[22] H. W. Schneider, *A History of American Philosophy,* New York, 1946,
p. 124.
[23] David Dudley Field, *Law Reform in the United States,* St. Louis, 1891,
p. 5.
[24] Hunt, *Life of Edward Livingston,* p. 281.

design of the association. It consequently recognises the greatest good of the greatest number, as the basis of the social compact '.[25]

Though no lawyer, perhaps because he was not, Everett went on to propose measures of codification. ' The past year was signalised, in the history of the Commonwealth, by a revision and re-enactment of the great body of the Statute law . . . it is confidently believed that by reducing to a uniform and continuous text and digesting under appropriate titles the mass of scattered laws, the administration of justice will be facilitated, a knowledge of the law made more accessible to the mass of the community, and public confidence in the judiciary thereby increased '. To say so much was, of course, only paying a deserved compliment to the great work just brought to completion by Justice Story. Everett went on, however, to propose measures with which Story disagreed. ' With every generation ', said Everett, ' since the settlement of the country, more and more of the perplexed and unprofitable technicalities of the English jurisprudence have been swept away, and the work of reform might possibly in some things be carried farther. The opinion is perhaps gaining prevalence, and on good grounds, that it would be expedient to incorporate into a uniform code, with the statute legislation of the State, those numerous principles of the Common Law which are definitely settled and well known, and which, without being reduced to the form of a positive and literal text, have been and still are left to be applied by the courts, as principles of common law, when the occurrence of cases requires it '. A year later, February 8, 1837, Governor Everett noted in his journal a remark not very different in tone from Bentham's animadversions on ' Judge & Co.' : ' The Clerk of the house called to inform me that the Committee of the Judiciary would report in favor of codifying the criminal law only. Several legal gentlemen in the house and senate are opposed to going further. Was it ever found that the members of the legal profession were in favor of legal reform? ' Everett's friend, Daniel Webster, objected even to what had been done already. Everett noted in his journal April 13, 1837, ' Mr. Webster of the party. He and I had a long argument on the subject of codification, to which he is bitterly opposed. I

[25] *Address of Edward Everett to the Two Branches of the Legislature,* January 6, 1836, Boston, p. 4.

mentioned the English law bill in 1730, with all the lawyers opposed. He said they were right—that the English Law Bill produced no benefit!'

The virus of Benthamism was spreading, however strongly the historical school might inveigh against it. In the same year, 1837, it reached the Supreme Court of the United States. Everett had been a Whig, the new Chief Justice, Roger B. Taney, was a Jacksonian Democrat. Yet in the majority decision on the Warren Bridge case, the Chief Justice asserted, ' The object and end of all government is to promote the happiness and prosperity of the community by which it is established, and it can never be assumed that the government intended to diminish the power of accomplishing the end for which it was created '.[26]

The question to be decided was one where Bentham (and Hobbes before him) joined issue clearly with the disciples of Blackstone and Coke. The Commonwealth of Massachusetts had granted a monopolistic franchise, first for a ferry and later for a bridge, to a group known as the Proprietors, who in turn paid Harvard University two hundred pounds a year out of tolls. Seventy years had gone by, the bridge had long since paid for itself, and the State granted a new franchise to the Warren Bridge Corporation for another bridge, without compensation to the Charles River Proprietors for the clear breach of contract. Should the Supreme Court overrule the State courts and hold the State to its contract? Taney argued that this was to bind the future against all change and progress, since any railroad would be faced by prohibitory claims from canal and toll road companies.

Justice Story, in his famous dissenting opinion, touched very briefly on the utilitarian claims for fulfilment of contract. ' The original bridge ', he said, ' had been a daring venture, across a span of tidewater greater than any ever before bridged. It had made possible the very community which now wanted more bridges. If the bridge had gone out with the first ice jam, only the proprietors would have suffered. That they had made money in the venture was irrelevant to the right of compensation for a breach of contract '. So far Story had argued as Bentham himself might have done. The performance of contracts, on the

[26] Charles Warren, *The Supreme Court in United States History,* Vol. 2, p. 308. The citation is 11 Peters, p. 420.

whole, does add to the greatest happiness of the greatest number. Story had too much learning, however, to let the matter rest on a basis of utility. He had to go back to Edward I, to the Year Books, to the fourteenth and fifteenth centuries, down to the Royal Fisheries under James the First. Law was historical; not a matter of fiat. 'I stand upon the old law', he concluded passionately,[27] 'upon law established more than three centuries ago, in cases contested with as much ability and learning, as any in the annals of our jurisprudence, in resisting any such encroachments upon the rights and liberties of the citizens, secured by public grants. I will not consent to shake their title deeds by any speculative niceties or novelties'. But the 'old law' had lost to the doctrine of utility.

A half century ago Dicey delivered the lectures at Harvard University which were published under the title of *The Relation of Law and Public Opinion in England during the Nineteenth Century*. He thought three main periods were evident in England in the century. The first was the period of Old Toryism, of Blackstonian optimism, from 1800 to 1830; the second from 1825 to 1870, the period of Benthamism or Individualism, the era of utilitarian reform; the third from 1865 to 1900, the period of collectivism, which favours the intervention of the State, even at the sacrifice of individual freedom for the purpose of conferring mass benefits. Despite the complications set up by slavery and the civil war, and by the U.S. constitutional system, it seems fairly clear that the United States has gone through similar phases in the same time.

It should be noted, however, that while Bentham's doctrines flourished in England during the period of individualism, they were equally capable of serving collectivist views. Bentham was very explicit in his statement that property is a creation made by law, that without law right does not exist.

In America, it is really only in the last twenty years that the entire climate in which government and courts have functioned has been avowedly utilitarian. The New Deal has been partly collectivist, but wholly Benthamic, for the most part without knowing it.

During the nineteenth century, however, the main reform that disciples of Bentham were able to accomplish was to modify and modernise the old law of procedure in the various states

[27] *U.S. Reports,* 11 Peters, p. 597.

of the Union. The name most closely identified with the Benthamite attempt to replace the precedents of the common law by apparently simple provisions of statute law is that of David Dudley Field (1805–1894). Field was admitted to the New York bar in 1825, and after ten years of practice he turned to the reform of the law. His published articles and essays at last brought about the appointment of a State commission, of which Field became a member.

Considering the fact that about one-third of the published work of Bentham deals with the matter of procedure, he should have been pleased with the changes brought about. The New York commissioners, headed by Field, reported to the legislature the first instalment of the Code of Civil Procedure in February 1848. It was enacted, and went into effect July 1, 1848. In Field's words, ' its essential features were the demolition of the forms of action, the abolition in that respect of the distinction between actions at law and suits in equity, and the substitution of one form of action for the enforcement or protection of private rights and the redress or prevention of private wrongs, in which one action should be determined all the rights of the parties, legal or equitable, in respect of the subjects in litigation '.[28]

The next year the Civil Procedure Code was adopted by the State of Missouri. California, under the influence of Field's brother, Stephen J. Field, Chief Justice of California, adopted the same code in 1851, and her example was followed by Kentucky, 1851; Ohio, 1853; Iowa, 1855; Wisconsin, 1856; Kansas, 1859; Nevada, 1861; Dakota, 1862; Oregon, 1862; Idaho, 1864; Montana, 1864; Minnesota, 1866; Nebraska, 1866; Arizona, 1866; Arkansas, 1868; North Carolina, 1868; Wyoming, 1869; Washington, 1869; South Carolina, 1870; Utah, 1870; Connecticut, 1879; Indiana, 1881; Colorado, 1887; and Georgia, 1889. During the same period the Field Code of Criminal Procedure was adopted by eighteen States and territories besides New York. The Civil Code (substantive) was adopted by Dakota in 1866; by California in 1873. The Penal Code (substantive) has been adopted by seven States besides New York: Texas, Utah, Idaho, Arizona, Oregon, Colorado and Wyoming.[29]

[28] Field, *Law Reform in the U.S.*, p. 12.
[29] M. E. Lang, *Codification in the British Empire and America*. Amsterdam, 1924.

From the fact that many of these adoptions were made by territorial legislatures in thinly settled regions, it seems ironically probable that the spread of Benthamism owed quite as much to inertia as to a burning desire for reform. A Livingston or a Field is fired with ambition to reform the entire body of law on Bentham's principles. He spends years in working out the details of the great codes, and more heart-breaking years in the attempt to get them enacted. Then, perhaps years later, a lazy judicial committee appointed by a territorial legislature saves itself months of work—by adopting the reform code *in toto*. This process, incidentally, was by no means limited to the United States. A friend in Nova Scotia wrote to Field in 1885, ' Perhaps you do not know that whole sections, and titles, from your work have been copied, almost word for word, into the legislation of Quebec, and what acknowledgment, if any, they may have made you privately I do not know, but there is not a word to indicate the sources of their draft '.[30] Apparently good work, well done, is never wasted.

Had Bentham lived sixty years longer, he would have found at least two States in the world attempting to live by codes he would have recognised as being of his manufacture. North and South Dakota were admitted to statehood in 1889, each, as already mentioned, with no less than six complete codes : the Political Code; the Code of Civil Procedure; the Code of Criminal Procedure; the Civil Code; the Penal Code; and the Justices' Code. Young Francis Gilmer's advice (already alluded to) to Bentham, back in 1818, had been proved sound in history. ' New territories and states are every year forming in America ', he had said. ' They imbibe in their origin, the principles most approved at the crisis of the foundation '.

The one great work of Bentham which as yet has had little influence, either in America or elsewhere, is his Constitutional Code. It may well be that states and nations, now being formed out of the Orient and out of colonial empires, may find among their lawyers a Field or a Livingston capable of adopting Bentham's constitutional principles to local circumstances. Talleyrand's phrase is still valid : ' Pillé par tout le monde, il est toujours riche '

30 Field, *op. cit.*, p. 16.

CHAPTER 10

BENTHAM, FOREIGN LAW AND FOREIGN LAWYERS

K. Lipstein

' His name is little known in England, better in Europe, best of all in the plains of Chili and the mines of Mexico. He has offered constitutions for the New World and legislated for future times. The people of Westminster where he lives hardly dream of such a person but the Siberian savage has received cold comfort from his lunar aspect '.[1]

IN this essay it is proposed to study three separate questions: first, it is proposed to investigate to what extent Bentham's writings became part of the legal literature of foreign countries; second, an attempt will be made to shed some new light upon Bentham's personal relations with foreign lawyers and statesmen, and third, it will be discussed to what extent Bentham was acquainted with foreign law.

I. EDITIONS IN FOREIGN LANGUAGES

The task of listing the editions of Bentham's works which were published abroad, and of comparing variant readings, was accomplished thirty-seven years ago when the late Professor Siegwart published an article on ' Bentham's Werke und ihre Publikation ',[2] upon which the present observations are based. It is not surprising that the first comprehensive edition in French consisted of Dumont's collected translations. It appeared in Brussels between 1829–1832, under the title *Oeuvres de J.B. editées par Hausmann* (3 vols.).[3] Shortly afterwards appeared a Spanish edition by A. Espinosa, *Colección de obras del célebre J.B., reunida y vertida al castellano con commentarios arreglados a las circunstancias y legislación actual de España*, Madrid, 1841–1832 (2 vols.).[4]

---

[1] Hazlett, *The Spirit of the Age*, 4th ed. 1886. I am indebted to Dr. Glanville Williams for having drawn my attention to this passage.

[2] *Politisches Jahrbuch der Schweizerischen Eidgenossenschaft*, Vol. 24 (1910), pp. 285–403; Compare Everett in Halévy, *The Growth of Philosophical Radicalism* (English ed. 1928), pp. 522–546.

[3] Siegwart, pp. 304, 403.

[4] Siegwart, pp. 304, 403.

Of the individual works, the faithful Dumont had published in 1802 what appears to be a translation of *An Introduction to the Principles of Morals and Legislation*,[5] supplemented by extracts from other manuscripts, one of which is known under the title ' Principles of the Civil Code ',[6] another as ' Principles of Penal Law ',[7] a third as ' Essay on indirect legislation '.[8] The core of ' A general view of a complete code of laws ' (1786) was also embodied,[9] together with ' A memoir upon the Panopticon scheme ' (1791),[10] and two essays entitled *Promulgation des Lois*[11] and ' On the influence of Time and Place in matters of Legislation ' (1782).[12]

Dumont's complete edition was subsequently translated into German[13] by F. E. Benecke and by another translator whose name appears to be unknown,[14] and into Spanish by Ramon Salas[15] and by Espinosa.[16]

It deserves special mention that two Russian and one Hungarian translation were completed, the first very soon after the publication of Dumont's edition,[17] the latter at a comparatively

---

[5] *Traités de Législation civile et pénale, précédés de principes généraux de législation, et d'une vue d'un corps complet de droit; terminés par un essai sur l'influence de temps et des lieux relativement aux lois,* 3 vols., Paris, 1802. Second edition revised, 1820; Third ed., 1830; London ed., 1858 (abbreviated). Compare *Revue Britannique*, Vol. 5 (1797), pp. 155, 277; Vol. 6, (1797), pp. 3, 281; Siegwart, pp. 314, 323.

[6] Bowring ed. 1, pp. 297–364; Siegwart, p. 318; Dumont, 1, pp. 1–140; 2, pp. 1–236.

[7] Bowring ed. 1, pp. 367–580; Siegwart, p. 319; Dumont, 2, pp. 239–434; 3, pp. 1–199.

[8] Siegwart, p. 319.

[9] Bowring ed. 3, pp. 155–210; Siegwart, p. 320; Dumont, 1, pp. 146–370.

[10] Dumont, 1, pp. 214–263; Siegwart, p. 321. Also published in 1791 by the Imprimerie nationale; Assemblée legislative, Secours public, No. 1.

[11] Dumont, 3, pp. 275–321; Siegwart, p. 322; Bowring, 1, pp. 155–168.

[12] Dumont, 3, pp. 325–395; Bowring, 1, pp. 169–194; Siegwart, p. 323.

[13] *Grundsätze der Zivil— und Kriminalgesetzgebung aus den Handschriften des englischen Rechtsgelehrten J.B. herausgegeben von E. Dumont, nach der 2. Auflage . . . bearbeitet . . . ,* 2 vols., Berlin, 1830. See Siegwart, p. 324.

[14] *Prinzipien der Gesetzgebung herausgegeben von E. Dumont, nach der neuesten Auflage uebersetzt,* Cologne, 1833.

[15] *Tratados de legislación civil y penal, obra extractada de los manuscritos del Señor J. B. par E. Dumont y traducida al castellano con comentarios por Ramon Salas con arreglo à la secunda edición revista, corregida y aumentada.* Madrid, 1821, 1822; 2nd ed., 8 vols., 1823, published in Paris by J. R. Masson; 3rd ed., 1838, published in Paris by Lecomte et Lassère; Siegwart, pp. 326, 327.

[16] Siegwart, p. 327.

[17] 1805—see Siegwart, p. 326, note 4; citing Bowring, 4, p. 507; Atkinson, p. 149; *Biographie Universelle 1843,* Vol. 3, p. 670. Codification Proposal, 1822, p. 51; Bowring, 4, p. 566.

late date.[18] According to Siegwart it is likely that Dumont's edition was also translated into Portuguese and into Polish,[19] but no evidence is extant.

Parts of Dumont's works were translated into Spanish by Toribio Nuñez [20] and by J. Esriche,[21] while ' the Codification Proposal ' (1822) was translated into Spanish directly from the English original.[22] When Dumont had published his version of the Codification Proposal in 1828 [23] it was immediately translated into Spanish by De Bustamente.[24] The *Rationale of Punishment* was first published in English in 1830,[25] and *The Rationale of Reward* in 1825,[26] but Dumont had brought out a French edition in 1811 [27] of which two Spanish translations appeared in 1825 [28] and in 1826.[29] According to Siegwart, Bentham's ideas on criminal law were taken up in Germany by Hepp, but were not published as a separate work.[30] According

[18] Bentham Jer. Munkai, *Polgári s. Büntetö Törvényhozàsi értekezések Bentham Jer. kezizataibol kiadta Dumont Istvan Francziábol Récsi Emil*, 2 vols., 1842–1844. Siegwart, p. 328.
[19] Siegwart, p. 328. For traces of a Portuguese edition see a letter to Col. Hall, folio 12, folder 7, and see below, notes 49, 74 and 112.
[20] (a) *Espiritu de Bentham: Sistema de la Ciencia social ideado por el jurisconsulto Inglés J.B. y puesto en ejecución conforme a los principios del autor original. . . .* Salamanca, 1820.
(b) *Principios de la ciencia social o de las ciencias morales y politicas. Por . . . J.B. ordenados conforme al sistema del autor original y aplicados a la costitución española . . .*, Salamanca, 1821. Siegwart, p. 327.
[21] *Compendio de los tratados de legislación civil . . . con notas . . .*, Paris, 1823, 2 vols.; Siegwart, p. 327.
[22] Bowring, 4, pp. 535–594; *Propuesta de Codigo dirigida por J.B. a todas las naciones que profesan opiniones liberales*, London, 1822; Siegwart, p. 331.
[23] *De l'organisation judiciaire et de la codification*, Paris, 1828. See Hausmann ed. 3, pp. 1–126; Siegwart, p. 331.
[24] *De la Organización judicial y de la codificación, extractos de diversas obras de J.B. par E. Dumont, traducida al español por Don J. L. de Bustamente*, Paris, 1828. For another version see Espinosa, Vols. 9 and 10. Siegwart, p. 332.
[25] Bowring ed. 1, pp. 388–525.
[26] Bowring ed. 2, pp. 189–296.
[27] *Théorie des peines et des récompenses, redigée an Français d'après les MSS de J.B. par E. C. Dumont*, London, 1811, 2 vols.; 2nd ed., Paris, 1818; 3rd ed., Paris, 1825; Hausmann ed., Vol. 2, pp. 1–238; extracts were published in *Bibliothèque Britannique*, 56 (1814), p. 413; 57 (1814), pp. 150, 281, 417; 58 (1815), p. 75; Siegwart, pp. 335–337.
[28] *Teoria de la penas legales*, 2 vols., Paris, 1825; *Teoría de las recompensas*, 2 vols., Paris, 1825; Siegwart, p. 337.
[29] *Teoría de las penas y de las recompensas, obra sacada de los manuscritos de J. B. por Et. Dumont, traducida al español de la tercera edición por D.L.B.*, 4 vols., Paris, 1826. Siegwart, p. 338.
[30] *Grundsätze der Kriminalpolitik, in einem Auszug und systematischem Zusammenhang dargestellt* von Prof. Dr. Ferd. Hepp, Tübingen, 1839; Siegwart, p. 338, note 1.

to the same writer it has been suggested, without evidence, that Bentham's treatise on the Panopticon [31] was brought out in Spain by Villanova in 1821.[32] 'Letters to Lord Pelham, giving a comparative view of the system of penal colonisation in New South Wales and the Home Penitentiary System'[33] was published in France shortly after it had appeared in England.[34]

'An Introductory View of the Rationale of Evidence' was published in a French version by Dumont in 1823,[35] and was translated into Spanish[36] and German.[37]

An early draft (1823) of the essay now known as 'The Constitutional Code' was published in London in the Spanish language.[38] According to Siegwart, Bentham was anxious to have this final draft of his Constitutional Code translated into French, but did not succeed.[39] Out of the 'Essay on Political Tactics', written in 1789 with an eye on the events in France, and a number of additional manuscripts, Dumont fashioned an independent work entitled *Tactique des Assemblées législatives, suivie d'un traité des sophismes politiques, ouvrage extrait des MSS de J.B.* (2 vols.), Geneva, 1816.[40] It appears that none of the works of Bentham found so many translators as this. The first part ('An Essay on Political Tactics') was translated into German in 1817,[41] into Spanish in 1824[42] and into Italian in

---

[31] 2 vols, Dublin and London, 1791.

[32] Siegwart, p. 342; citing Mohl, *Die Geschichte und Literatur der Staatswissenschaften* . . . Erlangen, 1858, p. 614, note 4.

[33] Bowring ed. IV, pp. 173–248.

[34] In '*Recueil de mémoires sur les établissements d'humanité*', No. 36, Paris, 1804; Siegwart, pp. 342–344.

[35] *Traité des preuves judiciaires. Ouvrage extrait des MSS de M.J.B.* par E. Dumont, 2 vols., Paris, 1823; 2nd ed., Paris, 1830; Hausmann ed., 2, pp. 239–481; Siegwart, p. 349.

[36] (a) *Tratado de los Pruebas Judiciales. Obra extraida de los manuscritos de Jer. B. escrita en Francés por Estevan Dumont y traducida al castellano por C.M.V.*, 4 vols., Paris, 1825.
(b) Same, *traducida de la secunda edición por Don J. L. de Bustamente*, 2 vols., Paris, 1838; Siegwart, p. 350.

[37] *Theorie des gerichtlichen Beweises aus dem Französischen* von Et. Dumont, Berlin, 1838; Siegwart, p. 350.

[38] *Principios que deben servir de guia en la formación de un codigo constitucional para un estado por J.B.* Extractado del *Pamphleteer No. 44*, London, 1824; Siegwart, p. 357.

[39] P. 359, citing *Journal des Economistes*, 5th Series, Vol. 2, p. 368.

[40] 2nd ed., 2 vols., Paris, 1822; Hausmann ed. 1, pp. 371–576. Also in part in *Bibliothèque Britannique* (or *Universelle*), Vol. 1, pp. 217, 329; Vol. 2, p. 213; Vol. 3, p. 3. Bowring ed. 2, pp. 299–373; Siegwart, pp. 361–362.

[41] *Taktik oder Theorie des Geschäftsganges in deliberierenden Volkständeversammlungen nach Bentham's hinterlassenen Papieren bearbeitet von Dumont*, Erlangen, 1817.

[42] *Táctica de las Asambleas legislativas*, Paris, 1824; 2nd ed., Paris, 1835,

1841,[43] in 1863 [44] and again in 1888.[45] There was also a Russian edition.[46]

The second part, now known as ' The Book of Fallacies ',[47] went through at least four separate Spanish editions [48] and was translated into Portuguese.[49] After the first English edition in 1824 another French edition appeared in 1840.[50] A ' Plan of Parliamentary Reform in the form of a catechism ' (1817) [51] was published several times in France.[52]

Of the open letters and pamphlets dealing with conditions abroad, ' Letters to Count Toreno on the proposed Penal Code delivered in the legislation committee of the Spanish Cortes . . ., 1822 [53] was translated into French soon afterwards.[54]

under the title: *Tactica de las Asambleas legislativas de J.B. Traducida al Castellano por F.C. de C.*, Madrid, 1835.

43 *Tattica delle assemblee legislative. Traduzione di Lor. Serazzi*, Turin, 1848 ; Siegwart, p. 363.

44 Naples, 1863.

45 *La Tattica Parlamentare, Note di Bentham e Dumont*, in *Brunialti, Biblioteca di Scienze politiche*, Vol. 4, Part 2, Turin, 1888 ; Siegwart, p. 363.

46 Siegwart, p. 363 ; Bowring, 10, p. 440.

47 Bowring ed. 2, pp. 375–487 ; cf. 2, pp. 489–534.

48 (a) *Tratado de los sofismas politicos*, Paris, 1824 ; 2nd ed., Paris, 1837.
(b) Same, *Nueva edición aumentada con el tratado de los sofismas anárquicos por el mismo*, Paris, 1838 (according to R. H. Valle, La Prensa, of May 25, 1947, this edition was published in Madrid, 1838).
(c) *Tratado de los sofismas, sacado de los manuscritos de J.B. por Et. Dumont*, 2 vols., Madrid, 1834 ; Siegwart, p. 366.
(d) ' *Tratado de los sofismas politicos* ', translated by Francisco Azala, Buenos Aires, Editorial Losario, 1945.

49 *Sofismas anarquicos: exame critico das diversas declarações dos direitos do homem e do cidadaô por Mr. B, traduzido por R.P.P.*, Rio de Janeiro, 1823. Cf. ' *Sofismas anarquicos de Bentham* ', translated by Evaristo Zenea y Luz, Havana, 1823.

50 *Sophismes parlementaires par J.B., traduction nouvelle* . . . par M. Elias Regnault, Paris, 1840.

51 Bowring ed. III, pp. 433–557.

52 (a) *Catéchisme de réforme électorale par J.B., traduit de l'anglais* par E. Regnault, Paris, 1839.
(b) *Des garanties d'aptitude législative* in *Opuscules législatifs contenant divers fragments inédits de Bentham*, Vol. 1, pp. 293, 341, 373 ; Vol. 2, pp. 22ff., Paris and Geneva, 1831. This work was a translation of articles which had appeared in the Journal *L'Utilitaire*, founded in 1829 in Geneva. See Siegwart, p. 390.
(c) *De l'influence ministerielle sur les élections en Angleterre*, Paris, 1818 ; Siegwart, p. 369.

53 Bowring ed., Vol. 8, pp. 487–554.

54 *Essais de J.B. sur la politique de l'Espagne, sur la constitution et sur le nouveau code espagnol, sur la constitution du Portugal*, Paris, 1823 ; Hausmann ed., Vol. 3, pp. 127–237 ; Siegwart, p. 340, who refers to the mention by Bowring, 4, p. 576, of a Portuguese edition but states that he has not found any evidence of such a translation.

The 'Draught of a new Plan for the judicial establishment in France, proposed as a succedaneum to the draught presented for the same purpose by the Committee of the Constitution to the National Assembly', 1790, had a varied fate at the hands of its English publishers, [55] and its fate in France was not less chequered. Part of the manuscript was published by Dumont in a periodical [56] and was reprinted separately. [57] Bentham's message ' to his fellow citizens of France on Houses of Peers and Senates', 1830 [58] appeared in French in 1837. [59] This French edition [60] also contains the ' Three Tracts relative to Spanish and Portuguese affairs with a continual eye to English ones ',[61] the first of which, entitled ' Letters to the Spanish Nation on a proposed House of Lords', was separately translated into Spanish by Bentham's friend Mora. [62]

It is unnecessary in this connection to set out the distribution in foreign languages of Bentham's writings on political economy, philosophy, religion and science. [63]

II. INFLUENCE UPON FOREIGN LAW AND FOREIGN LAWYERS

If the number of translations into foreign languages were a sure indication of a writer's influence upon foreign communities then Bentham would have to be regarded as one of the most powerful forces shaping the course of legal development all over the world. But such a conclusion is inadmissible, although it may be possible to conclude that the influence was small, if translations were few. There were hardly any translations into German, and indeed Bentham's influence in Germany appears to have been small. [64] That most of his works were published in French, many

---

[55] Siegwart, pp. 344–345 ; Bowring ed. 4, pp. 285–406.
[56] In the ' Courrier de Provence'. Siegwart, p. 345.
[57] Sur le nouvel ordre judiciaire en France ou extraits des dissertations de M. Bentham adressées par l'auteur à l'assemblée nationale, traduit de l'anglais, Paris, Imprimerie du Patriote français; Siegwart, pp. 345–346 ; Atkinson, p. 99.
[58] Bowring ed. 4, pp. 419–450.
[59] J.B. à ses concitoyens de France sur les chambres de Pairs et les sénats. Traduit de l'anglais par Charles Lefebvre, Paris, 1831.
[60] See also Hausmann, ed. 3, pp. 181–206 ; Siegwart, pp. 370–371.
[61] Bowring ed., Vol. 8, pp. 468–485.
[62] Consejos que dirige a las Cortes y al pueblo español J.B., traducido del inglés por José Joaquin de Mora, Madrid, 1820.
[63] Siegwart, pp. 373–390.
[64] Grünhut, Journal of Comparative Legislation (3rd ser.), 20 (1938), p. 165, at p. 174, note 2. See a letter to the King of Bavaria, Bowring ed. 10, p. 578.

of them before they were even published in England, is due not
to the interest shown in his works in France, but to the efforts
of Dumont as his editor.   Indeed it is not surprising that the
practical interest in Bentham was limited in France [65] and in
Germany, for France had received her great system of codes
only a few years before Bentham's works appeared, and the
position in Germany was, on the whole, not very different from
that in France.   It has been contended that the method of literal
and logical interpretation, which rejected all considerations of
policy, and which characterised the work of the French legal
writers in the nineteenth century, known as the ' école des interprètes ', had its origin in Bentham's writings.[66]   However, this
suggestion seems to be unfounded.   Bentham's preference for
legislation and for the strict interpretation of statutes was inspired
by the desire to reduce the law-making power of the judiciary.
The ' école des interprètes ' applied strict methods of interpretation because the new Codes had abrogated the old common law
with the result that gaps in the Codes could not be filled by a
supplementary common law.   Instead, the solution of every
question had to be found within the four corners of the statute.[67]
It is impossible not to agree with Halévy's opinion [68] that
Bentham's influence in France and Germany was infinitesimal.
On the other hand countries which were about to embark upon
large-scale legislation took a lively interest in the works of the
great reformer.   Spain, Portugal and the South American States
all fell into this category.   Spain and Portugal had not yet taken
steps to modernise their legal systems which dated largely from
the eighteenth century and before, while the South American
States were beginning for the first time to establish legal systems
of their own.   But it is noteworthy that many of the Spanish
editions were published in France and that the translators were

---

[65] See a letter by Dumont to Bentham, of February 22, 1821 ; Bowring ed.
10, p. 525.
[66] Gény, *Méthode d'Interprétation*, 1, pp. 25 note 2, 62 note 4 ; 2, pp. 280,
340 note ; Bentham, *Principles of the Civil Code*, Bowring ed. 1, p. 334.
Hatschek, *Die Geschlossenheit des Rechtssystems* in *Archiv für öffentliches
Recht*, 24 (1909), 26 (1910), and Lukas, *Bentham's Einfluss auf die
Geschlossenheit der Kodification, ibid.*, 26 (1910), were not available.
[67] The present writer, *Journal of Comparative Legislation* (3rd ser.), 28
(1946), pp. 34–44.
[68] *The Growth of Philosophical Radicalism* (1928), English ed., p. 296.

refugees.[69] Similarly, it must be noted that the first edition to be published in Italy appeared in the year 1848, while Bentham's fame in Greece is due to the emergence of Greek independence and to the attempts to establish new institutions of government and a new legal system. The popularity of Bentham's works is thus clearly related to the existence of or need for a movement of legal reform and to the conditions of political freedom in the countries concerned.

An investigation of Bentham's unpublished correspondence in possession of University College London confirms the impression that Bentham's influence was principally an indirect one through the medium of foreign statesmen and politicians and that his interest was concentrated upon his Constitutional Code, the Prison system and the freedom of the Press, with occasional excursions into the field of procedure and evidence. Rafael Heliodoro Valle, writing in *La Prensa* of May 25, 1947[70] appears to agree with this view, in so far as South America is concerned. Here Bentham made himself felt through the writings of Francisco de Miranda and of Simon Bolivar in Venezuela, of Bernardino Rivadavia in the Argentine and of José Cecilio del Valle in Guatemala, Francisco de Paula Santander in Colombia and José Maria Luis Mora in Mexico.

Stanhope, writing to Bowring from Pisa on October 25, 1823[71] says : ' Bentham's works are much admired on the continent. This will be still more the case in the next generation. The Professor of Law here, Carminiani, is of this mind. At the College of Bologna none but Greeks and foreigners are allowed to read this author '.

Bentham himself was much touched by the attention given to his works abroad. On May 9, 1821 he wrote to Toribio Nuñez[72] : ' From Salamanca such a book[73] as thine. From Coimbra marks of liberalism altogether correspondent! In the

---

[69] Bentham to José del Valle, November 10, 1826, Bentham MSS. University College, London, folio 12, folder 22.

[70] I owe this reference to the kindness of Prof. Ruiz Moreno and of Dr. M. Raitzin, of Buenos Aires.

[71] University College, London, MSS., folio 12, folder 11.

[72] Folio 13, folder 10. For Toribio Nuñez see Kenny in (1895) 11 *Law Quarterly Review*, 175, 179, 180 where the letter here quoted is set out without abbreviation.

[73] He wrote ' *Espiritu de Bentham o la ciencia social* ' por el doctor *Toribio Nuñez dedicado a las Cortes españolas* (Salamanca), 1820. See above, note 20.

University of Coimbra was Dumont's edition of my works almost
as soon as edited, an object of attention to the Carvalhos . . .
and the Rochas.   What Salamanca and Coimbra were before
that Oxford and Cambridge are still today '.[74]

GENEVA

Dumont in Geneva tried to put Bentham's ideas into practice
by drafting the New Penal Code according to the principles
outlined by his master,[75] and expressed the wish to see the recent
Penal Code of New Orleans to discover whether it was more
Benthamist than Bentham himself.[76]   In a letter of October 3,
1823 he mentions the question of the introduction of a Code of
Civil Procedure based on Bentham's Theory of Judicial
Evidence.[77]   In 1819 Dumont came to London to consult
Bentham on the drafting of the Penal Code,[78] and in 1821 he
thanks Bentham for his interest in the Code for which he must
have ' paternal affections'.   Bentham, in turn, mentions in a
letter to Bolivar that he has been invited to Geneva ' to draw up
a complete Code of Law for that Commonwealth' and that he
has offered that city to draw up ' an entire Code '.[79]   The discussion centred, however, around questions of classification
alone, and Bentham's advice was couched in terms of English
law.[80]   Dumont was puzzled where the ' crime d'usage de

---

[74] Carvalho was a member of the Portuguese Regency.   Bentham corresponded with him.   In a letter of June 12, 1821, he suggested that the
Portuguese Regents should get in touch with Dumont who was framing
a Code on the lines of Bentham's works, folio 13, folder 11.   On July 2,
1821, he asked Carvalho to collaborate in drawing up a Code ; folio 13,
folder 11.   For Carvalho's answer of August 24, 1821, see folio 13,
folder 12.   Rocha appears to have considered undertaking a translation
of some of Bentham's works.

[75] For the further history of this attempt see Grünhut in *Journal of the
Society of Comparative Legislation* (3rd series), 20 (1939), p. 165, at
p. 174, citing Dumont, *Note historique sur la législation pénale du
Canton de Genève*, in *Schweizerische Zeitschrift für Strafrecht*, 3 (1890),
pp. 178ff.

[76] Folio 10, folder 19 ; February 3, 1825.

[77] Folio 10, folder 19.   For the further history of this Code (1819) see
Grünhut, *loc. cit.*, quoting Schurter-Fritzsche, *Zivilprozess der Schweiz*,
2, 1 (1931), p. 20.

[78] Folio 10, folder 9, letter of February 6, 1821.   Bentham to Carvalho,
June 12, 1824 : ' Mr. Dumont . . . has for these two or three years been
hard at work in the endeavour to frame a Code upon the principles of
my works. . . '.   Folio 13, folder 11 ; Dumont to Bentham, February 22,
1821, Bowring ed. 10, p. 525.

[79] Folio 10, folder 3.

[80] Folio 10, folder 9 ; letter of November 3, 1817.

tabac' was to be placed. Was it a private, a public or semi-public delict? Again, where was the place for the crime of 'injures mentales' and of ' cruelty to animals'? [81] He informed Bentham that there was no freedom of the Press in Geneva and that it was useless to make provision in the criminal code safeguarding this liberty. Dumont was to come to England on a mission from his government to discuss the titles of the Geneva Penal Code which Bentham was to revise.[82] However, nothing came of Dumont's endeavours, and the law of Geneva was not adapted to the ideas of the great man in London.

FRANCE

Bentham's relations with French statesmen and politicians did not lead to any positive results either. A correspondence with the Duc de la Rochefoucauld and Baron Delassert dealt with the plan of a panopticon.[83] In a letter to Le Dieu dated July 30, 1821 he mentions that at the request of Bowring he has ordered ' instanter to be sent ten copies on the Liberty of the Press to the French Legation directed by his Royal Highness, the Duke of Orleans'.[84] The receipt of a copy of this work is also acknowledged by Benjamin Constant.[85] It would be tempting to examine whether the first French Press Law, which was also the first in Western Europe, was influenced by Bentham's work; but this task would exceed the limits of the present essay.

Bentham's interest was chiefly attracted, and his advice sought, by those countries which had recently gained their independence or which were passing from a state of absolutism into a more liberal era. Among these countries Greece, Spain and South America take first place.

GREECE

The official relationship between Bentham and the Greek Provisional Government is illustrated by the invitation conveyed in a letter of André Luriottis dated February 14, 1823 [86] to the following effect:

---

[81] August 12, 1823; folio 10, folder 19.
[82] Dumont to Bentham, February 6, 1821, folio 10, folder 9.
[83] Letters of November 28, 1820, folio 10, folder 6.
[84] Folio 10, folder 12.
[85] Letters of July 27, 1821; August 29, 1824, folio 10. For Bentham's opinion on Portalis, one of the draftsmen of the Civil Code, see Bowring ed. 10, p. 396.
[86] Folio 12, folder 8; Orlando wrote a flattering letter in a similar vein,

'En vous priant à donner à mon Gouvernement les observations que vous jugerez à propos sur (?) votre Loi Organique et sur le moyen de contribuer par votre Code Général au bonheur du Peuple Grec, je fais un service a ma patrie et un véritable plaisir à moi. Mon Gouvernement recueillera avec reconnaissance tout ce que vos lumières (?) pourront suggérer'. In return, Bentham asked E. Blaquière [87] on March 2, 1823 to have his advice to the Greek nation printed, and Blaquière in a letter dated Tripolitza, May 16, 1823 thus describes the scene when he conveyed Bentham's observations to the Greek Assembly:

'When I presented the philosopher's works . . . and observations . . . resolutions were immediately passed for translating the works. I have found a man who is likely to devote the remainder of his life to the study and prorogation of Mr. Bentham's principles . . . But there is not a single type in Greece, much less a press'.[88]

There is no doubt that the 'Constitutional Code' was sent to Greece.[89] Stanhope reports, in addition, that he waited in Geneva for Bentham's manuscripts which were to be delivered to the Greek Assembly.[90] In the words of Bentham: 'I sent them (the Greeks) accordingly some time ago a paper containing observations on their Constitutional Code in its present state; which paper has since been translated into Greek here, and I have some reason to think has by this time been translated into Greek there'.[91] Some manuscripts appear to have been handed to the Greek Assembly by Stanhope.[92] There followed abortive

dated May 12, 1823; folio 12, folder 16. Luriottis and Orlando were the agents of the Greek Government charged with raising a loan in London; see Bentham to Rivadavia, April 5, 1822, folio 12, folder 15. Bentham conducted a long correspondence with both and had personal contact with them. He repeats proudly that they addressed him as νομοδιδάςκαλος τοῦ ἐννεαδεκάτου ἔτους.

[87] For Blaquière see Bowring, 10, p. 474.
[88] Folio 12, folder 10. This folder includes two resolutions dated June 22 and July 4, 1823, passed by the Greek Assembly and signed by A. Mavrocardato. Two more resolutions were recorded on August 11 and 12, 1824; folio 12, folder 17.
[89] Bentham to the Hon. Leicester Stanhope, Ancona, October 21, 1823, folio 12, folder 11.
[90] Stanhope to Bowring, October 25, 1823, folio 12, folder 11.
[91] Bentham to Richard Rush, December 4, 1823, folio 12, folder 11. Bentham to Bolivar, July 14, 1825, folio 12, folder 19. See below, notes 98 and 100.
[92] Stanhope to Bentham, May 4, 1824, folio 12, folder 16.

negotiations for the publication of this translation,[93] but Bentham was not discouraged and suggested sending all his works to Stanhope to be translated in Greece.[94] Turning to the more practical aspects, Bentham suggested that everybody should have a knowledge of English, ' the only language from which tolerably adequate views of justice can at present be imbibed (?) and that were it only for the instruction afforded by the contrast, he should have some acquaintance with English legislation and English Judicature '.[95] He favoured a commission for drafting a Constitutional, Criminal and Civil Code and drew up in some detail plans for the establishment and composition of local Government districts. These were to consist of areas measuring between six and twenty-four square miles, containing one elementary school; their administration should include a Justice of the Peace, jurors, a constable and a company of militia with officers. Each district was to be responsible for its roads and police.[96] Meanwhile a new admirer turned up in the person of Dr. Negris, publisher of a newspaper, *The Greek Chronicle*, in Missilunghi. He pointed out that a Code for Greece must have the appearance of being Byzantine, but stated that Bentham's Code would be introduced if it were ready.[97] On September 21, 1824 Bentham offered his assistance once more to the Greek Legislative Assembly, pointing out that he had entrusted a Greek with the translation of his Constitutional Code.[98] Contrary to his earlier report [99] the negotiations for this translation were only taken in hand in 1824, when Dr. Corny, of Paris, undertook this work.[100] The gap between Bentham's view that the Greeks should learn English law and adopt Bentham's Codes, and the Greek view expressed by Negris that Bentham should make his Code more Byzantine was not rendered smaller when Bentham sent to the Greek Assembly an Ordinance in Spanish relating to Tactics of Legislation of the Republic of Buenos

---

[93] Stanhope to Bowring, Missilunghi, December 23, 1823, folio 12, folder 11.
[94] Bentham to Stanhope, February 10, 1824, folio 13.
[95] Bentham to Stanhope, February 10, 1824, folio 13.
[96] Bentham to Stanhope, March 14, 1824, folio 13, folder 14.
[97] Folio 12, folder 16; see also two letters of May 12/23, 1823, folio 12, folder 16, and of May 10, 1826, *ibid*. Bentham sent him his works— letters of September 21 and 22, 1824, folio 12, folder 18.
[98] Folio 12, folder 18.
[99] See above, note 91 and letter of December 4, 1824, folio 12, folder 11.
[100] Bentham to Corny, August 12, 1824, folio 12, folder 17.

Aires, a work which was based on Bentham's 'Technique des Assemblées Publics', and informed them that he was working on a Constitutional Code and a Code of Judicial Procedure.[101]

In the end Georg Ludwig Maurer, a Bavarian lawyer, ousted Bentham, and a legal system was developed (1832–1836) which drew heavily upon Roman, French and Austrian law.

SPAIN

Whatever Bentham's feelings were about the government of Spain [102] and the censorship of his letters addressed to friends in Spain,[103] he thought it all-important that he should be invited to draw up a Code to be presented to the Cortes.[104]   Cambronaro, formerly head of a department in the Spanish Ministry of Justice under Napoleon, informed him that he had a letter from Mendoza; 'you and your works are spoken of in the strongest possible terms, of the adjunct of immortal and some such token of superiority'.   He tells that he has completed a Spanish translation of the 'Traité de Législation' which is to be published and has given orders to a bookseller in Nimes to forward copies to South American governments.[105]   Not without pride Bentham writes to Edward Bell, quoting 'España Constitucional' of August 1820, p. 157: 'Se dice que las Cortes . . . se emplarán immediatemente en la formación del Código Civil y Criminal, nombrando para este objeto una comisión de 12 diputados los mas intelligentes . . . y que las proyectos de ambos códigos serán consultado con los primeras juristas de Inglaterra y Francia . . . que las Cortes consideran (?) al Jeremy Bentham por si se digne ir á España para contribuir con sus vastos conocimientos a la grande obra de nuestra legislación'.[106]   Some time later Bentham reports that he has 'expended no ordinary quantity of labour, time and paper' on an essay which has since been received in Spain by the intended

---

101 Bentham to the Greek Legislative Assembly, January 28, 1825, folio 12, folder 19.
102 To Samuel Bentham, folio 10, folder 8: "I am regarding democracy with disgust and taking refuge in monarchs and aristocracy'.   Cf. Kenny in (1895) 11 L.Q.R. 48.
103 Bentham to Blaquière, December 11, 1820, folio 10, folder 11.
104 See preceding note.
105 December 4, 1818, folio 13, folder 1; for Mendoza see below, note 107. For the sale of Dumont's translation in Spain see Bowring ed. 10, pp. 395–396.
106 Letter of August 5, 1820.   Cf. Bowring, 10, pp. 514, 516.

translator and is to his best knowledge in the course of publication.[107]   He informs Col. Hall that the Cortes have accepted the panopticon for Spain and the possessions overseas.   Mora asked for his view on the introduction of the jury system in Spain, but Bentham refused to commit himself in the absence of information as to what function juries were intended to fulfil and what types of courts were to be established.[108]   However, in a letter to Arguelles he sets out his objections to the jury system in England and France, in particular to juries in England who, in his opinion, were instruments of the government through the medium of grants of spoils, and merely a check upon the judge.[109] However, in a letter to Mora he suggests the introduction of common and special jurors in Spain.[110]   It is hardly necessary to point out that this meant transplanting English institutions into an alien land.   Suggestions of this kind seem to have drawn from Mora some remarks about the need for an indigenous legal system.   For shortly afterwards Bentham chastised Mora for suggesting that the Code for Spain should be unlike all others.   Instead, Bentham was emphatic that there must be a complete condification—it must be remembered that Spanish law relies to a certain extent on customary law to this day— and that he would undertake the work only on this condition. On the other hand he reaffirmed his readiness to help and stressed that, in order to be free, he had rejected an invitation from the Emperor Alexander of Russia to assist in the task of legislation there.[111]   It would not appear, however, that Bentham's influence made itself felt either in the Spanish Penal Code of 1822 or in the Constitutional Law of Spain.[112]   On the

---

[107] Bentham to Col. Hall, Colombia, May 17, 1822, folio 12, folder 7.   In a letter to Bolivar Bentham mentions that Pedro Barán Mendoza was engaged upon a translation of his works; folio 10, folder 2.

[108] September 9, 1820, folio 13, folder 13.

[109] April 7, 1821, folio 10, folder 10; to Mora, September 20, 1820, folio 13, folder 3.

[110] September 18, 1820, folio 13, folder 3.

[111] Bentham to Mora, November 13, 1820. Cf. Bowring ed. 4, pp. 514–528; 10, p. 406.

[112] The relations between Bentham and Portuguese statesmen are obscure. He invited Carvalho, a member of the Regency Council, to draw up a Code of Law (July 2, 1821, folio 13, folder 10; June 12, 1824, *ibid.*) and the Legislative Assembly of Portugal may have written to Bentham (Carvalho to Rocha, June 8, 1821; Carvalho to Bentham, August 24, 1821, folio 13, folder 11).   Bentham records an acceptance of his codification offer by the Assembly and hopes that Manuel Fernandez Thomas will persuade the Portuguese Cortes to introduce the panopticon. Letter to Col. Hall, May 17, 1822 (?), folio 12, folder 7. Cf. Bowring, X, pp. 525, 539.

other hand it has been conjectured that through the works of
Bentham's pupil Toribio Nuñez[113] the Spanish prison system
was modified in accordance with Bentham's ideas.[114]

SOUTH AMERICA

It appears that Bentham's connection with South American
statesmen was much closer than with their Spanish counterparts.
Some aspects of these relationships have recently been examined
by South American writers.[115] From Bentham's papers it is
possible to reconstruct the following picture.

He conducted a correspondence with Bolivar, in which he
informed Bolivar that Rivadavia was contemplating a translation of his works. Bolivar's letter, sent after a delay of two years
(1822), was non-committal but flattering : ' The name of the
preceptor of legislators is never pronounced, even in these savage
regions of America, without veneration and without gratitude '.[116]
At the instance of Miranda in Venezuela Bentham drew up a
Code for the liberty of the Press in that country,[117] but he was
aware that the country was governed by a dictatorship. Further
he contemplated drafting a new comprehensive Code for
Venezuela, for he believed that the Spanish law there in force
was ' bad in substance (?) and matter '. The possibility that
this Code, as yet unwritten, might be adopted by Venezuela
encouraged the additional hope that other South American
States would also adopt it : ' Among the advantages that would
result from such an intercommunication of laws would be . . .
that the several States might resort to each other for judges '.[118]
Colonel Hall, an Englishman in the service of Colombia, received
Bentham's ' Codification Proposal ',[119] and a draft of titles for

---

[113] See above, notes 20, 71 and 72.
[114] R. H. Valle in *La Prensa* of May 25, 1947.
[115] Mariano Picón Salas : ' Miranda ' ; Alberto Palcos y Ricardo Piccirilli on
Rivadavia ; Carlos Finesta : ' Braulio Carillo y su tiempo ' ; R. H. Valle :
' Cartas de Bentham a José del Valle ', Mexico, 1942. See R. H. Valle
in *La Prensa* of May 25, 1947.
[116] Folio 10, folder 3. In a letter dated April 20 (29?), 1823, to Bolivar
Bentham offered advice on the system of instruction in schools ; folio 12,
folder 8. On July 14, 1825, Bentham sent him a copy of his ' *Principios
que deben servir en la formación de un Código Constitucional* ' and
several other works ; folio 12, folder 20.
[117] Bentham to Dumont, November 3, 1817 ; February 6, 1821, folio 10,
folder 8.
[118] Folio 12, folder 1.
[119] Bentham to Hall, May 17, 1822, folio 12, folder 7. See also Bowring,
10, p. 457.

a Colombian Constitutional Code (1821) is to be found among Bentham's papers.[120] Hall's reply was not encouraging : ' You will scarcely expect . . . that with its hands as full as they are at present, the Government should be well disposed to turn much of its attention towards your excellent plans of Prison Reform. In fact they have much to reform here (before they?) come to the Prison—schools, churches, courts of justice '.[121] Another copy of the ' Codification Proposal ' went to General Martin in Peru, with the advice to relinquish absolute power and to establish a constitutional government.[122] In a letter to Rivadavia he refers to the Spanish and Greek translations of the ' Constitutional Code ' and sends Rivadavia some of his works. He reports that objections have been raised against the ' Constitutional Code ' on the ground that it was unintelligible and concludes by stating that even if the charge were justified as regards the ' Codification Proposal ' it would not matter much.[123]

From Guatemala José del Valle asked for Bentham's assistance [124] in codifying the laws of Guatemala, and Bentham responded by sending him his works, some in Spanish translation.[125] He also sent through Prospero Herrera, the first Central American minister to France, and a nephew of Del Valle, an extensive and interesting reading list.[126] When Del Valle mentioned that he was interested in federal government, Bentham replied : ' My Constitutional Code has not . . . any arrangements for the use of the federative government '.[127]

Yet this account of the relations between Bentham and Del Valle should not obscure the fact, recorded by a recent South American writer, that Bentham's ideas have undoubtedly influenced the draft of the first Guatemalan Constitution.[128]

UNITED STATES

Bentham's relations with leading personalities in the United States cannot be investigated here, but some points from his

---

120 Folio 12, folder 7.
121 Bogota, October 17, 1822, folio 12, folder 7.
122 March 31, 1822, folio 12, folder 7.
123 April 5, 1822, folio 12, folder 15. Cf. Bowring, 10, pp. 500, 513.
124 D. H. Valle, *La Prensa*, of May 25, 1947, quotes a letter of August 3, 1821 ; see a letter of April 18, 1827, Bowring ed. 10, pp. 558–559.
125 November 10, 1826, folio 12, folder 22.
126 Folio 12, folder 22 ; see below.
127 March 18, 1827, folio 12, folder 22.
128 R. H. Valle in *La Prensa*, of May 25, 1947.

correspondence may be mentioned. In a letter to Bolivar he states that Illinois, Alabama and Georgia have abolished usury laws in accordance with his writings, and expresses confidence that New Hampshire and others will soon follow suit.[129] From the same letter it appears that he was in touch with several governors through the offices of Quincy Adams, and that he sent Adams a number of his works to be forwarded to the President, Vice-President, the Secretary of the Treasury, twenty Governors and to Professor Cooper.[130] A note from J. Adam Smith, although it expresses great expectations for the future influence of Bentham's writings, does not record any concrete achievements: ' I am happy to see Governor Plumer's letter to you, and I believe it is only a specimen of the successive acknowledgment you are yet to receive from the gratitude of my countrymen for your devotedness to the interests of mankind and to the immediate improvement of the condition of our happy country '.[131]

III. BENTHAM'S ACQUAINTANCE WITH FOREIGN LAW

So far it has been shown that Bentham, in propagating his ideas, was spreading at the same time the principles of English law and government. This account would be incomplete, however, if no mention were made of Bentham's interest in legal developments abroad and his wide reading in foreign juridical literature. Nor does the matter rest there. He put his knowledge to good use, for the purpose of bringing out the character of local institutions at home and of promoting reform.

The list of books which he prepared for Del Valle [132] contained a considerable number of French legal works,[133] including some which must be regarded as early works on comparative law.[134] From America he received, at his own request, the first

---

[129] Folio 10, folder 3.

[130] Folio 12, folder 2.

[131] December 1, 1817, folio 12, folder 3. For Bentham's relations with Egypt see Nys, *Revue de Droit International et de Législation Comparée*, 19 (1887), p. 446.

[132] November 10, 1826, folio 12, folder 22.

[133] Berriat, *Cours de Procédure Civile*, 2 vols. ; Pigeau, *La Procédure Civile des tribunnaux de France ; Annuaire de Législation et de Jurisprudence*, 1824–1826 ; *Projet d'un Code Pénal pour la Louisiana*.

[134] *Reflexions sur les lois pénales de France et d'Angleterre,* by Fallaindier (?) ; M. Rey, *Des Institutions judiciaires de l'Angleterre comparées avec celles de la France,* 1826.

volume of the laws of the United States [135] and a copy of the
amended Constitution of New York,[136] and he made inquiries
concerning the frequency of prosecutions for libels in the United
States, especially libels against the Government.[137]   From the
Argentine came the gift of a copy of the Constitution of Buenos
Aires.   He quotes Heineccius,[138] Grotius, Pufendorf, Bur-
lamaqui,[139] D'Aguesseau :   Oeuvres (1773),[140] Swift's Laws of
Connecticut,[141] Sonnenfeld's Police of Vienna (1777)[142] and
Beccaria.[143]

A cursory examination of Bentham's works shows that he
made extensive use of his knowledge of foreign law.   He had
a sufficiently intimate knowledge of foreign legislation and codes
to quote from the following : —

The Prussian Codex Fridericianus (1750)[144] ;   The Code
Noir of Louis XIV [145] ; The Virginian Declaration of Rights of
June 1, 1776[146] ; The Austrian Codex Theresianus [147] ; Austrian
legislation under Joseph II [148] ;   The French Constitution of
1814[149] ;   The French Code Penal of 1810[150] ;   and the
Code Civil of 1804[151] ;   Danish [152] and Dutch legislation [153] ;
The American Sedition Act, 1798[154] ;   The Spanish Constitution [155] ; The Polish Constitution.[156] Often a reference to foreign
law discloses an antiquarian interest or a desire to note a legal
curiosum.   Thus he discusses corporal punishment in Russia,

---

[135] Rush, United States Minister to Great Britain, in a letter to Bentham,
August 5, 1821, folio 12, folder 4.
[136] J. Adam Smith to Bentham, January 21, 1821, folio 12, folder 6.
[137] To W. Vaughan, folio 12, folder 2 ; cf. Bowring, Vol. 10, p. 512.
[138] *Elementa Juris Civilis*, Bowring, 1, p. 460, note.
[139] Bowring, 3, p. 158.
[140] *Ibid.*, 1, p. 149, wrongly described as d'Auguessau.
[141] 2, p. 472.
[142] 2, p. 536.
[143] *Ibid.*, 2, p. 224.
[144] Bowring, 1, p. 7; 2, p. 229.   Professor Jolowicz informs me that the
Prussian Code of 1794 was also known to Bentham : folio 97, folder 220.
[145] *Ibid.*, 1, p. 143 note.
[146] *Ibid.*, 1, p. 154.
[147] *Ibid.*, 1, pp. 414, 554, 560.
[148] *Ibid.*, 1, p. 532.
[149] *Ibid.*, 2, p. 315 note.
[150] *Ibid.*, 2, p. 31.
[151] *Ibid.*, 2, p. 70.
[152] *Ibid.*, 2, pp. 47, 309.
[153] *Ibid.*, 2, p. 321.
[154] *Ibid.*, 2, pp. 277–278.
[155] *Ibid.*, 2, pp. 277–278, 285.
[156] *Ibid.*, 2, pp. 328, 369.

Poland and China,[157] such as cutting nails (ancient China) or beards (ancient Russia) or slicing or cutting off noses, or shaving adulterous women (ancient France).

Not infrequently a closer examination of a rule of foreign law by the author discloses an absence of more than a superficial familiarity with the foreign legal system under review. Thus in 'Anarchical Fallacies' he misinterprets the French doctrine of expropriation,[158] and the usual continental definition of ownership.[159] He misunderstands the extent of the overriding powers of the police on the continent and the importance of restrictions upon those powers [160] which by their nature were preventive rather than remedial. Again his account of the French law of torts is not quite accurate.[161] But these are trifling blemishes and generally he makes skilful use of his material.

He tackles problems of method, such as whether laws can be transplanted,[162] and shows how the same rules operate differently if applied by different communities.[163] Nevertheless he admits that valuable lessons can be obtained from the experience of other countries.[164] The general topics of comparative law are treated, such as the importance of *Travaux préparatoires*,[165] the place of a general part in a Code,[166] the relation between law and equity,[167] canons of interpretation [168] and the need for a common terminology.[169] Again individual questions, whether touching upon policy or upon technical details, are discussed with the help of the comparative method. In this paper it is only possible to indicate some of the more interesting points which received Bentham's attention. Among these are : Trust and *Fideicommissum*,[170] parental consent to marry,[171] divorce,[172] land

[157] His authority for Chinese law was Sir G. T. Staunton, *Penal Code of China*, Bowring ed. 1, p. 415.
[158] *Ibid.*, 2, p. 521, Art. XVII.
[159] *Ibid.*, 2, p. 524.
[160] *Ibid.*, 2, pp. 513, 515.
[161] *Ibid.*, 2, p. 76.
[162] *Ibid.*, 1, p. 171 ; cf. p. 162.
[163] *Ibid.*, 1, pp. 171–177, 185.
[164] *Ibid.*, 1, p. 39 ; 2, p. 229.
[165] Bowring ed. 1, p. 160 ; 2, pp. 337–341 ; 3, p. 207 ; see however, 2, p. 339 for a somewhat mistaken view.
[166] *Ibid.*, 3, p. 161.
[167] *Ibid.*, 1, p. 60.
[168] *Ibid.*, 1, p. 325.
[169] *Ibid.*, 1, p. 149.
[170] *Ibid.*, 1, p. 106.
[171] *Ibid.*, 1, p. 349.
[172] *Ibid.*, 1, p. 355.

registration,[173] the repression of insults,[174] usury,[175] the *société en commandite*,[176] habeas corpus and the *actio ad exhibendum*.[177] Criminal Law, Punishment, Prison Systems and Constitutional Law offer a particularly fertile ground for the application of the comparative method, and Bentham made constant use of it.

Contrary to the practice of the generation of comparative lawyers who flourished in France during this period, Bentham never employed the study of foreign law as an end in itself. The task of setting out foreign law he was content to leave to others. He used foreign law for the purpose of promoting reforms and, incidentally, as a means towards the better understanding of his own law. In so doing he did not avoid the pitfalls which still beset modern students of comparative law, insufficient information and uncritical eclecticism, but he did not fail to draw inspiration from the study of foreign law.

[173] *Ibid.*, 1, p. 552 ; 10, p. 350.
[174] *Ibid.*, 2, pp. 277–278.
[175] *Ibid.*, 3, p. 4.
[176] *Ibid.*, 3, p. 42.
[177] *Ibid.*, 3, p. 204.

CHAPTER 11

BENTHAM AND THE INDIAN CODES

S. G. Vesey-FitzGerald

' THAT a compleat and explicit body/code/system [1] of laws, if well imagined and expressed, is the greatest blessing any country can possess is a truth which I suppose there will be no occasion to demonstrate : that the British possessions in Indostan have at present a more particular need of such a system is what your Lordship, I imagine, as well as every other man who has at all attended to the late transactions in that country is fully sensible of : such a Code as far as it depends upon the best efforts of a man whose whole life has been employed upon the subject of legal policy/legislation [1] it is the purpose of the present address to offer to your Lordship '

So wrote Bentham [2] in or about the year 1782 ; even at that early date he was already aware of the need for a uniform system of law in India. He went on to say that he would work from [Halhed's] Gentoo Code [1st ed. 1776] which is ' so explicit and so neatly drawn ' [high praise which that work does not normally receive] ' that I could possibly by way of proportional . . . [words illegible] reduce it to my own method, preserve its excellences, and point out its defects '.[3] Finally ' By selecting out of the system of British jurisprudence such laws as are the delight and pride of Englishmen and rejecting such as they sigh to be relieved from [4] want only to be known in order to be approved '. In the same box is a curiously magniloquent *Exordium Codicis Indicæ* commencing ' Worshippers of Christ, followers of Mahomet, children of Brama, hear and attend ! ' This was intended to be prefixed to the Code which Bentham hoped to draw up. In it with his usual contempt for shams he speaks plainly of the downfall of the Mughal Empire : he asserts unequivocally the sovereignty of King George and the delegation

[1] Bentham's MSS. drafts contain many instances of alternative phraseology, no alternative being struck out.
[2] MSS. CLXIX, Folders 11, 6, and 15.
[3] *Ibid.*
[4] The anacoluthon is Bentham's.

of its exercise by the King to the East India Company. We may be amused at the spectacle of George III (and Bentham as his mouthpiece) speaking *ore rotundo* as an Oriental despot. But, in fact, democrat though he was and advocate of parliamentary reform though he later became, the idea of the benevolent despot, the philosopher king, was never uncongenial to Bentham. At various dates he was even hopeful of converting Mahomet Ali of Egypt, the Bey of Tripoli and the Russian Tsar to his ideas.[5]

Further evidence of Bentham's deep interest in Indian affairs at this date (1782) and of the care and understanding with which he studied them is to be found in the ' Essay on the influence of Time and Place in matters of Legislation '. This essay of which a translation appeared in Dumont's *Traités* (1823) and the full English text for the first time in the *Collected Works* (1843, Vol. i, pp. 171 *et seq.*) contains passages of Bentham's finest English.[6] The work of a root-and-branch reformer, it none the less exhibits a statesmanlike regard—some might say, in view of what has since happened, almost too great a regard—for the danger of any sudden break with old-fashioned prejudices. Indeed, in this respect it is curiously unlike much of Bentham's purely English work. But only a very thoughtful and unprejudiced observer of Indian affairs could have written it. The following passages may be taken as almost prophetic :

' The problem as it stands at present is this : the best possible laws for England being established in England ; required, the variations which it would be necessary to make in those of any other given country in order to render them the best possible laws with reference to that other country '

' To draw up in a perfect manner a statement of the difference between the laws that would be the best for England and the laws that would be the best for Bengal would require three things. First, the laws which it is supposed would be the best for England must be exhibited *in terminis ;* next, the leading principles upon which the differences between those laws and the laws for Bengal appear to turn must be displayed ; lastly those

---

[5] Indeed, even in a Parliamentary democracy, reforms so sweeping as Bentham had in mind require the prestige of a great name to carry them through ; and his appeal to the Duke of Wellington is inspired by similar feelings.

[6] It is not free from those oddities of thought and expression which give so piquant a flavour to Bentham's wisdom.

principles must be applied to practice by travelling methodically over the several laws which would require to be altered from what they are [? ought to be] in the one case in order to accommodate them to the other. According to this plan, were it rigorously pursued, a complete code of laws for England accompanied with a collection of all the laws for Bengal which would require to be different from those which are for England would form a part only of the matter belonging to the present head. The impracticability of this plan is such as need not be insisted upon '.

' I would venture to lay down the following propositions: first, that the English law is, a great part of it, of such a nature as to be bad everywhere [7]; second, but that it would not only be but appear worse in Bengal than in England; third, that a system might be devised which while it would be better for Bengal would also be better even for England '.

Scattered up and down Bentham's unpublished correspondence are letters and papers which show that his interest in India continued throughout his life. The most important from our present point of view are in 1829, when he made three long drafts (the last of which may perhaps have been dispatched) of a letter to Lord William Bentinck, at that time Governor-General of Bengal, calling for legislative reform. Although it is true that the reforms which he urges were not those which eventually obtained priority, yet many competent observers agreed with him in pressing procedural reform. The letter was timely. Codification was on the doorstep, and its great progenitor rang the bell.

On July 10, 1833, the year after Bentham's death, Macaulay, at that time Vice-President of the Board of Control, introduced the Bill which became the Charter Act of that year. It provided *inter alia* for the post of Law Member of the Governor-General's Council and for the setting up of a Commission to prepare a complete Code of Laws for India. Other parts of the Bill were hotly contested, but these two proposals appear to have gone through with hardly a dissentient voice. It is worth while noting

---

[7] This is preceded by striking praise of the British Constitution ' probably the best beyond comparison that has hitherto made its appearance in the world, resting at no very great distance perhaps from the summit of perfection '.

the words which Macaulay used for they echo those which had been used by Bentham half a century before : [8]

' As I believe that India stands more in need of a Code than any other country in the world, I believe also that there is no country on which that great benefit can more easily be conferred. A Code is almost the only blessing—perhaps it is the only blessing—which absolute governments are better fitted to confer on a nation than popular governments '

At this point it may be instructive to compare Bentham's influence in England and in India. So far as English law is concerned, his work was rather destructive than constructive : he cleared away a vast amount of rubbish, particularly in the law of evidence and civil procedure. He has been compared to Hercules turning the cleansing waters through the Augean stables, or (by FitzJames Stephen) to an exploded bomb. buried in the ruins it has made. But the ideal of codification—of anything, that is to say, which Bentham would have recognised as codification—remains, save in a few isolated topics, as remote as ever. Even his hope that the experience of Indian codification might ultimately result to the benefit of England has not been realised. The Indian Negotiable Instruments Act and the English Bills of Exchange Act are both the work of Mackenzie Chalmers; but though the former is slightly earlier in date, it cannot be said that the English Act would have been any different had the Indian Act never been drafted. FitzJames Stephen's disappointment after his return from India over the projected codification of English Criminal Law and Law of Evidence is well known.

But in India it has been otherwise. The gap was there, and it had to be filled. With but small exceptions the law of India is a codified law; and (again with exceptions) the method by which the codes were fashioned, though it was not pursued with the meticulous attention to detail which Bentham, even while he desired it, rightly saw to be impracticable, was in the main that which he had laid down—namely to take the law of England, reform it so far as a small committee of the ablest lawyers of the day working with an absolutely free hand thought that it required reform; then to inquire how far the resultant draft required modification to suit Indian conditions; and finally to

[8] Hansard H.C., July 10, 1833, 3rd ser., Vol. 19, p. 533.

clothe the product of these inquiries with the force of an Act of the Indian Legislature.[9]

There are, of course, exceptions to the general statement that English law is the quarry from which the Indian codes have been hewn. A long list might be made of provisions in all the codes from the Indian Penal Code to the latest Partnership Act which appear to have had their origin north of the Tweed. Distinguished Scots had a hand in all or nearly all of them. For the Land Revenue and Tenancy Laws of the various provinces, indigenous laws and customs, Hindu and Moslem, have provided perhaps the major part of the material. Within the limits permissible in an essay of this sort we cannot deal with more than one code nor even with that in any detail. Let us confine ourselves to the greatest puzzle of all : where did the framers of the Indian Penal Code, the first of the codes, get their material? How far were they indebted to English Criminal Law on the one hand and to Bentham on the other?

They themselves, by implication at least but none the less emphatically, deny that they were enacting English Criminal Law; ' we have not thought it desirable to take as the groundwork of the Code any of the systems of law now in force in any part of India. . . . We have taken suggestions from all '. Those systems included not only the regulations of the three Presidencies but the English Criminal Law administered as such by the Supreme Courts at the Presidency towns. They go on to acknowledge a debt to French law, and to Livingston's Louisiana Code. It is tempting to suggest that Livingston was one channel by which the influence of Bentham might have reached them : for it is clear from the correspondence not only that Livingston was an admirer of Bentham, but that Bentham was equally alive to the merits of Livingston. It is difficult, however, as Sir George Rankin has pointed out, to trace any real debt to Livingston : his code embodied many of the most complicated provisions of

---

[9] Even outside the enacted law, the same process was applied to the residual principles of ' justice, equity and good conscience ' which is normally interpreted as meaning ' the rules of English law if found applicable to Indian society and circumstances ' (*per* Lord Hobhouse in *Waghela Rajsangji* v. *Masludin* (1887), 14 I.A. 89). The interpretation is however elastic. A judge might, for instance, in a suitable case import a rule of Roman law ; Hindu law has been applied to Syrian Christians and Burmese Buddhist law to Chinese domiciled in Burma by the application of the same principle.

English Common Law (*e.g.* in regard to larceny) and, in depart-
ing from it as they freely did, the framers of the Indian Penal
Code departed also from English law. The Commissioners
acknowledge also in general terms a debt to the ' most celebrated
systems of Western jurisprudence '—so far as available to them
in India. Of one such system we shall have more to say.

In spite of this disclaimer FitzJames Stephen, a great admirer
of the Indian Penal Code, whose opinion was echoed by
Sir Frederick Pollock, thought that the Code was substantially
the Criminal Law of England ' freed from all technicalities and
ambiguities, systematically arranged and modified in a few
particulars ', and a similar opinion has been expressed, though
in much more guarded terms, by Sir George Rankin. The fact
is that reminiscences of English Criminal Law are frequent in
the main provisions of the code : but in many such cases the
common law doctrine is merely set up in order to be knocked
down again (' asportation ' in the law of theft is a particularly
good example). The differences from English law—notably in
the two examples which Rankin has selected, theft and defamation—go to the root of the matter ; the likenesses are in many
cases only superficial. That the Indian Penal Code is founded
on English Criminal Law is true only in the sense in which it
might be contended that without a Blackstone to excite his
critical faculty we might never have had a Bentham. Macaulay
(accepting the traditional view that the covering letter and the
notes to the first draft are from his pen) is never so happy (indeed
one might almost say gleeful) as when pointing out the absurdity
of this or that rule of the English law.

Is it irreverent to suggest that English Criminal Law,
' freed from all technicalities and ambiguities and systematically
arranged ', has undergone such a metamorphosis as to be an
entirely new thing ? Fortunately, there has always been an
ample supply of lawyers in England whose minds were so
inherently clear and logical that they could take the contradictions, the archaisms and the chaos of the law in their stride. Of
such was FitzJames Stephen. British juries, too, from at least
the time of Blackstone to the present day, have exercised an
unacknowledged criminal equity to tone down the asperities of
the law, particularly in such matters as provocation and the
doctrine that death accidentally caused in committing a felony

or misdemeanour is respectively murder or manslaughter. But let any one who is disposed to think of the Penal Code as being substantially English law compare it with such a textbook as the framers of the Code might have used—an early edition, for instance, of *Russell on Crimes*.[10] He will find a chaotic jumble with no clear list of punishments, no list of general exceptions, no clear statements of rules. Discussions of case law begin from nowhere and lead to nothing. Blasphemous, seditious and defamatory libel are still varieties of the same offence. ' Usury and Illegal Brokerage ', ' Offences relating to Dead Bodies ' and ' Going armed in the night-time for the destruction of game and assaulting gamekeepers ' jostle one another under the general head of ' offences principally affecting the government, the public peace or the public rights '.[11] Or if that be considered an unfair comparison, let him ponder these words of FitzJames Stephen's sons in editing their father's *Digest* (seventh edition, 1926, preface).

' Practically nothing of substance has been added to the law relating to such offences as treason, murder, theft, perjury and forgery since 1861 ; and as far as the main framework of the law is concerned, this period may be prolonged to the time of Blackstone if not to that of Hale or even Coke. . . . A glance at Chapters 36 and 37 of this work [*Embezzlement and Stealing*] will suggest to any intelligent reader the needlessness of many of the obscurities that still encumber the criminal law '. Those obscurities, be it said, do not exist in the Penal Code, under which the well-known crux of *R.* v. *Ashwell* (1885), 16 Q.B.D. 190, *R.* v. *Hehir* (1895), 2 Q.B. 709, and *R.* v. *Middleton* (1873), 2 C.C.R., on which law students are invited to sharpen their teeth, simply does not exist. Ferri once said (and we have seen the remark quoted with approval by Kenny) that English courts make up for the archaic character of their criminal law by the humane spirit in which they administer it. But the law remains at any rate in theory archaic, and it is these archaisms which the Penal Code rejects.

In one curious point, however, the influence of English Criminal Law is clearly traceable. The Code provides no

---

[10] The attempt to codify English penal law began concurrently with, not anterior to, the work of the first Indian Law Commission.
[11] Even today the substantive criminal law of England is contained apart from the common law in over three hundred different statutes.

punishment for incest, though both the Scots and the Muhammedan Criminal Law did so. It seems probable that this offence was overlooked because in England prior to the Incest Act, 1908, punishment of it was left to the ecclesiastical courts and it did not form part of the ordinary criminal law of the realm.

The first Indian Law Commission as originally constituted consisted of five Scotsmen : Macaulay, Macnaghten, Macleod, Anderson and Cameron. Macnaghten never took his seat, and an Englishman, Millett, was appointed in his place. Cameron was ill during a great part of 1836 and 1837 and was not one of the signatories to the submission of the Draft Code in 1837 ; but he continued to be a law commissioner for at least ten years longer, and with Eliott (another Scot) was responsible for the first (1846) and second (1847) reports on the Code. With such a gathering of the clans, the Penal Code could hardly fail to contain many traces of Scots law. The subject is too large for discussion here, and is one on which anybody but a Scots lawyer would be rash to dogmatise. In the Penal Code, culpable homicide by the free consent of the victim where the victim is legally capable of giving consent ; culpable homicide in exceeding the right of private defence ; culpable homicide in discharging a public duty with excessive zeal or mistaken means, are not murder.[12] On all these points the code appears to be nearer to Scots than to English law. There are other points too in which the same influence may perhaps be traced. ' Theft ', for instance, was not at that date a technical term of English, though it was of Scots, law, and the Penal Code seems here also to be nearer to the Scots than the English law. It is not necessary in Scotland to describe the person from whose possession the property is stolen as an owner, and the resultant fiction of ' special property ' is therefore unnecessary. If the thief intended to take without consent, the fact that unknown to him the owner consented in laying a trap for him will not destroy the criminal character of his act. In these and other respects the Penal Code, though it goes beyond the Scots law in penalising *furtum usus,* was nearer to the Scots than the English definition. It was also nearer to Bentham.

[12] The existing provisions regarding murder and culpable homicide which have been universally censured for their undue complexity are not the work of Macaulay and his colleagues. The original draft was even nearer to the Scots law.

Of the original framers of the Code two only, Macaulay and Cameron, were members of the English Bar. Both belonged to Lincoln's Inn, that liberal-minded society which in 1817 had called Bentham to its Bench—surely a unique compliment to one who had not been a practising lawyer for well-nigh half a century and had criticised the law, the lawyers and the judges with the freedom which Bentham allowed himself. Macaulay was an admirer, Cameron a professed disciple of Bentham : and we should certainly look for traces of Bentham's influence in their work. Such traces there undoubtedly are. Macaulay's ' Note J on the chapter of offences relating to religion and caste ' and parts of his ' Note M on offences against the body ' particularly those relating to provocation by mere words echo in detail views of Bentham in the Essay already quoted, as does such a passage as the following :

' That on these subjects our notions and usages differ from theirs is nothing to the purpose. We are legislating for them, and though we may wish that their opinions and feelings may undergo a considerable change, it is our duty while their opinions and feelings remain unchanged to pay as much regard to those opinions and feelings as if we partook of them. We are legislating for a country where many men, and those by no means the worst men, prefer death to the loss of caste ; where many women, and those by no means the worst women, would consider themselves as dishonoured by exposure to the gaze of strangers ; and to legislate for such a country as if the loss of caste or the exposure of a female face were not provocations of the highest order would in our opinion be unjust and unreasonable '.

Nevertheless, in the details of the Code the influence of Bentham is seldom directly traceable. The idea of a penal code was with him throughout his life. It appears not only at a number of places in his *Collected Works,*[13] and in Dumont's draft Penal Code for the Republic of Geneva (1821), but also in outlines and unfinished drafts scattered through his unpublished work from about 1780 to at least 1826. None of these drafts, however, published or unpublished, had the essentials of a workable code ; and to have enacted any of them would have made

---

[13] *E.g.* (1843 ed.), Vol. 1, pp. 60–151, 164–168 and 365–580 ; Vol. III, pp. 163–176.

even the English Criminal Law of the eighteen-thirties more complicated and difficult (albeit more logical and humane). Their classifications are often complicated and unpractical, their generalisations too sweeping in character (Bentham, for instance, included crime and tort in a single *nomen generalissimum*) and their definitions rudimentary and inadequate. He expressly says, for instance, ' that my unlawful occupation of your immovable property is just as much theft as my consumption of your movable property '. His definition of defamation involves the imputation of an act : the imputation of a state (*e.g.* that X is a congenital imbecile or a leper) may be equally damaging but would escape Bentham's net. Insanity he defines as the total loss of reason : if this were all, at least nine-tenths of the certified lunatics in England would have to be released, and nearly all those who escape punishment on the ground of insanity would have to be sentenced ; though in his system hallucination like any other belief honestly held would be an extenuation or even a complete defence.

Bentham indeed for all his oddity is at rock-bottom a thorough John Bull. He is at his best when dealing with practical abuses and suggesting practical remedies for them. Nevertheless, arid and remote from reality though much of his more abstract thinking is, it would be a grave mistake to under-estimate its importance. Others before him, Hale, Blackstone, Foster, had presented the law attractively and clearly as a purely empirical set of rules ; and it is worth noting that his famous tribute to Blackstone as having ' taught jurisprudence to speak the language of the scholar and the gentleman ' was repeated years later in his ' View of a Complete Code of Laws '.[14] But it was Bentham's peculiar merit that he taught lawyers—at any rate lawyers of the high quality of those who framed the Indian Codes—to think always of the law as a symmetrical and logical whole and of the law not merely as it is but as it ought to be ; to dissect every idea ; to base themselves always on first principles and to ask of every rule, ' what useful purpose does this serve ? '

---

[14] *Works* (1843 ed.), Vol. 3, p. 163. ' Blackstone, who confined himself to making a picture of the laws of England, has only sought to arrange the technical terms most frequently used in English jurisprudence. His plan is arbitrary, but it is preferable to all those which have preceded him. It is a work of light in comparison with the darkness which previously covered the whole face of the Law '

He also inculcated a simplicity of language which he himself sometimes failed to maintain. That the result of his teaching was something very different from his own codes does not detract from the value of the lesson he taught. The care with which the Indian Penal Code (avoiding the vague term *mens rea*) distinguishes between the various mental states which may be ingredients in crime is a good example of the influence of this part of Bentham's work.

The last three paragraphs of the second report (1847) on the Penal Code may fairly be attributed to the pen of Cameron and breathe the spirit of Bentham :

' It is not the least of the many advantages of a Penal Code of which the principles are purely rational and of course always consistent with each other that a student may become master of it without the aid of any extrinsic learning. The English Criminal Law cannot be fully understood without a considerable share of historical and antiquarian knowledge. Knowledge of that kind is no doubt an elegant and even a useful accomplishment. But it is no more necessary to the comprehension of a penal law founded solely on principles of morality and jurisprudence than an acquaintance with the biography of Euclid is necessary to a comprehension of the problems and theorems of Geometry '.

Here and there in England are manor houses of the Georgian or Queen Anne period which stand on the site of earlier Tudor or medieval dwellings. The Gothic building, save perhaps for a wall or two, was pulled down, and an entirely new building erected by architects of the school of Wren ; not a single room, perhaps, is the same. This is what has happened in the case of the Indian Penal Code. The

' Rich windows that exclude the light
    and passages that lead to nothing '

are gone. Some of the materials used may be the old materials ; but the edifice is a new edifice by architects of the school of Bentham.

PART FIVE—LEGAL THEORY

CHAPTER 12

BENTHAM AND MODERN LEGAL THOUGHT

W. Friedmann

THE estimate of great thinkers, especially of politicians, jurists and social reformers, is bound to vary with the times and their changing values. Hobbes, for example, once celebrated, and then despised in an era of expanding liberalism and democracy, is again coming to the fore in another age of deep social and political trouble. Little more than a century has elapsed since Bentham's death; but in that time the machinery of the modern state and of social organisation, which was in its infancy during his life, has developed immeasurably. Economic ideas and social conditions have changed beyond recognition; above all, the primacy of reason in a world developing towards greater freedom and international cohesion has given way to a world profoundly irrational, swayed by hatreds and emotions and torn by suicidal antagonisms, political, racial, religious, which are utterly against reason but are nevertheless real.

It would not be surprising, therefore, if Bentham's greatness today were mainly a matter of history, of grateful remembrance of many legal and social reforms owed to his courage and initiative but no longer a matter of active controversy or inspiration. Even now, only the most hard-boiled anti-democrats would wish to undo such developments as the reform of prisons, of the English judicial system, of criminal law, the democratisation of election procedure, the vast improvements in efficiency and integrity of the Civil Service, and the abolition of imprisonment for debts. Bentham is the spiritual father of all these reforms and of a host of others.

Such a tribute would, however, be grossly inadequate. Some of Bentham's ideas and assumptions are today discredited; but the inspiration of his main ideas and the clarity of his analytical thought is perhaps clearer and more vital today than in his own time.

The first and fundamental necessity in any appreciation of Bentham's thought and work is to see his work as a unity. Bentham was, above all, a moralist, a jurist and a social reformer. Any critique of any one of these three aspects of his work torn asunder from the others is bound to be one-sided and misleading.[1] It is fundamental to Bentham's thought that every piece of legal analysis or social reform is derived from basic principles and ultimate value assumptions. A general moral philosophy, without its implementation in practical precepts, would have appeared no less futile to him than a series of isolated proposals not held together by a fundamental belief. This does not mean that the various aspects of his work are of equal value. The weaknesses in particular of Bentham's moral theory and of his economic assumptions are today so evident as to be trivial. They have nevertheless been a real and essential inspiration for other and more lasting aspects of his work. This interconnectedness of theory and practice is indeed the first of the messages which Bentham has for our own time. Whereas every one of his innumerable proposals for codification, poor law reform, criminal procedure, was tested and inspired by his ultimate beliefs, subsequent generations of jurists have lost sight of this vital connection. For almost a century, English jurisprudence became the monopoly of legal craftsmen competent and knowledgeable but devoid of greatness because they thought increasingly that legal science could be divorced from legal theory, that the law as it is and the law as it ought to be were two worlds entirely separate from each other and that the lawyer's concern was only with the former. The decline started with the greatest of Bentham's disciples, Austin, and it went on almost unchecked until the deep disturbances of our own time revealed again the deep connection between ultimate values and technical legal doctrines.

BENTHAM'S MORAL PHILOSOPHY

Bentham's basic philosophy remained unshaken throughout his

---

[1] A characteristic example of this is Professor J. W. Allen's essay on Bentham in Hernshaw's series of *Great Social and Political Thinkers*. Ignoring completely Bentham's juristic thought and reform proposals, Professor Allen has not much difficulty in exposing the theoretical weaknesses of Bentham's utilitarian philosophy. This had been done a century earlier by John Stuart Mill; but Mill, like any true student of Bentham, knew well the absurdity of treating Bentham's utilitarian theory as if it were the whole of his work.

life. It is a combination of the principle of utility with the ideal of the greatest happiness of the greatest number. Utility means a redefinition of good and evil in terms of pleasure and pain. The greatest happiness principle means the pursuit of pleasure and avoidance of pain for the greatest number. The spiritual father of the former is, above all, David Hume, whose analysis is, however, part of an infinitely more comprehensive and profound philosophic system that Bentham attempted to develop. The principle of the greatest happiness has been formulated in different ways by Hutcheson, Helvetius and Beccaria. Its underlying faith is the belief in the equivalence of man regardless of class, wealth, race or nationality.

Some cruder and long discredited critics have accused Bentham of sensualism, materialism and hedonism. Bentham was certainly a materialist and empiricist in the philosophical sense. He professed to reject *a priori* principles, although, like so many other philosophers, he unconsciously substituted another *a priori* principle himself. The reproach of hedonism is absurd; for Bentham's categories of pleasures and pains hide a number of principles which other philosophers would express in terms of duty or ideals. Along with the pleasures of sense, riches and power, we find the ' pleasures ' of friendship, piety and benevolence. It was with the help of these principles that Bentham could, without apparent contradiction to his basic philosophy, pursue the life of a single-minded social reformer more devoted to duty and work than many philosophers who have proclaimed high-sounding principles of duty and self-denial. In his wish to have a clear-cut philosophy as the basis of all other work and thought, Bentham, like other great thinkers, became the victim of an intellectual self-deception. He forced everything into categories of pleasure or pain, just as Hegel overcame the conflict between individual interest and community by the introduction of the ' rational ' will, or as Duguit pretended to derive every legal principle from a completely fictitious social fact which he called ' solidarity ' and which was nothing but a natural law ideal in disguise.

This obvious weakness, which friends and critics alike were quick to discover, has not much diminished the value of his thought and work as a legal and social reformer. It is, however, responsible for two major weaknesses in his work. Bentham's belief that all values, motives and actions could be expressed in terms of pleasure and pain prevented him from seeing man in all his complexity, from appreciating fully all his conflicting emotions and motives, the mixture of materialism and idealism, of egoism and altruism, of nobility and baseness, which forms the unending theme of history. Closely connected with this is Bentham's refusal to see the reality of conflict between the individual interest and that of the community. The adjustment of these two has been the guiding problem of legal philosophy and is apparent in the definitions of law by the vast majority of legal philosophers.[2] Bentham's attempt to gloss over the problem is astonishingly similar to that of Hegel, whose premises were exactly the opposite of Bentham's. Bentham thought that the interests of an unlimited number of individuals were automatically conducive to the interests of the community. Hegel thought that the interest of the individual was automatically contained in the service to the community. Both deceived themselves by using an almost verbally identical formula : ' Meantime, this function of interests, how can it be fixed ? The nature of the case admits of one method which is of destroying the influence and power of whatever sinister interest the situation of the individual may expose him to the action of ; this being accomplished, he will thereby be virtually divested of all such sinister interests ; remains, as the only interest whereby his conduct can be determined, his right and proper interest, that interest which consists in the share he has in the universal interest, which is the same thing as to say, that interest which is in accordance with the universal interest, taken in the aggregate '.[3]

In almost identical terms Hegel, in his philosophy of law, harmonised the will of the individual with that of the community by substituting the term ' rational will '. The delusion is fatal in both cases, although the practical effect of Hegel's delusion has been infinitely worse than that of Bentham's. Throughout the many volumes of Bentham's work, one fails to discover a really thorough explanation why the happiness of a number of

[2] See Kant's definition : ' Law is the aggregate of the conditions under which the arbitrary will of one individual may be combined with that of another under a general inclusive law of freedom ', or Spencer's : ' Each man may do what he likes, provided he does not injure the equal freedom of others '.

[3] Bentham's *Constitutional Code*, p. 7.

individuals taken as such should automatically increase that of the community. Bentham evaded this examination by a rather naïve economic theory. He believed, without critical examination, that the development of industry and trade through the unfettered initiative of the individual would automatically produce a more equal distribution of property. ' It is worthy of remark that, in a nation prosperous in its agriculture, its manufactures, and its commerce, there is a continual progress towards equality. If the laws do nothing to combat it, if they do not maintain certain monopolies, if they put no shackles upon industry and trade, if they do not permit entails, we see great properties divided little by little, without effort, without revolution, without shock, and a much greater number of men coming to participate in the moderate favours of fortune. . . . We are at no great distance from those ages of feudality when the world was divided into two classes : a few great proprietors who were everything, and a multitude of servants, who were nothing. These pyramidal heights have disappeared or have fallen ; and from their ruins industrious men have formed those new establishments, the great number of which attests the comparable happiness of modern civilisation '.[4]

It is true that today the distribution of property is relatively more widespread and equal than in the early days of the industrial revolution. But far from being the automatic result of industrial and commercial development, this has been achieved through the deliberate intervention of the State, on behalf of the community, in order to mitigate the evils of growing inequality in wealth and power which unfettered industrial and commercial development have brought about. Ironically enough, this intervention was in no small measure due to Bentham's own untiring activities, translated into practice by such followers and sympathisers as Romilly, Brougham or Shaftesbury. Dicey, in his *Law and Public Opinion in England,* has pointed out the paradoxical development by which Bentham's reformist activities, strengthening the legislative machinery in order to achieve an equality of status and opportunity which the law and constitution of England failed to provide, led to the positive State actively controlling and regulating the social life of the community. This is more than a matter of historical dialectics. The contradiction

[4] *Theory of Legislation,* p. 123.

is inherent in Bentham's own theory. While professing to follow solely the principle of economic self-interest, Bentham followed in fact a different principle when describing the limitations and objects of government. In his proposals for the reform of the Poor Law, for example, Bentham says, ' The notion which insists upon disinterestedness . . . as an indispensable qualification . . . in the instance of a person bearing a part in the management of such a concern, is a notion respectable in its source but the most prejudicial in its tendency of any that can be imagined. . . . That principle of action is most to be depended upon, whose influence is most powerful, most consistent, most uniform, most lasting, and most general among mankind. Personal interest is that principle '.[5] This observation was made in connection with the management of the Houses of Industry which Bentham proposed as productive workhouse centres for the poor and which were to be conducted according to commercial principles. Yet, in his proposals for the reform of public administration, Bentham proclaimed the principle of disinterestedness, ' Parsimony and frugality are the main objects in public administration '. Repeatedly Bentham postulates not only economy in the public service but the deliberate depression of salaries and emoluments and the utmost diffidence in the activities of government. This is a sound enough principle in itself, but it fails to be practical unless the respective spheres of government and private industry are clearly and permanently defined. For the absolute individualist it might be easier to say that government should be confined to the most elementary protective functions; but few people demanded more actively than Bentham deliberate action of the State in order to promote greater economic equality. ' The principle of equality requires that so far as may be, without taking away the inducement to productive industry and frugality, the opulent few should be prevented from doing injury to the indigenous many, by means of the power necessarily and properly attached to opulence . . . hence opportunity should be taken of breaking down large masses into smaller ones '.[6] The pursuit of this principle has demanded ever-increasing action of the State to prevent the accumulation of power and the consequent doing of injury by the ' opulent few '. Its consequence has been a steady

[5] *Pauper Management Improved,* p. 55.
[6] *Constitutional Code,* p. 34.

increase of the public service, accompanied by the need to raise its status in every respect.   The proper adjustment between the public and private fields of economic activity is still one of the most urgent economic and social problems.   The present-day systems of the U.S.A., the Soviet Union, and of Great Britain, show three different attempts to solve this problem.   No one would pretend that this problem, or in particular the adjustment of self-interest and incentives on the one hand and of dis-interested service to the community on the other hand, has been satisfactorily solved, but at least the problem is seen in all its complexity.   Bentham laid the foundations but precluded him-self by fallacious assumptions from seeing the deeper implica-tions. Bentham the practical reformer was at odds with Bentham the theorist.   It is, however, only by comparison with the pro-phetic insight which Bentham showed into so many other problems that these failures stand out.

BENTHAM THE JURIST

The limitations of Bentham's moral and social philosophy have not greatly impeded the value of his juristic thought.   For, as he himself so clearly points out, jurisprudence and legislation are concerned only with a limited sector of morality.   Bentham's assessment of human motives and actions in terms of interests formed a powerful foundation for the science of legislation.

Hitherto, Bentham's importance as a jurist has been mainly seen in his theories about the ends of law, that is to say, in his contribution to legal philosophy.   Such a conception now needs fundamental revision, after the epoch-making discovery, by Professor Everett, of Bentham's hitherto unpublished *The Limits of Jurisprudence Defined*, which reveals Bentham as one of the greatest analytical jurists of all time.

As a legal philosopher, Bentham has made a destructive and a constructive contribution, both of which are of un-diminished significance today.   His destructive contribution lies in the merciless exposure of inarticulate premises, clothed in natural law formulas, inalienable rights, and similar phrases. Bentham himself never ceased to emphasise that his own ultili-tarian philosophy was a matter of faith and postulates, not themselves capable of deduction.   ' Has the rectitude of this principle ever been formally contested? . . . Is it susceptible of any direct proof? It should seem not; for that which is used to prove everything else, cannot itself be proved; a chain of proofs must have their commencements somewhere . . . to give such proof is as impossible as it is needless '.[7] Bentham attacked not only the use of natural law phrases in the early drafts of revolutionary French Constitutions; he was consistent in refusing to invest the rights of liberty and property—both of which he valued highly—as natural rights. The right of property he regarded as a creation of positive law, an expectation of enjoyment conferred by the law.[8] Liberty he regarded as subordinate to security, which was the main object of law. All this constitutes an immense advance on the identification of a particular political faith with permanent legal principles which is characteristic of the different natural law schools, both old and modern. Bentham, in fact, anticipated the criticism of Kelsen and his school by a century and a half. Bentham's constructive contribution lies, above all, in his establishment of the foundation of a theory of balance of interests as the object of legislation. All his powerful contributions to the science of criminal as well as civil legislation—some of which are the subject of other contributions to this volume—are based on an appreciation of a weighing of interests by the legislator. All legal policy could still be defined in terms of the four basic values which Bentham gives as the object of civil law, that is to say subsistence, abundance, equality and security, although Bentham's own elaboration of these four values is largely out of date. Again, Bentham's minute investigation of the means of punishment and of criminal procedure in general is based upon a weighing of the different interests which the legislator has to bear in mind. Underlying this balance of interests is the balancing of pleasures to be achieved and pains to be avoided. There is no space to analyse in detail the many fruitful conclusions which Bentham derives from these premises. One example, among hundreds, is his reasoning against the punishment of homosexuality. The development leads from Bentham to Ihering, and from there to the modern sociological theories of law, of which Pound, Gény and Ehrlich are outstanding exponents. The scale of values has shifted in accordance with the development of modern legal and social problems, but the foundation was laid by Bentham.

[7] Introduction to the *Principles of Morals and Legislation,* p. 4.
[8] *The Limits of Jurisprudence Defined,* p. 84.

Bentham's no less powerful contribution to analytical jurisprudence has failed to have the same practical influence, through
the accident of history which left the second part of his *Principles of Morals and Legislation* unpublished until 1945, buried
among the manuscripts preserved at University College, London.
The discovery and publication of this work [9] shows beyond
doubt not only that the most powerful of Austin's contributions
to analytical jurisprudence must have been based on Bentham's
teaching but also that Bentham has, in many respects, anticipated
the discoveries of subsequent generations of jurists. A detailed
analysis of this work, written in 1782, and characterised by a
transcendent lucidity of thought as well as of style, deserves a
separate study.   It must suffice to mention a few of its outstanding features.

(1) Bentham defines as a Sovereign ' any person or assembly
of persons to whose will a whole political community are (no
matter on what account) supposed to be in a disposition to pay
obedience : and that in preference to the will of any other
person '.[10] This must have inspired Austin's celebrated definition of sovereignty.

(2) With the insight of genius, Bentham defines law so as to
include its different manifestations, not only through subordinate
and delegated legislation but also through administrative regulations. ' Under the term " law " . . . we must include a judicial
order, a military or any other kind of executive order, or even
the most trivial and momentary order of a domestic kind, so
that it be not illegal '.[11] . . . ' With equal propriety (according to
the definition) would the word " law " be applicable to a temporary order issued by any magistrate who is spoken of as exercising
thereby a branch of executive power, or has exercised the
functions belonging to any department of administration '.[12] . . .
' They are all referable ultimately to one common source : they
have all of them alike their subjects and their objects, their local
extent and their duration : in point of logical extent as it may
be called they must all of them be either general or particular,
and they may in most instances be indefinitely either the one or
the other '.[13]

[9] *The Limits of Jurisprudence Defined.* Edited by Charles Warren Everett,
Columbia University Press, 1945.
[10] *Op. cit.,* p. 101.
[11] *Op. cit.,* p. 90.
[12] *Op. cit.,* p. 91.
[13] *Op. cit.,* p. 96.

These definitions were narrowed down by subsequent generations of jurists. Law became identified with a specific form of legislation, or with judgments of law courts. Bentham anticipated the criticism of such modern jurists as Duguit and Kelsen; his definition is applicable to the political realities of 1947, while the definitions of Austin, Holland, Gray or Salmond are out of date.

(3) The modern analytical school which bases itself upon Hohfeld and which finds increased recognition in the United States, has been at pains to break down the loose and often misleading use of the words ' right ' and ' duty ' into more exact categories. Its main distinctions, especially that between powers and rights, between duties and immunities, between privileges and liberties, are anticipated by Bentham, although he had to work with much more limited material.[14]

(4) The famous theory of the Vienna school which analyses the law as a process of gradual concretisation (*Stufentheorie*) is anticipated by Bentham : 'An administrative order, judgment, a contract are all manifestations of law deriving their authority from the Sovereign. If a man engages or covenants to mend your coat for you, and such an engagement is valid, it is because on the part of the Sovereign a mandate has been issued, commanding any person upon the event of his entering into any engagement . . . and thereby that particular person in consequence of his having entered into that particular engagement . . . to perform it . . . thus then in all cases stands the distinction between the laws which belong to the legislator in the way of conception and those which belong to him in the way of preadoption. The former are the work of the legislator solely; the latter that of the legislator and the subordinate power wholly in conjunctivity, the legislator sketching out a sort of imperfect mandate which he leaves it to the subordinate power wholly to fill up '.[15]

These few examples reveal the whole greatness of Bentham's analytical mind, and it is a tragedy that generations of lawyers have been unable to benefit from it. Bentham is less happy on the subject of judicial interpretation. He believed in the possibility of rational legislation based on scientific principles to a

[14] Cf. in particular, *The Limits of Jurisprudence Defined,* p. 57 *et seq.*
[15] *Op. cit.,* pp. 108, 109.

degree which would make the liberal judicial interpretation unnecessary. The subsequent development of law in all countries has shown that a liberal interpretation must be complementary to even the best piece of legislation. Bentham's view is largely due to his understandable mistrust of the English judicial system of his time and his contempt for the judge-made common law, as put forward in Blackstone's *Commentaries*.

BENTHAM'S SIGNIFICANCE TODAY

Jeremy Bentham, resuming his labours in 1948, would probably be a puzzled and a sad man. He might regard with satisfaction the immense growth and improvement of legislative machinery, the spread of democratic rights, the quick response, by public opinion and the elected representatives of the people, to crying social evils. He would see almost all of his specific proposals for legal reform adopted. A significant exception would be the codification of English Law, a matter of much greater urgency than in Bentham's time but still a distant aspiration of a few law reformers, except in certain specified fields such as sale of goods, negotiable instruments or, in substance if not in form, criminal law.

Bentham's disillusionment, however, would certainly far outweigh his satisfaction. His neglect of history, of the irrational character of man, his underestimate of the difference of peoples and civilisations, his dogmaticism, were outstanding weaknesses even in his own time, but Bentham lived and worked at a period when the gradual expansion of the liberty of the individual and of the community of nations, above the differences of race, religion and history, were generally believed to herald the inevitable progress of mankind. Bentham drew his inspiration from the belief in reason as the guiding principle in an age of progress. While not ignorant of the influence which time and circumstances had on peoples and laws [16] Bentham believed in ' Man ' as the transcendent unit.[17] Today Bentham would see these very foundations shattered. Sovereignty and the technique of legislation are less and less the agents of individual liberty or of international understanding. Against all rational necessity,

---

[16] Cf. his Essay on ' The Influence of Time and Place in matters of Legislation '.

[17] Cf. Sir Leslie Stephen's *The English Utilitarians,* Vol. 1, p. 299.

differences of race, religion, nationality and tradition are tearing the peoples of the world asunder and plunging them into economic misery.

This makes the essentials of Bentham's work neither less vital nor less inspiring. We certainly cannot accept his individualism, his utilitarianism, or his views on the respective functions of government and individual without many qualifications. But his basic principles, the persistence and courage with which he translated them into practical precepts and proposals, the unity of thought and action, which gave him courage to attack the most powerful persons and institutions of his time—monarchy or judiciary, the House of Lords or the oppressors of the poor—these more than any specific doctrine should be a source of inspiration to all those who have not yet entirely given up the struggle for the survival of civilisation.

CHAPTER 13

THE PRINCIPLE OF UTILITY

A. J. Ayer

'THE law-giver should be no more impassioned than the geo-
metrician. They are both solving problems by sober calculation '.
The quotation is from Jeremy Bentham's *Deontology*,[1] and it
gives a measure both of his peculiarity and his importance as a
moral philosopher. His peculiarity was that he believed that
morals and politics could be made into a branch of science : his
importance lies in the way in which he worked this theory out.

In its main outlines his system was very simple. He accepted,
apparently without question, the psychological hypothesis that
every man acts only with a view to his own interest; and this
self-interest Bentham identified with happiness. Happiness he
defined as ' the possession of pleasures with the absence of pains,
or the possession of a preponderant amount of pleasure over
pain '.[2] These pleasures and pains, which he laboriously classified, might be of various sorts. In saying that every man pursued
his own happiness, Bentham did not mean to imply that every
man was an egotist, in the narrow sense of the term. He allowed
the existence of natural human sympathies which would lead
men to promote the happiness of others, and among the conscious principles of human action he included ' principles of
benevolence '. It was, indeed, one of his main objects to recommend these principles of benevolence : like Bishop Butler, he
maintained that to pay attention to the happiness of others was
a mark of enlightened self-interest; it was the surest way of
securing one's own. But the fact that men were capable of
active benevolence did not seem to him to be inconsistent with
his assumption that they acted always with a view to their own
interest. If someone behaved, as we should say, unselfishly, he
thereby showed that the pleasure which he derived, or expected
to derive, from his unselfish action, even if it were no more than

[1] Vol. 2, p. 19 (Bowring's edition).
[2] *Deontology*, Vol. 2, p. 19.

the pleasure of giving pleasure to someone else, seemed to him greater on balance than the pleasure he would derive from act-ing ' selfishly ', or indeed from acting in any other way than the way in which he did. He might, of course, be mistaken. It might be that the result of his benevolence was ' to confer upon others a smaller portion of happiness than he himself sacrificed ', and in that case, Bentham held, his conduct ' would not be virtue—it would be folly '. ' It would not be effective benevolence, it would be miscalculation '. It would, indeed, be ' a course of action which could not intentionally have place '. A man might make a sacrifice of his own happiness to the happiness of others, but ' unless in some shape or other he derived more pleasure from the sacrifice than he expected to derive in abstaining from making the sacrifice, he would not, he could not, make it '.[3]

From these psychological premises Bentham inferred that ' pleasure is in *itself* a good; nay, even setting aside immunity from pain, the only good '; and that ' pain is in itself an evil; and indeed, without exception, the only evil '. ' Or else ', he adds, ' the words good and evil have no meaning '.[4] The logic of this reasoning is not very clear, but I suppose that Bentham, like his disciple John Stuart Mill, conceived of ' good ' as the object of desire and ' evil ' as the object of aversion; and from this, on the assumption that things were sought only for their tendency to give pleasure or avoided only for their tendency to give pain, it would follow that pleasure was a good, and indeed the only good, and that pain was an evil, and indeed the only evil. If this was his reasoning, Bentham was more consistent than Mill. For Mill was inclined to allow that one pleasure might be qualitatively preferable to another.[5] He spoke of ' higher ' and ' lower ' pleasures in a way which suggested that he recognised another standard of value than the mere preponderance of pleasure. He seemed to imply that there was somehow more intrinsic value in the enjoyment of a ' higher ' pleasure than in the enjoyment of a ' lower ' pleasure to an equal amount. This may indeed be unfair to Mill. He may have meant only that what he called the higher pleasures were the more intense, or

[3] *Deontology,* Vol. 1, p. 191.
[4] *Introduction to the Principles of Morals and Legislation,* Chap. 10, s. 10 (Vol. 1, p. 40 in Bowring's edition of *Works*).
[5] *Vide* J. S. Mill, *Utilitarianism* and G. E. Moore, *Principia Ethica,* pp. 77–81.

possibly that the total consequences of pursuing them were in general more felicific than the consequences of pursuing 'lower' pleasures. And if he did mean only this his talk about quality of pleasure, though certainly misleading, was not inconsistent with his principle that pleasure alone was good. But whereas Mill's language is ambiguous on this point, Bentham's is quite clear. He held that in comparing the value of two pleasures the only relevant consideration was the quantity of pleasure involved in either case, and this he characteristically brought under seven headings : the intensity of the pleasure, its duration, its certainty or uncertainty, its propinquity or remoteness, its fecundity, by which he meant its chance of being followed by further pleasures, its purity, by which he meant its chance of not being followed by pains, and finally, in cases where a number of persons are involved, its extent.[6] How one of these factors is to be weighed with another is never made clear, but if we allow, what Bentham seems never to have doubted, that there could be some practical method of scoring, then by the terms of his theory the pleasure that obtained the highest score would be the most valuable. Indeed, to say of one pleasure that it was more valuable than another could mean nothing else for Bentham than that when marked by these standards it had obtained a higher score. Naturally, these assessments would vary from person to person, but this would not affect their validity. Bentham's standard of value is objective in the sense that his rule that pleasure is the only good and pain the only evil is supposed to hold equally for all sentient beings ; but, in a derivative sense, it makes different things good for different persons, in so far as in all matters of pleasure and pain, different persons have different tastes. Neither was there any question for Bentham of their not being entitled to their respective tastes. A man might be mistaken in his estimates of what would bring him happiness, and in such a case he might

---

[6] *Vide Introduction to the Principles of Morals and Legislation,* Chap. 4 (Bowring, Vol. 1, p. 16). To enable his readers to memorise these points, ' on which the whole fabric of morals and legislation may be seen to rest ', Bentham puts them into verse. Thus

' *Intense, long, certain, speedy, fruitful, pure*
Such marks in *pleasures* and in *pains* endure.
Such pleasures seek, if *private* be thy end :
If it be *public,* wide let them extend.
Such *pains* avoid, whichever be thy view :
If *pains* must come, let them *extend* to few '

The italics are his.

benefit from advice. It might be that the sources of his pleasure were productive of greater pain to others, and then, as we shall see, the legislator might be called upon to intervene. But as regards the value of any actual experience it seemed obvious to Bentham that the person who was having the experience was the best, indeed the only sure, judge of whether it gave him pleasure or not. And in so far as it did give him pleasure it was to that extent good.

Now if it is true that the only object that any person is capable of seeking is his own happiness, then clearly there can be no sense in saying that he ought to seek any other. For any individual such questions as What ought I to do? What is it my duty to do? What is it right for me to do? are all reducible to the question What will make me happiest? Which of the courses of action open to me will secure for me the greatest preponderance of pleasure over pain? From the point of view of the individual, therefore, there can be no distinction between morality and expediency. If the most expedient action is defined as that which will in fact procure him the greatest measure of happiness, then it is also the action that he ought to do. To recommend him, on so-called moral grounds, to do any other would be either to deceive him about his chances of happiness, or else to bid him act in a way of which *ex hypothesi* he is psychologically incapable.

The case is different, however, when it is considered not from the point of view of the individual but from the point of view of the community. Admittedly, the community is nothing apart from the individuals who belong to it. As Bentham says, ' the community is a fictitious *body,* composed of the individual persons who are considered as constituting as it were its *members* ', and he adds that what is called ' the interest of the community ' is nothing but ' the sum of the interests of the various members who compose it '.[7] Nevertheless it does not follow that the interest of any given member of the community at a given moment will be the same as that of the community as a whole. It may in general be true that a person consults his own interest best by consulting the interests of others, but this rule is not infallible. Occasions may arise in which the effects of a certain course of action are such as to bring more happiness to the agent

[7] *Introduction to Principles,* etc., Chap. 1, s. 4 (Bowring, Vol. 1, p. 2).

himself than those of any other course of action that was open to him, but are·not such as to bring more happiness to the total number of persons who are affected by it. And this is especially likely to be true in cases where the agent occupies a position of power; for in such cases the other members of the community have a smaller chance of taking reprisals, and so rendering his selfishness unprofitable to him.

Consequently, what is right for the individual is not necessarily right for the community, and it is because of this that there is in Bentham's system both an opening and a need for a science of morality. The standpoint from which he considered all questions of right and wrong, justice and injustice, and so forth, was not personal but social; and it is only when this is understood, as it has not always been by his critics, that one is able to deal correctly with his Principle of Utility.

The principle of utility is simply this. Let us say that the value of an action is positive if the total quantity of pleasure that it causes to all the persons in any way affected by it is greater than the total quantity of pain; and let us say that its value is negative if the total quantity of pain that it causes is greater than the total quantity of pleasure. If it causes an equal amount of pleasure and pain it may be said to have neutral value. Then, in any case in which the value of an action A exceeds that of another action B, it may be that both are positive but that the margin is greater in the case of A, or that while A's value is positive B's is neutral or negative, or that A's is neutral and B's negative, or that while the value of both is negative the margin is greater in the case of B. In all these cases let us say, for the sake of brevity, that A produces a greater quantity of happiness than B does. Now the principle of utility is that of any two actions which differ in value, by these criteria, the more valuable is to be preferred. In other words, that action is to be chosen which will cause the greater quantity of happiness in the sense defined. And if the amount of happiness that they will respectively cause is equal then there is no reason for choosing one of them rather than the other.[8]

Thus the principle of utility is defined in terms of happiness,

[8] This formulation of Bentham's principle is more precise than any that he actually gives himself. I am largely indebted for it to G. E. Moore. *Vide* his *Ethics*, pp. 40–42.

which is itself defined by Bentham in terms of pleasure and pain. But since the word 'utility' does not in itself convey any very strong suggestion of happiness or pleasure, Bentham often preferred to speak explicitly of 'the greatest-happiness principle'; and it is under this title that the principle of utility commonly figures in his later works. He also used the expression 'the greatest happiness of the greatest number', which is the one most frequently quoted. Thus in his *Introduction to the Constitutional Code*[9] he wrote 'The right and proper end of government in every political community is the greatest happiness of all the individuals of which it is composed, say, in other words, the greatest happiness of the greatest number'. The objection to this, however, is that the use in such a context of the words 'the greatest number' may suggest that a new criterion is being introduced, which would not necessarily coincide with the criterion of pleasure. It might be thought that one was required to consider not merely the total quantity of happiness that an action produced but also the way in which that happiness was distributed; so that an action which produced a greater quantity of happiness might not be preferable to one that produced a smaller quantity, if in the case of the less felicific action the happiness was more widely enjoyed. I am fairly sure, however, that this was not what Bentham meant. I think that he held, as he must have held to be at all consistent, that the right action was that which produced the greatest measure of happiness, no matter how it was distributed; and that in speaking of 'the greatest happiness of the greatest number' he intended only to emphasise the point that one of the most important factors by which the total quantity of happiness would be determined was the number of persons whom the action affected, and that no matter who these persons might be the interests of all of them were alike to count.

As I have said, the principle of utility is a social principle; it refers to the interests of individuals only in so far as they combine to constitute the interests of the community. At the same time it is put forward by Bentham as a criterion of morals. Thus he says: 'Of an action that is conformable to the principle of utility, one may always say either that it is one that ought to be done, or at least that it is not one that ought not to be done. One may say also, that it is right it should be done; at least

[9] Section 2 (Bowring, Vol. 9).

that it is not wrong it should be done; that it is a right action; at least that it is not a wrong action. When thus interpreted the words *ought* and *right* and *wrong,* and others of that stamp, have a meaning: when otherwise they have none '.[10]

At this point, however, a difficulty arises. The object of Bentham's definition is to give words like ' right ' and ' wrong ' a purely descriptive meaning. It is assumed that there are various possible ways of acting in any given situation, and that one has to decide which of them is right. But this is equivalent to asking which of them produces the greatest quantity of happiness; and this, according to the theory, is a plain question of fact. Thus to say of two alternative actions that one is right and the other is not is simply to describe their respective consequences. It is to assert a proposition which is supposed to be objectively verifiable. Either the one action will produce more happiness than the other or it will not. And this might seem to justify Bentham's claim that he succeeds in putting morals onto a scientific basis. But let us suppose that I am actually faced with a choice of actions, and that of the various actions that I can choose there is one that will in fact produce a greater quantity of happiness than any of the others; and let us suppose, what is evidently questionable, that I can know this to be so. Then this action will be right, according to Bentham's definition, and I may know that it is right. But is that any reason for my doing it? As the word ' right ' is ordinarily understood, this might seem a strange question to ask. It might be thought that the fact that I knew the action to be right would be a sufficient reason for my doing it. But this by no means follows from Bentham's argument. According to his principles, the only motive that I can have for doing any action is that I think it will secure my own greatest happiness; and from the fact that an action is right, in the sense that it brings the most happiness collectively to all those who are affected by it, it does not follow that it brings the most happiness to them severally; in particular, it does not follow that it brings the most happiness to me. Consequently, the fact that an action is right, and known to me to be right, is not a ground for my doing it.[11]

---

[10] *Introduction to Principles,* etc., Chap. 1, s. 10 (Bowring, Vol. 1, p. 2).
[11] Except in so far as the thought that I am doing right may happen to give me pleasure. I recur to this point later on.

For, as we have already seen, the only ground that I am allowed to have for doing any action is that I think that it will be in my own best interest, that it will bring the greatest quantity of happiness, not to the world at large, but simply to myself.

To some extent we have already met this objection by distinguishing between the personal and the social uses of words like ' right ' and ' wrong ', and by pointing out that it is only with the social uses that Bentham is concerned. Nevertheless the difficulty remains that every action, if it is to be done at all, has to be done by some person, and that, on Bentham's principles, it will not be done by any person unless he conceives it to be in his own interest. Consequently, while Bentham may have succeeded in finding a descriptive meaning for the ethical terms that he uses, it appears to be at the cost of sacrificing their normative force. If I adhere to Bentham's system, I shall no longer judge of right and wrong merely by my own sentiments; I am furnished with an objective rule. And this is the great argument that Bentham urges in its favour; that it takes moral judgments out of the nebulous realm of sentiment, in which other moral philosophers had placed them, and brings them under the control of reason. But of what use is my objective rule if it governs neither my own actions nor those of anybody else? We shall all continue to pursue our several interests : there is *ex hypothesi* nothing else that we *can* do. Consequently, all that I obtain by my acceptance of Bentham's principles is a new way of *describing* a certain class of actions, namely those that conduce to the greatest happiness of my community. I shall now say that these actions are right, which I might not have said before. But I shall not thereby be any more inclined to do them, unless I have reason to believe that the action which conduces to the greatest happiness of the community is also that which conduces most greatly to my own.

Bentham's solution of this difficulty is not so much theoretical as practical. It is to try to make the interest of the individual and that of the community coincide. The point of view which he takes up is that of a law-giver. He assumes that this law-giver has the power to enforce his legislation upon the community, and the question that he raises is, What laws shall he impose? Now here again it may be objected that, if Bentham is to be believed, the law-giver will in fact do whatever he thinks will bring the greatest happiness to himself; so that the question of what he ought to do is not of any practical importance. But Bentham skilfully removes the ground from this objection by assuming that his legislator is a person who happens to find his own greatest happiness in promoting the happiness of those for whom he legislates.[12] Thus, by psychological necessity, he will in fact set out to make such laws as will secure 'the greatest happiness of the greatest number': he is morally obliged to do so by definition, though if his psychology were different this would not count for much; and the only question that remains is, How is this end to be achieved?

The answer to this question is complicated in detail: in one form or another it occupies almost the whole of Bentham's exceedingly voluminous works. But in essentials it is simple. On the one hand people must be encouraged, by precept, by their education, and by social as opposed to legal sanctions, to find their sources of pleasure in activities that conduce to, or at least do not detract from, the happiness of others. And on the other hand the laws must be so devised that anti-social activities become unprofitable. There will probably always be people who are naturally disposed to take their pleasure in ways that run counter to the interests of the community: but these dispositions can be checked if the operation of the law makes the total consequences of such activities to the agent himself a lesser source of pleasure than of pain. Such at least was Bentham's opinion. He assumed, what is not altogether borne out by experience, that the knowledge that he stood to suffer by them more than he would gain would be sufficient to deter the prospective 'criminal' from following out his natural inclinations. Accordingly, Bentham attached very great importance to the question of legal punishment. Since punishment consists in the infliction of pain, he was obliged to regard it as in itself an evil. The only, but sufficient, justification for it was that it made his 'offences' unprofitable to the offender and so deterred both him and others from repeating them. The problem then became to find the degree of punishment that would in every case most economically achieve these ends. Too great a degree of punishment would diminish the general happiness by causing an unnecessary amount of suffering to the criminal; too small a degree

[12] *Vide Introduction to the Constitutional Code.*

of punishment would improperly favour the criminal at the expense of the community. But how to discover the mean? The answer, as Bentham recognised, would depend to some extent upon the circumstances of each particular case, but he still thought it possible to lay down certain general rules, and in his usual systematic way he set about discovering them. How near he thereby came to solving his problem is a matter that does not here concern us; but it may very well be doubted whether the problem, as Bentham conceived it, is capable of any precise solution.

We have remarked that one of the ways in which the benevolent legislator operates is by encouraging people to pursue their happiness in ways that will not conflict with the happiness of others; and we may now add that this seems to be the primary purpose of Bentham's own moral system. And by this I do not mean merely that he sets out to depict the rewards of benevolence in such a manner as to make them appear as attractive as possible. He does do this but he also pursues his end in a very much more subtle way. Like all moral philosophers, he writes for an audience which is already conditioned to respond in a certain fashion to the use of moral terms. Thus, most people are brought up in such a way that they like on the whole to think of themselves as doing what is right and do not like to think of themselves as doing what is wrong. That is to say, it gives them pleasure to be able to tell themselves that they are acting rightly and pain to feel that they are acting wrongly. Thus the fact that an action is *called* ' right ' does provide a motive for doing it, just as the fact that an action is called ' wrong ' provides a motive for avoiding it. Now what Bentham does is to appropriate these moral terms for his own purposes. By defining right action as that which promotes ' the greatest happiness of the greatest number ', he tries to get people to transfer to this notion of promoting the greatest happiness the feelings that they already have about doing what is right. He does not, indeed, himself appear to be aware that this is what he is doing. He talks of his definitions as if they were purely and simply descriptive, but in fact they are not so much descriptive as persuasive. The principle of utility is not a true, or even a false, proposition; it is a recommendation. Strictly speaking, it is a recommendation to use words in a certain fashion, but the point of it is that by this use of words people may be brought to act in the way that Bentham wishes. If the principle of utility were to be regarded as a true or false proposition, then its validity would turn on the question how words like 'right' and 'wrong' were actually used; and Bentham does in fact maintain that people do very commonly use such words in a way that conforms with his principle. His evidence is that when people dispute about questions of morality the considerations that they adduce, in so far as they are rational at all, are considerations of utility. But sometimes these considerations are not rational. In many cases, as Bentham himself admits, people's use of moral terms does not follow any principle. It merely reflects their more or less arbitrary sentiments of approval or disapproval. Bentham's comment on this is that it does not affect his argument; for, in such cases, the moral terms are being used without any factual meaning. But if his object really were to describe the current use of these terms this answer would be nothing to the purpose. For why should he not conclude, in conformity with the evidence, that words like 'right' and 'wrong' were sometimes used in accordance with the principle of utility, sometimes in accordance with some other, say some religious principle, and sometimes without any factual meaning at all? The reason is that his object was not to discover exactly how such words are used. His object was to *give* them a meaning, which should be sufficiently in line with ordinary usage to serve the practical end that he had in view. What he was trying to do, whether he was aware of it or not, was to make the best of two worlds; to turn judgments of value into judgments of fact and at the same time to retain their emotive force, so that they would actually cause people to do what they were understood to describe. Unless the use of words like 'right' and 'wrong' was primarily emotive, this aim would not be achieved. And that is why I said that Bentham's definitions were not so much descriptive as persuasive.

Are we then to be persuaded by them? The stock objection to Bentham's system is that it is based upon a false psychology.[13] Not all human action is purposive; and of those actions which are purposive it is not true that they are always such as the agent thinks will bring him the most happiness. For the most

---

[13] For elaborations of this criticism *vide* G. E. Moore, *Principia Ethica*, Chap. 3, and F. H. Bradley, *Ethical Studies*, Chap. 3.

part people aim at particular objects; they set out to accomplish certain tasks, to indulge their emotions, to satisfy their physical needs, to fulfil their obligations, to outwit their neighbours, to gratify their friends. These, and many others, are their ends and while they are engaged in pursuing them they do not look beyond them. It may be that the achievement of these ends will actually give them pleasure, but this does not imply that they have had this pleasure in view all along. It is, indeed, possible to pursue an object, say that of gratifying a friend, not even immediately for its own sake, but solely for the sake of the pleasure that one expects oneself to derive from its attainment; but this is a sophisticated attitude, which even in the case of purely selfish action furnishes the exception rather than the rule. Nevertheless, it may be objected, whatever ends a person may in fact pursue, it is surely the case that he would not pursue them unless he liked doing so. And to say that he does what he likes is to say that he acts with a view to his own happiness, whether he be conscious of doing so or not. But now the question is, By what criterion are we to establish that a person is ' doing what he likes ' ? If our measure of what a person likes is simply what he does, then to say, in this sense, that every man acts with a view to his own happiness is just to assert a tautology. It is to say no more than that every man does what he does. But if, on the other hand, our criterion of a person's liking one thing better than another is his saying to himself that he will derive more pleasure from it, then the proposition that every man, who acts purposively, does what he likes best is psychologically false; and so, consequently, is the proposition that every man seeks his own greatest happiness.

I think that this objection is certainly valid against Bentham, but I do not think that it is so fatal an objection as some of his critics have supposed. For one thing, it is still possible to hold that pleasure is the only thing which is good in itself, even if one gives up the contention that it is the only thing which is ever actually desired. One can still encourage people to pursue pleasure, and nothing but pleasure, as an end, even while admitting that there are other ends which they can pursue. But I do not think that many people would be inclined to take this view, unless they also held the psychological doctrine that there could be no other end but pleasure. Once this psychological doctrine was shown to them to be false, I think that they would mostly not take pleasure as their only value. They would say that pleasure was sometimes to be aimed at, but sometimes not; and that some types of pleasure were more worth having than others. There is, however, a more subtle way of preserving the essential part of Bentham's system, and that is to maintain his proposition that every one seeks happiness, not in the way that he maintained it, as a psychological generalisation, but as a tautology. Thus, we may agree to understand the word ' happiness ' as referring, in this context, not to some particular object of desire, but to any object of desire whatsoever. That is to say, we can identify the ' happiness ' of a person with the class of ends that he in fact pursues, whatever these may happen to be. No doubt this is not quite what is ordinarily meant by happiness, but that does not matter for our purpose. Then Bentham's principle of utility becomes the principle that we are always to act in such a way as to give as many people as possible as much as possible of whatever it is that they want. I think that this interpretation preserves the essence of Bentham's doctrine, and it has the advantage of making it independent of any special psychological theory.

A much more serious objection than the one that we have just now tried to meet is that Bentham's criterion is not practically workable. For, in the first place, it is impossible for any one to estimate *all* the consequences of any given action; they may extend over centuries. If Bentham had not written as he did, I should not now be writing this. I do not know in what way my writing will affect the ratio of pleasure to pain that Bentham's actions have so far produced; but presumably it will alter it in some way, if only for its effect upon myself; yet this is not a circumstance that Bentham could conceivably have taken into account. Besides we are required to consider not merely the actual consequences of our actions but also what would have been the consequences of the actions that we might have done in their place. Ought Brutus to have murdered Cæsar? Would someone else have murdered Cæsar if Brutus had not? Suppose that but for Brutus Cæsar would not have been murdered, what difference would this have made to the history of the Roman Empire? And what further difference would that have made to the history of Europe? Would Shakespeare still have existed? If he had still existed, he presumably would not have written the play of *Julius Cæsar* in the form in which he did. And how much difference would that have made to the general happiness? Plainly the whole question succumbs into absurdity.

It is clear then that if we are to make any sense at all of Bentham's principle we must confine its application to a limited number of the consequences of our actions, namely to those consequences that the agent can reasonably be expected to foresee. And, in fact, if Bentham's principle is to be regarded, as I think that he himself wished it to be regarded, not as a rule for passing moral judgments after the event, but as a practical guide to action, we are bound to interpret it in this restricted way. For to a man who is considering how he ought to act the only consequences that can be relevant are those that he foresees. Even so, when it comes to the assessment of these consequences, the problem is by no means as straightforward as Bentham seems to have assumed. Suppose that I am hesitating between two courses of action, both of which, so far as I can see, will affect only five people. And suppose that I have reason to believe that if I do action A three of these people will obtain some satisfaction from it, whereas only two of them will be satisfied if I do action B. But suppose also that the amount of dissatisfaction that I shall cause to the remainder is likely to be somewhat greater in each instance if I do action A than if I do action B. How, even in such a simplified example, can I possibly work out the sum? In virtue of what standard of measurement can I set about adding the satisfaction of one person to that of another and subtracting the resultant quantity from the dissatisfaction of someone else? Clearly there is no such standard, and Bentham's process of ' sober calculation ' turns out to be a myth.

Here again the answer is that to do justice to Bentham's principle we must consider it as applying not to individuals but to a society. The amount of happiness that is likely to follow from any particular action cannot be calculated with any nicety, though even so it will often be reasonably safe to judge that one course of action will produce more happiness than another; and in these cases there will be no difficulty in making Bentham's principle apply. But what can be judged with very much greater

certainty is that the general observance of a certain set of rules
throughout a given society will contribute more to the happiness
of the members of that society than will the general neglect of
those rules, or the observance of some other set of rules which
might be adopted in their place. Our proposition is, in short,
that the members of a given community will be more likely to
obtain what they want on the whole, if they habitually behave
towards one another in certain ways rather than in certain other
ways, if they are, for example, habitually kind rather than cruel.
And it seems to me that this is a type of proposition that can be
practically verified. It is not indeed a question that can be
settled by mathematical calculation. Our estimates of what it
is that people 'really' want and how far they are satisfied are
bound to be somewhat rough and ready. Nevertheless I think
that by observing people's behaviour one can become reasonably
sure that their general adherence to certain rules of conduct
would on the whole promote the satisfaction of their wants.
And it is just the discovery and application of such rules that
Bentham's principle of utility recommends.

My conclusion is then that, while he did not succeed in
setting either morals or politics ' upon the sure path of a science ',
Bentham did produce a guide for action which it is possible to
follow, though not perhaps exactly in the form in which he
stated it. Whether one follows it or not is then a matter of taste.
If any one chooses to adopt what Bentham called the principle of
asceticism and set about making himself and every one around
him as miserable as possible he can be remonstrated with but,
strictly speaking, not refuted. For if all that he is doing is to
take up a peculiar moral attitude, no question of truth or falsehood arises. It is, however, unlikely that he would now get very
many people to agree with him. Again it might be urged against
Bentham that the question which we have to consider is not what
people actually want but what they ought to want, or what they
must be made to want; and I suppose that there is something to
be said for this point of view. But Bentham's attitude is simpler
and, from the practical standpoint, I think it is to be preferred.

TABLE OF CASES

TABLE OF STATUTES

TABLE OF TREATIES

INDEX

266 JEREMY BENTHAM AND THE LAW